THE UNIVERSITY OF
WINCHESTER

Martial Rose Library
Tel: 01962 827306

To be returned on or before the day marked above, subject to recall.

Understanding Disability Policies

Robert F. Drake

MACMILLAN

First published 1999 by
MACMILLAN PRESS LTD
Houndmills, Basingstoke, Hampshire RG21 6XS
and London
Companies and representatives
throughout the world

ISBN 0–333–72426–7 hardcover
ISBN 0–333–72427–5 paperback

A catalogue record for this book is available
from the British Library.

This book is printed on paper suitable for recycling and
made from fully managed and sustained forest sources.

10 9   8   7   6   5   4   3   2   1
08 07 06 05 04 03 02 01 00 99

Editing and origination by
Aardvark Editorial, Mendham, Suffolk

Printed in Hong Kong

This book is dedicated to my parents
Robert and Audrey Drake

Contents

Acknowledgements

Our universities are underfunded and undervalued. Increasingly, research is judged in terms of the money it brings in rather than the benefits it confers. One feels deep gratitude therefore for being given the space and time to attempt a volume that may be assayed on its own merits. In particular, I appreciate the support of my colleagues at the Department of Social Policy, University of Wales, Swansea. Notwithstanding the inordinate pressures confronting them, Ken Blakemore, Anthea Symonds and Mike Sullivan gave freely of their advice, wisdom and experience, and heartened me throughout the whole process of writing this book. Equally, our social policy students relished the chance to turn the tables and criticise early drafts of chapters, and the magnificent Eryl Evans, with her usual serenity and aplomb, held back the administrative tide that threatened to swamp us all.

According to the pre-eminent Greek scholar H.D.F. Kitto, Aeschylus described his own work as being 'slices from Homer's banquet'. I have no hope of approaching Aeschylus' greatness, but may perhaps emulate his modesty by recognising how much my studies owe to the solicitous help of several distinguished colleagues. I should particularly mention the encouragement I have received over many years now from Professor Michael Oliver, Professor Len Barton, Dr Tom Shakespeare and Dr Colin Barnes. I am equally grateful to a host of other friends, some disabled, some not, in the academic, statutory and voluntary sectors here in Wales who freely gave me their advice and offered new insights. They discussed some of the thorny issues addressed in the book and challenged my misconceptions and prejudices. Accordingly, whatever degree of understanding this volume reveals, they have taught me. Any errors are, of course, entirely my own.

Next, I must thank several colleagues from library and information services who aided my search for much of the material used in the book. I am especially grateful to Lis Parcell at Swansea University Library, Sue Johnson at the Policy Studies Institute, Philip Pinto at the Commission for Racial Equality, Brenda Ellis from the Greater London Association of Disabled People, and Claire Williams at Mind Cymru.

Third, formal acknowledgements are due to those who granted permission to use copyright material. I am particularly grateful to

Harvester Wheatsheaf for allowing me to adapt some of my ideas in the book *Understanding Equal Opportunity Policies* and to Carfax Publishing Limited (PO Box 25, Abingdon, Oxon, OX14 3UE) for permission to use material from my article on power and disabled people first published in *Disability and Society*. My thanks also go to the Office for National Statistics for permission to reproduce Tables 7.1 and 7.2, and to Dr Tom Shakespeare for allowing me to quote from two of his works, as well as for his kindness in reading and commenting on Chapter 8. I also owe thanks to Bill Bytheway for extensive and helpful comments on the material I use in Chapter 10.

For her infinite patience and sage advice, I am especially grateful to my editor at Macmillan, the superb Catherine Gray, and last but not least, I must also acknowledge the forbearance and support of my family – my parents and my partner Gillian – all of whom have now heard enough about disability policies to last them a lifetime.

ROBERT FRANCIS DRAKE
Swansea 1998

1

Introduction

The word 'disability' conjures up images of a kind that few would consider enviable. On hearing it, a typical reaction may be to think of wheelchairs, charity collecting boxes and individuals constantly in need of medical care. Indeed, until very recently, any discussion of disability policies may have gone little further than an inventory of the welfare benefits and social services available to help 'those less fortunate than ourselves'. Academics have even published papers on how to 'break the bad news' to parents when their baby is born with an impairment (Krauss-Mars and Lachman, 1994).

Latterly, however, images like these have been increasingly and determinedly challenged by disabled people themselves, who have declared, first and foremost, that they take pride in who they are, and second, that disablement arises not from physiological or cognitive impairments but from a host of social and environmental disadvantages. For example, Simon Brisenden (1986: 176) argues that:

> We are disabled by buildings that are not designed to admit us, and this in turn leads to a range of further disablements regarding our education, our chances of gaining employment, our social lives and so on. The disablement lies in the construction of society, not in the physical condition of the individual.

This debate about the meaning of disability is crucial if we are to comprehend the attitudes and policies of the past and respond to the ambition of disabled people to achieve full citizenship and equality now. My prime purpose in writing this book is to provide the reader with a critique of disability policies in Britain so that he or she may more readily recognise the nature of that struggle.

The structure of the book

The book is, in essence, a journey. It begins with an exploration of the way in which the norms and values that stand dominant in any society arise from particular conceptualisations of 'reality'. These definitions constitute, *de facto*, an exercise of power, but more than that, they provide the context in which policies and organisational structures are created by governments. Tangible consequences flow from these dominant social understandings, and the book goes on to describe a wide range of potential policies and their related outcomes. I am saying, then, that the definition of a 'problem' and the political response to it (both in terms of policy formulation and subsequent practice) lead ultimately to specific impacts on particular citizens, and the final leg of our journey traces the results of extant policy and practice for disabled people, especially those in Britain.

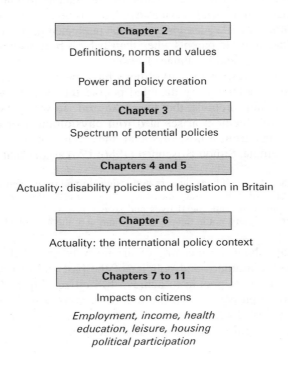

Figure 1.1   From values to impacts – the shape of the book

To guide us on our way, the book has three main sections. Part I explains differing theoretical approaches, in particular the medical and social models through which the concept of 'disability' may be understood, and explores in detail the main arguments about the origins of disablement. I have said that the ascendancy of one or other of these models depends on the distribution of power within any society and on the norms and values that govern the processes of policy creation. In Part II therefore, I elaborate a broad band of possible disability policies and argue that the point on the spectrum occupied by any particular society at any given time will depend on a variety of economic, social and political factors, as well as the extent to which disabled people can exercise influence over, or participate in, the governance of that society. To relate theory to current practice, Part III surveys the impacts of contemporary policy on various groups of disabled people in Britain.

In line with this overall plan, Chapter 2 explores different understandings of the term 'disability' and considers how the exercise of power may determine not only society's standpoint, but also the very definition of the term 'disability' itself. The chapter addresses two more fundamental questions: how is policy made, and what influence may disabled people command in that process?

Chapter 3 discusses the different sorts of purpose that policies may fulfil. The key proposition here is that where governments have regarded disability as being a personal tragedy affecting an 'unfortunate' few, they have often responded by devising policies intended to support individuals in specific circumstances (who qualify for help by dint of some medical evaluation of their condition). This approach has resulted in the emergence of a wide range of specialised interventions, for example various kinds of medical procedures, day care projects, social security benefits and particular forms of institutional accommodation. On the other hand, where it has been accepted that disability arises from the contours of the physical and social environment, governments have been more ready to establish legal powers for disabled people so that they may compel changes in society. Only by ending discrimination and removing physical barriers can their exclusion from so many areas of everyday life be remedied.

In reality, current British legislation owes something to both these strands of thinking, but I will argue that, until very recently, the 'civil rights' approach remained poorly represented, so that the 'personal tragedy' view retains the upper hand even today. In order to understand why this may be, and why disability policy in Britain is shaped as it is, Chapters 4 and 5 trace the development of policy since Victorian times and assess the contemporary impact of social institutions such as education, housing, work, social security and the health and social services. Both chapters illustrate the consequences for disabled people (as users of services) that arise from the configuration and *modus operandi* of these institutions. In order to judge the circumstances in which disabled people now stand, Chapter 6 sets contemporary British policy in an international context. Using the spectrum of policy models set out earlier in the book, I compare the United Kingdom's approach with (*inter alia*) the strategies adopted by governments in Sweden, Australia and the United States.

Part III (Chapters 7–11) weighs the impact of disability policies on specific groups within the disabled community. Having argued earlier in the book that policy making is a particular example of exercising power, I focus in Chapter 7 on social class and explain how the unequal distribution of life chances produces (and is produced by) norms, values and social structures configured to the detriment of disabled people. So, for example, access to education is problematic, and this in turn makes it harder to gain the kinds of job that provide comfortable levels of income. There is, of course, a knock-on effect in terms of ability to travel, to obtain good quality housing and to pursue more personal matters such as the opportunity to socialise and start a family. Within the total population of disabled people, these disadvantages fall with differing degrees of severity and express themselves in different ways. Accordingly, Chapters 8, 9 and 10 consider the unique impacts of disability policies as mediated by the age, gender and ethnic origins of those affected.

Increasingly, disabled people are refusing to accept the disadvantageous circumstances in which they have been placed, and Chapter 11 outlines the methods they have used in order to overturn such policies and practices as may compound, rather than ameliorate, their social ostracism. By highlighting the social causes of disadvantage, disabled people have focused attention on what amounts to a denial of their citizenship. The final chapter provides a summary of the key outcomes of contemporary policy in Britain and an assessment of future prospects for disabled people in their search for civil rights and equality of opportunity.

There are three further points to be clarified. First, my underlying assumption is that the goal of disability policy should be to enhance the lives of disabled people. It is against this yardstick that legislation must be measured. For this reason, the book identifies *citizenship* as its pivotal concept. The notion of citizenship is central to explaining the inclusion or exclusion of disabled people from society as a whole, and it is crucial in any attempt to judge whether policies counter, or indeed erect, barriers to their emancipation.

The second main point concerns geographical focus. Although I have gathered evidence from several parts of the world, the book is crucially concerned with the development of disability policies in the United Kingdom. Accordingly, international data are used in order to highlight the particular approaches shared by successive British governments. Both Sweden and the United States have developed disability policies in much greater depth than many other countries, and it is to these that the book refers most often. However, Canada, Australia and some African states have also enacted disability legislation, and these examples are introduced where appropriate. In order to show how negatively societies have treated disabled people, I have also drawn historical material from Nazi Germany and China, but would make the point that, as in most other places, contemporary conditions in these countries bear little resemblance to those in the past.

Third, while age, ethnicity, gender and social class have their own chapters, the reader will find that the issue of sexuality and sexual orientation has been subsumed within the chapter on gender, and the influence of religion is discussed in Chapter 2 of the book (the experience of disability may be substantially affected by religious interpretations of impairment). The limits of time and space have not allowed a more generous treatment of these particular aspects, but I do not wish to deny their importance in shaping people's lives.

By the end of the book, the reader should be in a position to understand the values and assumptions that underpin disability policies, recognise their intended effects and actual outcomes, and evaluate their efficacy in terms of promoting (or hindering) the citizenship of disabled people. To begin with, however, we must recognise the nature of the link between the exercise of power within society and the definitions of the norms, values and beliefs that constitute the currency of such power. It is to this subject that I now turn.

The Meaning of Disability and the Creation of Policy

Part I

The Meaning of Disability and
the Creation of Policy

2

Theoretical Understandings of Disability

Introduction

In this chapter, I introduce two key concepts: policy and power. My argument is simple. Our understanding of, and everyday response to, phenomena such as 'disability' or 'poverty' is profoundly shaped by values and beliefs brought to general acceptance by powerful social groups and actors. I should say immediately that I am not seeking to peddle any sort of 'conspiracy theory', nor am I proposing some simplistic account of rule by a privileged or malign élite. However, except in unusual circumstances, there are far more non-disabled people than disabled people in any given population, and there can be little surprise therefore that prevailing norms and values reflect the interests of the majority and may subordinate those of the minority. These same norms comprise the warp and woof of contemporary disability policies.

The chapter begins with an analysis of the different ways in which 'disability' has been defined. First, I introduce the medical and social models of disability and argue that which of these prevails depends on the exercise of power. Second, I argue that it is the exercise of power within the state that connects the act of definition with the process of policy creation. As I show in the third part of the chapter, what is less clear is whether policies are shaped more through the actions of *individuals* or by the pressures and constraints of state *structures*. Partly in order to address that question, and partly to gain a better understanding of the development of disability policies, the fourth part of the chapter enquires into the nature of policy itself and the processes through which it comes into being. Finally, I argue that these several questions of power and process are crucial to the relationship between citizenship, disabled people and disability policies in Britain. This preliminary theoretical discussion is necessary because, in subsequent chapters, I use these same concepts to enunciate a spectrum of possible approaches to disability policy and assert that the concept of citizenship is central to policy evaluation.

Defining disability: the 'personal tragedy' model

'Disability' has been defined in different ways. The explanation that has prevailed in Britain (and much of the developed world) for most of the twentieth century has become known as the medical or 'personal tragedy' model. It is supported by the world's major religions and pervades society. More recently, however, a competing account has emerged: the social model of disability. This second, more radical view of disablement has been used by disabled sociologists in their critique of the personal tragedy narrative and, as we will see, also informs the activism of the disability movement.

The personal tragedy model of disability arises from, and is an integral part of, Western medicine. During the 1970s, the World Health Organisation adopted a typology that distinguished between the terms 'impairment', 'disability' and 'handicap'. *Impairment* was taken to refer to some psychological or anatomical disorder, or might result from the loss of physiological, cognitive or anatomical structures or functions. The word *disability* was used to refer to the impact of impairment upon everyday living. For example, a leg injury might reduce a person's ability to walk or climb stairs. The term *handicap* was used to designate the social disadvantage that accrued from disability.

Disabled sociologists express serious dissatisfaction with this kind of definition. First, they point out that it fails to reflect the reality of disabled people's experiences. Second, by concentrating on the workings of the body, it omits entirely the non-medical causes of disadvantage and promotes the idea that impairments equate with 'abnormality' (Oliver, 1990). As a result, unwarranted assumptions are made about what is, and what is not, 'normal'. The notion of normality is crucial in this area of debate, since those with the power to define 'normality' are also able to specify what constitutes deviancy and what sanctions or remedies might subsequently be applied to transgressors.

Medically orientated definitions of disability are formulated within societies constructed and governed by non-disabled people. As a result, the majority of changes that take place involve impaired individuals accommodating themselves to prevailing social norms and built environments rather than the social and physical fabric of the community being altered in order to accommodate the needs of particular groups of individuals. Medical definitions, then, fail to take sufficient account of the fact that as environmental circumstances vary, so the consequences of impairment become more or less acute. In a world perfectly suited to a disabled person, although the physiological impairment still remains, he or she is no longer *dis*abled.

Ethics and the personal tragedy model

Medical understandings of disability are buttressed not only by religious beliefs, but also by the broader scientific background from which medicine has sprung, especially the field of genetics. These sources have played a significant part in augmenting the influence that the 'personal tragedy' model has enjoyed.

Religion

> The priest asserted that only the devil within us prevents each and every one from immediately acquiring a perfect body. (Owen, 1991: 16)

Little research is available about the influence of religion on the formulation of secular disability policies. It is nevertheless clear that the world's major religions reinforce the idea that disablement represents a deviation from some sort of 'able-bodied' norm and that segregation, rehabilitation or cure is an appropriate response. In Christianity, for example, the power and goodness of the Messiah is illustrated by the curing of the sick, the recovery of the lame and the restoration of sight to the blind. Equally, within Islam, the Koran permits dispensation from certain duties (such as fasting) for disabled people. Similarly, the Talmud adjures that the sick should receive charity and benevolence. In Japan, however, the Shinto traditions of cleanliness and ritual purity have reinforced the segregation of some disabled people. For example, notwithstanding the fact that leprosy has been treatable since the 1950s, only now is the 88-year-old Leprosy Prevention Law to be repealed and the mandatory quarantine of about 5800 lepers ended. The health ministry has recently given a formal apology for the suffering endured by the Act's victims (Parry, 1996). Beyond any moral influence on policy formulation, then, the world's major religions clearly subscribe to the notion that disabled individuals are different from other members of the community and require special treatment or consideration.

Work in genetics

Medicine has invested a great deal of effort in genetic technologies. Indeed, the Human Genome Project has set out to map all the genes found in human DNA, and the understanding of how genes work is advancing almost daily. Increasingly accurate techniques are being developed to identify (and replace) 'flawed' genes that give rise to specific impairments and diseases. Work is also being done on human embryos, and increasingly precise tests are being developed in order to discover, at an early stage of pregnancy, whether a fetus manifests any unusual features. If impairments (particularly severe impairments) are found, the fetus may well be aborted.

It is clear, first, that the medical model of disability is fundamental to this kind of approach towards the human body, and second, that the judgement of certain genetic conditions as 'flawed' causes great disquiet for disabled people. As Saxton (1984, quoted in Kallianes and Rubenfeld, 1997: 214), a disabled woman speaking of pregnancy, argued:

> How can I, a disabled person myself… regard this option to end the life of another one disabled?… I question the practice of systematically ending the life of a foetus because it is disabled.

The place of genetics in the lives of disabled people is discussed in greater detail in Chapter 8, but the main point here is that we must recognise the increasing tendency of science to 'geneticise' difference, that is, to explain physiological and cognitive differences between human beings in terms of their genetic make-up and, more crucially, to attach differing (social) values to embryos, fetuses and human beings according to the particular configuration of their genetic (and therefore bodily) structure. The premise on which work in genetics is based – that disability results from malfunctioning physiology – fundamentally underpins medicine's (and thus society's) understanding of the causes of disability and the prevailing response to it.

The social model of disability

During the 1970s, a number of disabled people formed the Union of Physically Impaired Against Segregation (UPIAS) (1976: 3–4) and developed their own vocabulary directly to challenge the medical model of disability. UPIAS defined *impairment* as 'lacking part or all of a limb, or having a defective limb, organism or mechanism of the body'. However, *disability* was the disadvantage or restriction of activity caused by a contemporary social organisation that took no or little account of people who had physical impairments and thus excluded them from the mainstream of social activities. Here, then, the emphasis rested on the impact of society: its values and norms; the way in which it was organised; its architecture; its laws and institutions. The key question from this perspective was whether a society served the needs of all of its members equally, irrespective of their physical shapes and differing intellects. Where it did not, the result for some of its members was disablement.

Clearly, our understanding of disability governs and informs our approach to policy making. In a society where a medical model of disability prevails, the emphasis will be on trying to change individuals, typically through care, therapy and treatment. But where the social model has the upper hand, the prime focus for change rests on the disabling impacts of society itself, and it follows from this perspective that a more appropriate response is to provide disabled people with the power necessary to compel environmental changes in order to put an end to disabling social conditions. However, in a state that subscribes to the medical model – a state that believes that people are rendered incapable through personal impairments – it is much less likely that power will be ceded to them for such purposes.

Which of these scenarios best describes the situation in Britain? Is British policy designed to change individuals or environments? In writing about their experiences with the state, disabled people have consistently argued that, far from having been given the opportunity to shape the policies and institutions that so immediately impinge on their lives, they have instead felt themselves to be subjected to the exercise of power by the non-disabled (Lindow, 1990; Church and Reville, 1988; Pagel, 1988).

The exercise of power

The medical and social models represent two fundamentally opposed ways of understanding disability. The successful assertion of one definition over the other depends on which set of antagonists is the more powerful in any particular time and place. We must consider therefore how power is exercised in a conflict of this kind, and such an analysis begins with an attempt to clarify what is meant by 'power'. This is no easy task. Bierstedt (1950: 730) argues that 'in the entire lexicon of sociological concepts none is more troublesome', and his view is borne out by the many ways in which writers have tried to pin the idea down. Some, like Dahrendorf (1959), equate power with the use of force and coercion; others (Weber, 1947) see it as a characteristic of authority exercised within some hierarchy; and yet others represent power as a bipolar concept entailing supremacy for some at the cost of dependency for others (Emerson, 1962). Many analysts conceive of power as a systemic attribute, functioning in a way similar to the circulation of money in an economy (Parsons, 1964; Giddens, 1968) or as a facet of social exchange (Blau, 1964; Heath 1968). Some have even attempted to understand power by the use of mathematical equations (Riker, 1964; Passigli, 1973).

However, one of the most powerful tools for explaining the relationship between power and social policy has been Gramsci's doctrine of *hegemony*. According to Gramsci, the ascendancy of a class or group rests on its ability to translate its own world view into a pervasive dominant ethos (Femia, 1985; Gramsci, 1971). This idea stands at the heart of Lukes's (1974) three-dimensional analysis of power. In the first dimension, power is an active concept: the direct exercise of power may occur in the form of decision making or, more dramatically, by the use of force or the imposition of authority (Dahl, 1957; White, 1972). Lukes's second dimension includes this active sense, but also introduces the notion of the 'deliberate non-decision', which is 'a decision that results in suppression or thwarting of a latent or manifest challenge to the values or interests of the decision maker' (Bachrach and Baratz, 1970: 39). Here, essentially, the passivity of the power-holder is sufficient to prevent a certain outcome. In so far as the inactivity is deliberate, this too is an exercise of power. For example, the concept of a deliberate non-decision has been applied to policy making by Hill (1997), who argues that just as governments may act vigorously and in a concerted way towards a particular goal, so they may also adopt a strategy of intentional silence – remaining inert, agnostic or uncommitted – either because they are genuinely ambivalent about an issue or because by doing nothing at all they achieve by default their *real* (as opposed to *publicly stated*) objectives. In the course of this book, the reader will detect many such 'silences' or 'absences' of policy towards disabled people. Governments have often been prompted to remain inactive by fear of the possible costs of taking action and the potentially adverse impact on the public sector borrowing requirement.

It is, however, the account of the third dimension of power that most closely resembles Gramsci's hegemony. Lukes (1974: 24) asks:

> is it not the supreme and most insidious exercise of power to prevent people, to whatever degree, from having grievances by shaping their perceptions, cognitions and preferences in such a way that they accept their role in the existing order of things because they can see or imagine no alternative to it, or because they see it as natural and unchangeable, or because they value it as divinely ordained and beneficial?

Lukes not only explains the mechanism by which such a construction prevails, but also enunciates specific ways of testing for its existence. The difficult problem facing such an account is that an imposed or constructed social reality is, by its very nature, identical in appearance to one of genuine consensus. Lukes (1974: 39) acknowledges that, where there is apparent consensus, the detection of an exercise of power is very difficult, but contends that merely because it is 'difficult or even impossible to show that power has been exercised in a given situation', we are not free to conclude that it has not. Accordingly, he seeks to address this problem by describing a way of differentiating between these two outwardly indistinguishable phenomena. He proposes that where power is exercised by means of a social construction of reality, there exists a latent conflict, which he defines as a:

> contradiction between the interests of those exercising power and the *real interests* of those they exclude. These latter may not express or even be conscious of their interests... the identification of which... ultimately always rests on empirically supportable and refutable hypotheses. (Lukes, 1974: 24–5)

So, for Lukes (1974: 33), the identification of real interests is for those excluded from power to determine 'under conditions of relative autonomy and, in particular, independently of the group which holds power, for example through democratic participation'. For Lukes, the exercise of power always implies a relevant counterfactual. B would have acted differently, made some other choice, pursued his or her *real* interests, but for A's hold over him or her. Accordingly:

> we need to justify our expectation that [the subordinate individual or group] would have thought or acted differently; and we also need to specify the means or mechanism by which [the dominant individual or group] has prevented, or else acted (or abstained from acting) in a manner sufficient to prevent [the subordinate individual or group] from doing so. (Lukes, 1974: 41–2)

We may apply this idea to disability policy by showing how disabled people in the disability movement have developed an understanding of disability alien to, and contradictory of, received wisdom. They have autonomously enunciated their 'real interests'.

Benton (1981) has suggested that the notion of 'real interests' may be better described as 'real objectives', in order to stress that it is for the subordinate group, rather than some external observer, to decide what the real interests in question may be. Other writers have articulated accounts that share Lukes's analysis. Fowler *et al.*, in their work concerning language and communication, have asserted that:

> a major function of sociolinguistic mechanisms is to play a part in the control of members of subordinate groups by members of dominant groups. This control is effected... by the creation of an apparently 'natural world' in which inequitable relations and processes are presented as given and inevitable. Power differentials provide the underlying semantic for the systems of ideas encoded in language structure. (Fowler *et al.*, 1979: 2, quoted in Manning, 1985: 6)

Brown (1978: 376) offers a similar conceptualisation with regard to organisational hierarchies, arguing that:

> In hierarchical organisations... elites exercise their powers more broadly, control-ling complex interconnections over an ever widening field... There comes to be not only a concentration of control over the contents of reality (the means of production) but also over the definition of reality (that is, foundational assump-tions concerning what constitutes 'property', 'rights', 'obligation', 'legitimacy', and so on).

To summarise then, Lukes's third dimension of power involves the imposition of a prevailing and all-pervasive ethos by a dominant social force upon a subordinate one. The environment so created (in this case, the medical or personal tragedy model of disability) appears to the subordinated (and thus disadvantaged) group to be natural, God-given and preordained (that is, if the resulting environment is thought about at all). Lukes proposes that this situation is one of latent conflict, which arises from a contradiction between the interests of those exercising power and the 'real interests' of those they exclude.

Gaventa (1980) argues that a common result in such situations is that the subordinate group becomes 'quiescent'. Because they cannot recognise that they are oppressed, subjects continue to acquiesce in, or even actively support, those very structures and mechanisms which impose and consolidate their oppression. This occurs even when the fount or basis of power of the dominant group has diminished or disappeared altogether, because, where the exercise of power went unrecognised in the first place, it is unlikely that the change of circumstance (the loss of power) will be perceived either. In this way, power may be self-perpetuating. There are many examples of where disabled people, and more especially carers, unthinkingly accept the medical model of disability and thus strive for individual rather than environmental change. Conductive education is a case in point.

In the 1970s and 80s, parents of 'motor impaired' children were keen for them to receive conductive education, a method developed by Dr Mari Hari at the Peto Institute in Hungary. The method sought to enable patients to function in society without special apparatus such as wheelchairs, ramps or other artificial aids. It was claimed that the method could bring about changes in the central nervous system of the patient. Oliver (1989) argued not only that there was no evidence such changes actually occurred, but also that the premises on which the method was based were fundamentally unsound, using as it did an uncritical concept of normality 'symptomatic of the gap... between the consciousness of the able-bodied staff of many disability organisations and the disabled people they are supposed to serve' (Oliver, 1989: 198). The central point for the present discussion is that the prevailing orthodoxy was (and remains) that 'motor impaired' people lacked the 'normal' ability to walk, and the way to help them was not to build an environment suited to all modes of human movement but to intervene at the individual level with the purpose of altering the physiology of 'patients'. So strong was the acceptance of conductive education as a potential 'lifeline' that Oliver's criticism met with a fierce rejoinder from a parent who had taken her daughter to the Peto Institute some time previously (Beardshaw, 1989). However, the independent evidence about the efficacy of conductive education falls on Professor Oliver's side of the argument (Bairstow *et al.*, 1993).

This example reveals the strength of Lukes's idea of the third dimension of power (the imposition and internalisation of a dominant ethos). It is particularly helpful to us in understanding the dominance achieved by the medical model of 'disability', in understanding how 'normality' is defined (and by whom) and, indeed, how various states of being are judged against that presiding definition (as well as by whom such judgements are made).

Clearly, Lukes's account of the exercise of power finds resonances in the work of those sociologists discussed in the earlier part of the chapter who propose that the notion of disability is socially constructed. The immediate advantage of the Lukesian model of power is that it is processual rather than mechanistic. That is to say, power shapes not just discrete events to a measurable degree, but also perceptions, understandings and beliefs that may in themselves not be tangible but nevertheless exert a continuing influence over the social environment in which disability policies are formulated and implemented.

The state, power and the creation of policy

Human values and aspirations are realised by an exercise of power channelled through some process, system or conduit, and that which converts understandings and definitions of disability into tangible policy is *the state*. It is through the vehicle of the state that meanings are sanctioned and intentions given effect. However, we must at once acknowledge that 'the state' is itself a problematic term. Scholars have moulded various theories on what constitutes a 'state', and they have disagreed in their understandings of how it operates. In this part of the chapter, I review (albeit in a very summary fashion) three major accounts that have attracted considerable attention – the pluralist theory of the state, the structural theory, and the bureaucratic model – and I then go on to describe the constituent organs through which policy is made in Britain. My task in what follows is to explain how political entities translate power, through the medium of policy, into legislation that gives rise to effects, whether these effects be acts of social definition, the creation of institutions, the formulation of operational structures or attempts to regulate the behaviour of citizens.

Theories of the state

From Schwarzmantel (1994), we learn that pluralist theories describe states (more specifically, liberal-democratic states) as being made up of a variety of powerful political groups and interests who, both in competition and through the formation of alliances, negotiate a political environment sufficiently flexible to allow each to pursue its own aims within certain agreed bounds. In these circumstances, diversity is treated as a positive dimension of social and political life. Clearly, within a pluralist state, especially where the centre is weak, there may be times when interests become incompatible and irreconcilable. Factions war with each other, and there is a danger of fragmentation or, at the extreme, total disintegration. More probable in a democracy, perhaps, is that there would take place a paradigmatic shift in the distribution of power, bringing new forces, groups and alliances into play. A second point, then, is that pluralist accounts of the state must be dynamic in order to explain how inequalities in the exercise of power permit some interests to override others (McLennan, 1989).

Pluralist accounts of how states work also assume that structures (authority, hierarchy, class relations and institutions) are outcomes of the negotiation of the contours of the state by competing power blocs. In a sense, inequalities of power precede (and thus continually construct and reconstruct) the structures of the state.

However, other theorists, the most notable being Karl Marx, recognise that existing structures profoundly influence the relative positions of social classes, groups and individuals, reinforcing the power of some while excluding others. It would be a mistake, however, to believe that Marx was 'super-structuralist' in the way described by Poulantzas (see below). In *Das Kapital,* Marx argued that the state was an abstraction and that only 'the people' was a concrete idea. So if structures alone are not responsible for determining the distribution of power within a society, what other factors may be at play? Hill (1997) argues that structural perspectives of the state lay particular emphasis on economic determinism; that is, capital and the intrinsic nature of work exert a fundamental influence on social divisions, the distribution of power and therefore policy choices.

While pluralist theories are concerned centrally with questions of action (how various interest groups exercise power to create a state, its governance and its policies), structural models are more concerned – as the term implies – with questions of how power is related to the structures of the state, how it is channelled almost irrespective of human volition. Poulantzas (1969), for example, argues that both the state and social class were to be comprehended:

> as objective structures, and their relations as an objective system of regular connections; a structure and a system whose agents 'men' [sic] are in the words of

Marx 'bearers' of it – *träger* [whereas] Miliband constantly gives the impression that for him social classes or groups are in some way reducible to interpersonal relations... (Poulantzas, 1969: 70)

Poulantzas (1969: 73) argues that it is the state itself which:

determines the domination of one class over the others [and that] the participation, whether direct or indirect, of this class in government in no way changes things... If the function of the state in a determinate social formation and the interests of the dominant class coincide, it is by reason of the system itself. The direct participation of members of the ruling class in the state apparatus is not the cause, but the effect.

In his reply, Ralph Miliband (1969: 57) calls Poulantzas' position 'super-structural determinism', arguing that his:

exclusive stress on 'objective relations' suggests that what the state does is in every particular and at all times determined by these 'objective relations', in other words, that the structural constraints of the system are so absolutely compelling as to turn those who run the state into the merest functionaries and executants of policies imposed upon them by the system.

These two positions, although they exhibit stark disagreement, need not be irreconcilable. It is entirely possible to conceive that the nature of the state at any particular time is determined by the interplay between structures and human volition. We may envisage a continuing cycle in which the exercise of power by (temporarily) ascendant groups leads to the formation of certain social institutions and political structures, and these in turn influence and channel the subsequent exercise of power, for example through policy making, planning and implementation. Such a symbiosis allows for the dynamic evolution of relationships between the state and social classes or groups of people. This synthesis also reconciles forces for change (recognising the pivotal influence of individuals and groups), with the natural inertia of structure and custom (see for example Giddens, 1993, on action and structure, and Berger and Luckman, 1967, on the social construction of reality).

Clearly, then, structural and pluralist theoreticians disagree about the extent to which policy makers can exercise power to actualise their interests and affect the relative positions of various groups in society. This academic disagreement notwithstanding, the question is a crucial one because it is through the creation and application of policy that the circumstances of so many disabled people in our society are determined.

The task for the next section of the chapter, then, is to clarify the nature and process of policy making, and it is to that topic that I now turn.

What is policy?

The *Oxford English Dictionary* describes a policy as 'a course of action adopted by a government, party, ruler, statesman, and so on... any course of action adopted as advantageous or expedient'. Levin (1997: 15–18) detects four possible interpretations of the term. First, 'policy' may represent stated intentions, as set out, for example, in the manifestos of the political parties just prior to general elections. Second, the term may be used to refer to some current or past action; it may describe the principles guiding a government's work. In this sense, a term such as 'education policy' includes the accretion of previous decisions as well as those to be taken in the here and now. This account concurs with Heclo's (1972: 85) argument that 'a policy may be usefully considered as a *course of action or inaction* rather than specific decisions or actions' (italics added). Third, it may be used to denote organisational practice – how an organisation commonly responds to or treats some particular event or circumstance. This account squares with the views of Friend *et al.* (1974: 40), who see policy as 'essentially a *stance* which, once articulated, contributes to the context within which a succession of future decisions will be made'. Finally, Levin argues that 'policy' may be intended to indicate the formal or claimed status of a past, present or proposed course of action. Here, there is a sense of laying down principle and guidance for the future conduct of government and institutions in specific regards.

Levin (1997: 20–3) also provides us with a useful classification of the various sorts of purpose for which policies are developed. First, there are legislative measures that confer, remove or modify powers and entitlements. Second, policies are created to guide levels and purposes of public (that is, governmental) expenditure. Third, together with subsequent legislation, policies are used to create or remove organisations or structures, thus, for example, creating the Child Support Agency or disbanding the Greater London Council. Finally, policies control management activities such as making appointments or setting targets, for example through charters or codes of practice. As we have seen, however, the formulation of intentions and the working-up of proposals may be a less tangible process than the formal routes to law and practice I have just described.

Disability policies

Clearly, this book is concerned not with the universality of government action but with a specific area that I have chosen to call 'disability policies'. The use of this term is not without its difficulties. Unlike housing policy or social security policy, there is neither a single department of state nor any real tradition of policy making to which I can attach the label 'disability policy'. Before the Second World War and certainly before the twentieth century, disabled people were substantially hidden away from view, and the state either had nothing at all to say or made pragmatic dispositions for the institutional 'care' of disabled people, and this sufficed as policy. In the decades after the Second World War, several departments of state produced limited and, for the most part, unconnected measures (often in contexts other than disability), which affected disabled people's lives. In the post-Second World War period, we began to see a marshalling of policies towards disabled people under the social welfare banner, but it is only very recently that policy makers have begun to consider the need for coordinated legislation in response to disabled people's situations *as citizens*. For these reasons, it is difficult to establish boundaries of what does, and what does not, constitute disability policy. However, for a working definition, I have tried to consider those policies (and the resultant legislation) that have had an impact on the lives of disabled people, irrespective of the (departmental) origins of those policies. Kleinman and Piachaud (1993) define 'social policy' as government interventions that are designed to affect individual behaviour or command over resources, or are designed to influence the economic system so as to shape society in some way. The term 'disability policy' may share this same definition but with two qualifications. First, our interest lies in the impact of government policy on disabled individuals rather than the population at large. Second, we must consider how or whether the reshaping of society renders it more or less *disabling* in the lives of impaired individuals.

How is policy made?

Scholars hold different views about the creative processes through which policy comes into being. For some, such as Simon (1957), policy making is a reasoned process of decision making employed by informed actors in pursuit of rational ends. The process involves the enunciation of strategy and the following of logical steps towards a planned conclusion. Others, such as Lindblom (1959, 1977), would not deny the desirability of strategic planning for desired ends but believe that the reality of policy making is less tidy, comprising a series of incremental advances made through hard bargaining in a real world of competing players with differing objectives and varying degrees of power and influence. A good example of this sense that politicians command, at best, only partial control of events appears in the memoirs of Dennis Healey (1989: 570), who recorded his own experience of government in these words:

> Human behaviour is infinitely diverse and unpredictable. A politician can hope only to play some part in moving society broadly in the right direction: he must accept the inevitability of error and the need to change his course when things are going wrong.

Just as in theorising the state, we encountered doubt about the relationship between (and relative influence of) action and structure, there is similar uncertainty about the nature and degree of influence wielded by bureaucracy in the mechanics of policy making and implementation. Such uncertainty makes it difficult accurately to assess the impacts that policy decisions will have, particularly on planning processes, institutions and individuals.

There are at least three reasons for this uncertainty. First, since policies (and this is particularly true of disability policies) arise in different departments of state, and at different times, their objectives may be contradictory, so that in practice choices would have to be made between them. Second, notwithstanding the provision of policy guidance from the centre, planning and operational decisions are taken principally at local level, and this may lead to inconsistencies in application. Third, decisions involve a number of players with differing interests. MPs and local councillors have political as well as social imperatives to consider. Civil servants and other officials may take an approach related more to professional identity than to political expediency. The extent to which discretion is exercised may vary widely from authority to authority.

Adapting the work of Bramley *et al.* (1995), we may theorise policy making in four main ways. First, a 'welfare economics' account has been proposed by writers like Le Grand *et al.* (1992), Walker (1981) and Jenkins (1978). Here the rationale behind policy making stems from the outcome of a cost–benefit analysis. Such an analysis would produce a measurement of both the equity and efficiency of any particular policy direction, so the aim would be to maximise both these measures. Put simply, any economic and other advantages would be measured against any costs in bringing them to fruition. A decision would therefore be based on a view of whether the overall benefits outweighed the liabilities or vice versa.

A second model of the policy process accords with analyses by sociologists such as Dahl (1961) and Ham and Hill (1984), and economists like Laver (1979). This *pluralist politics* account assumes that policy implementation takes place within a decentralised, democratic system of government. Decisions are therefore taken by politicians who bear in mind the impact of such choices on their subsequent electoral chances. They may be especially sensitive to the views and wishes of voters in marginal constituencies. If there is a natural conservatism and wariness of innovation, the likelihood is that the natural political instinct is for resistance to change.

However, there will also be special circumstances in which a party's major supporters expect certain concessions (political favours) in return for their continued goodwill and funding contributions. This brings us neatly to a third theoretical standpoint proposed by Winkler (1977) and Middlemas (1979). Neo-Marxist in origin, this account stresses the power of élites who have privileged positions in the political process. If this theoretical model is correct, and certain groups exercise a predominant influence over policy planning, then these groups may wish to see development rather than the preservation of the *status quo*, in which circumstances the balance shifts away from inactivity towards change in some specified direction.

A final theory of policy formulation and implementation is the *bureaucratic* model. Rather cynical in tone, this model is based on the premise that policy is made and carried out in the interests of politicians and bureaucrats themselves. Tullock (1997: 87) argues that bureaucrats are ordinary people and as such:

> they will make most (if not all) their decisions in terms of what benefits them, not society as whole. [Like others] they may occasionally sacrifice their own well-being for the wider good, but we should expect this to be exceptional behaviour.

The constant aim of bureaucrats is the accretion of power. Accordingly, administrations seek to secure their own positions, increase their staffing, enhance their budgets and extend their sphere of influence. They are averse to taking too much risk and prefer to advance incrementally rather than in a revolutionary way. In this model, the desire for standard but complex operating procedures vies with the bureau-crats' desire to retain discretion for themselves in their decision making. Clearly, a strong regulatory framework gives bureaucrats hefty bargaining power, so the natural inclination of a planning process that reflects this model is towards the *status quo* except where change promises distinct advantages for the administration.

These different theories of the formulation and implementation of policy are capable of synthesis. All four accounts will be in play most of the time. Politicians will pursue their ends, bureaucrats will seek to protect their departments, powerful outsiders will look to apply leverage to bring about advantages in their own particular direction, but all will be aware that the (normally somnolent) populace can be roused if its interests are outraged. In reality, then, those who make policy decisions will often (albeit unconsciously) attempt to strike a balance of some sort between preservation and development, between cost and benefit, and (bearing in mind the relative strength of the competitors) between the various interests whose hats have been thrown into the ring. Whether policies are real or ersatz, whether they emerge out of rational planning or the uncertain processes of bargaining, or, as it were, 'by accident', the actual steps through which policies are devel-oped, and the legislative framework through which policies are intended to take effect in Britain, are relatively clear.

Policy development

In considering the mechanics of policy development, Hogwood and Gunn (1984) identify a number of stages or congruent activities in the creative process. These include:

- deciding to decide (agreeing that there is something about which a decision is needed);
- deciding how to decide (agreeing the method to be used in coming to a decision about the matter under consideration);
- defining the issues (agreeing what the issue is and the points on which decisions must be taken);
- forecasting (identifying what is to be achieved in relation to the issues, and identifying the possible range of outcomes);
- setting objectives and priorities (agreeing the actual aims to be pursued, and their relative importance, in relation to the matter under scrutiny);

- options analysis (agreeing the best way[s] to achieve the desired ends);
- policy implementation, monitoring and control (putting plans into operation);
- evaluation and review (ensuring that policy is making progress towards desired ends and adjusting policy in the light of changing circumstances);
- policy maintenance, succession and termination (keeping on course, deciding when and whether aims have been met, seeing whether something must be done next or whether a policy can be ended).

These stages are merely analytical tools rather than a representation of the actual practice of policy making, but they fit well with Easton's (1965) perspective that explains policy making processes using a biological analogy. Political systems, like living organisms, take in the 'raw material' of demands, information and support, and process these in order to produce policies, decision making and action. Hill (1997) reminds us, however, that the secrecy that surrounds government in Britain makes it difficult to assess the middle element of Easton's model: the actual workings of the mechanism that converts the inputs of support, pressure, demands, information and knowledge into the outputs of policy, institutions and practices. Policy models are all very well, but how in practice is social policy made in Britain, and by whom?

How is policy made in Britain, and who makes it?

At national level, policies are made manifest through law. The giving of royal assent to a bill, and the subsequent enforcement of the new act of parliament as law, comes at the end of a long and complex process that has both formal and informal components. In formal terms, perhaps the most usual route through which a statute is created begins with either a commissioned piece of research or inquiry, or the publication of a Green Paper, a document inviting discussion on a given topic about which the government of the day is considering the need for legislation. After considering responses to its proposals, a government then finalises its own intentions, published in a White Paper (usually put before parliament as a Command Paper) and introduces a bill containing specific measures intended to become law. The bill is discussed in both the House of Commons and the House of Lords, having three readings, a committee stage and a report stage in each

House. During this time, the bill is scrutinised (line by line, unless there is a guillotine motion) and amendments are made to it. Assuming a successful passage through the Houses of Parliament, the bill finally receives royal assent and passes into law as an act of parliament. I should note in passing that not all bills are introduced by the government of the day. There are also private members' bills, and these are introduced by back-benchers of the governing party and by opposition MPs who have been successful in a ballot for the right to put forward proposals. Without government support, however, such measures stand little chance of enactment.

Many acts permit ministers to make detailed regulations without further reference to the House, and these are called statutory instruments. Also, an act may allow ministers to set up bodies such as boards or commissions (quasi-governmental organisations or 'quangos'). Clearly, if a government enjoys a large majority in parliament it may, through these methods, give its ministers very large areas of discretion in which to act without requiring the consent of parliament as a whole. In doing so, however, a government may face charges of acting undemocratically and may antagonise the electorate on which, ultimately, it depends. The formal processes I have just described are, of course, not the whole story. All governments are subject to several competing pressures from beginning to end of the policy formulation process.

In the first place, the cabinet itself may be deeply split over an issue, and the line taken by the government may be one desired by practically none of the members, being the result of a compromise deal. Again, policy may represent the victory of one 'faction' over another, but it may therefore not enjoy the backing of the entire government. Second, a government's intentions may be modified in the light of the resistance (or approval) of members of the parliamentary party. Especially when its majority is slim, just a few rebels abstaining or voting with the opposition can be enough to scupper a government's plans. Again, when a government has a small majority, it may be 'ambushed' by the opposition parties who force through amendments or wrecking motions when they know that a number of MPs from the governing party are going to be away from Westminster and will not be able to vote. Outside parliament, a government has workers ('activists') up and down the land whom it would not wish to alienate, and it has influential backers and fund raisers without whose support it would be hard pressed at election time. Clearly, then, a government must take a realistic view about the impact of any legislation on its own key supporters.

Beyond their immediate supporters, governments are increasingly subject to pressure from career lobbyists who have been paid to put across the fears and desires of influential extra-parliamentary groups of various kinds. Lobbyists seek to point out the benefits of legislation conducive to their employers' views, and the detriments of proposed legislation that runs contrary to their interests. A different kind of persuasion (sometimes associated with moral standpoints) is exercised by pressure groups. Many of these are voluntary associations fighting on a single issue. They seek to convince governments that they should do the 'right' thing. But pressure also comes from the professional groups who work in the organisations through which policy and law are turned into practice: doctors, nurses, probation officers, teachers, local government staff and so on. These may be represented by staff associations or trade unions. Local authorities themselves are represented by bodies such as the Association of Metropolitan Authorities or the Association of District Councils, and these too have a direct interest in the work of central government. It is frequently the local authorities that must work to, and implement, the decisions taken at national level.

Beyond these direct approaches, politicians pay close attention (especially at election times) to less immediate but powerful influences such as 'public opinion', which is often filtered through the distorting lenses of the electronic media and the press. Indirect influence may also be expressed through opinion polls, demonstrations, petitions and marches. For example, although Mrs Thatcher's government had a large majority when the poll tax (community charge) was introduced, opinion polls showed support for the Conservatives ebbing away so dramatically that the tax had to be replaced with a new system, the council tax. The scope for government action may also be constrained by the feasibility of what it wishes to do. In recent years, economic pressures (as well as political dogma) have played a significant role in shaping governments' attitudes towards public spending and borrowing.

In addition to the several and diverse pressures within Britain, policy making is also subject to supranational influences. As a member of the European Union, NATO and the United Nations, and as a signatory to the Geneva Convention, a government's leeway to make policy may also be constrained by international law and obligations under various treaties and other agreements. Of these external constraints, the agreement by governments of the European Union reached at Maastricht, to ready their domestic economies for the possibility of a single currency before the end of the century, has brought significant burdens. The conditions that must be met, *the convergence criteria*, have placed tight restrictions on the freedom of government to fix the level of public spending as a proportion of the gross national product (GNP) and have constrained a government's ability to borrow money in order to fund public spending deficits.

Finally, a government's policies may be influenced by the administrative machinery itself: the civil service. The civil service commonly provides ministers with documents setting out a raft of policy options and a series of costings associated with the possible expenditure impacts of various proposals (these are known as *compliance cost assessments*). As in the case of the Disabled Persons (Civil Rights) Bill, these analyses can be vigorously contested by pressure groups and opposition parties, first, because the practice has been to assess the costs without taking into account any benefits that may offset expenditure, and second, because some of the figures are speculative rather than based on hard evidence.

In sum, the creation of policy can be a rumbustious process open to many influences and pressures. In his account of this subtle and intricate reality, Hill (1997), like Dennis Healey, adjures us to recognise that policy making can frequently be disorganised and disjointed, and it may be as much a response to events as a means of controlling them. Equally, the announcement of policy can, on occasion, have more to do with creating the appearance of endeavour than representing a genuine commitment to action. Similarly, policies may be firm, clear and comprehensive, or may be so shadowy as to be 'little more than an orientation' (p. 7). Accordingly, Hill argues that the student of public policy should 'be wary of taking policy makers too seriously' (p. 22). Nevertheless, we should recognise that, however imperfect the process, power has been exercised and policies have been formulated that have had a direct and fundamental impact on the lives of disabled people in Britain, as much to their detriment as to their advantage.

The process of policy making and disabled people

Whichever model of the state (pluralist, structural or bureaucratic) proves to be nearest the truth, it is evident that none of these accounts is particularly helpful to disabled people. Policy produced in a 'structuralist' state of the kind envisaged by Poulantzas both reinforces and reflects existing relations between powerful and powerless groups. Policies towards disabled people, as a marginalised group, are thus unlikely to enfranchise or liberate them. In a pluralist state, where policy is the product of competing interests and power blocs, disabled people, as a minority group, are likely to command only limited power, and their sway in the production of policy will, *ceteris paribus*, be relatively limited. Finally, the absence of disabled people from critical positions in the working mechanism of the state (the executive and the administration, both of which incline naturally to the *status quo*) will make it difficult for them to overcome bureaucratic inertia. I will discuss the impact of class and the lack of equality of opportunity in more detail in Chapter 7; however, the arguments I have set out here may usefully be borne in mind as, in Chapters 4 and 5, we observe and assess the development of disability policies in Britain over the past 150 years and the policy montage that prevails in the United Kingdom today.

The scope of policy making

I have discussed the concept of power and the creation of policy, but before moving on, it is important to consider one further aspect, namely the *scope* of policies. As we have seen, 'policy' may be the name given both to amorphous desires and to highly specific intentions. Policy makers may use a broad brush applied to a very large canvas or the finest *petit point* to embellish the most intricate cameo. Policies can thus take a very comprehensive view of a substantial range of issues or may be very closely defined in order to treat only a particular and, perhaps, specialised matter.

Where in any particular field the focus of policy is narrow and leads to highly specific legislation (such as the provision of a benefit to aid an individual's mobility, or relief for blind persons from payment of the television licence), the danger is that the outcomes in the field as a whole will be piecemeal. There will be both gaps and duplications, as well as laws contradictory in their effects. For example, in the area of social security, the general policy intention has long been that the state should support unemployed individuals and their families to prevent them from starvation, but not to be so generous that they have little incentive to find work. Historically, however, the implementation of the fragmented and poorly coordinated rules informed by this policy has led, perversely, to the creation of a poverty trap, in which the tapered withdrawal of benefit has been so steep that if claimants accepted work at the levels of pay commonly available to them, they would actually become worse off than they were on benefits.

Where narrow and specific approaches carry the danger of creating a patchwork quilt of policy initiatives, it would appear that broader policy objectives offer the possibility of more coherent, coordinated and comprehensive outcomes. However, the critical question here is: in what direction? As we will see in later chapters, there has been (and there continues to develop) a struggle between those who advocate the need for disability policies to promote 'care' and those who support the need for civil rights and the guarantee of citizenship. (While these may not be precisely opposing aims, there are certain incompatibilities of both ideology and practice.) Clearly, whether policies be general or specific, they may bring about different results according to the objectives that originally informed them.

Conclusion

In this chapter, I have argued that there is a close relationship between the way in which power is distributed, disability is defined and social values and norms are created. These processes have a fundamental impact on the subsequent articulation of disability policies and their consequences for disabled people. Hitherto, prevailing concepts of disability have owed much to medical understandings of the human being, and we cannot be surprised therefore that the history of disability policy in Britain has involved the differentiation, containment and treatment of disabled people within a medical context. However, other countries have adopted quite different approaches, and it is to the development of disability policies in Britain and elsewhere that I turn in Part II.

Disability Policy, Models and Development

PART II

Disability Policy, Models
and Development

3

Models of Disability Policy

Introduction

In the previous chapter, I suggested that disability policies are shaped by an exercise of power. I argued that dominant groups subscribe to particular norms, values and conceptual definitions, all of which they employ in the building of the policies that they desire to advance. The aims of these policies are, naturally, congruent with the beliefs and attitudes of their authors. Equally clearly, the specific goals of disability policies will hinge on the values of the governments who formulated them. Accordingly, the central questions for this chapter are: what kinds of disability policies may exist, and how are we to measure the impact of various kinds of policies on disabled people?

Governments formulate and implement policies, in part, to give concrete expression to their ideologies, values and beliefs, and each administration creates and promotes policies that resonate with its own particular understanding of 'disability'. It follows that the way in which a government conceives of disability has a profound effect on the eventual shape that a country's laws and institutions will take, as well as on the quality of life that disabled people can enjoy.

Some states place the notion of disability at the heart of a coherent legislative programme, but others subsume it under more tangential areas of legislation. The effect of the latter approach is to create a patchwork of laws that overlap in some places but leave significant gaps in others. Moreover, some administrations may not develop disability policies at all, leaving disabled people to make their own way in the world as best they can. In effect, then, we may visualise a spectrum of possibilities. At one extreme, policies are actually detrimental to the well-being of disabled people, while at the other, the rights of citizenship are guaranteed. In between, policies may seek to achieve some aims, for example the provision of health services, but leave out others, like ensuring access to public transport.

Only a policy model that secures equal rights and equality of opportunity for disabled people can affirm and secure their citizenship. Such an outcome hinges on not only the aims of disability policies, but also their coherence, their scope, the extent to which they are enforced, their capacity to bring about social and environmental change, and (through their implementation) the practical differences (if any) that they make to daily life. It may be helpful to list the spectrum of policy models considered in the chapter (starting with the least positive):

- *The negative policy model* is found in states that seek actively to deny the human and civil rights of disabled people.
- *The* laissez-faire *policy model* occurs where a state plays a minimal part in the lives of disabled people, or indeed in the lives of any citizens, who are therefore left to fend for themselves.
- *The piecemeal approach to policy making* describes a position in which the state makes some response to disablement but only in a reluctant and haphazard way, perhaps being provoked to action as a result of pressure and circumstance rather than through any desire to construct and implement a cogent and carefully planned strategy.
- *The maximal policy model* constitutes one such strategic approach. The state's purpose here is to identify and respond to the several disadvantages caused by disability. Because, even in this model, the state still sees disability as stemming from individual impairments rather than the configuration of society itself, the focus remains on the need for changes in the physiology of disabled individuals, and the response involves the construction and maintenance of a web of services aimed at the palliation and amelioration of individuals' conditions. Even services aimed at integrating disabled people begin by identifying and labelling them, *ipso facto* segregating them (conceptually if not spiritually) from society at large.
- *The social or rights-based policy model* is founded on principles entirely different from those of the individual basis so far highlighted. Here the state accepts that it has a responsibility to serve all its citizens and recognises that disablement is a product of a society and environment designed by non-disabled people for non-disabled people. As indicated above, the product of such an approach is the guarantee of citizenship, and in the latter part of this chapter, the concept of 'citizenship' is explored in some detail with an eye to its

use as a test of the merits of varying policy models in general and British disability policy in particular.

A spectrum of approaches to disability policy

I have said that the shape and purpose of policy will depend fundamentally on the values and understandings that governments and influential others have brought to bear during the 'manufacturing process'. In particular, these values and understandings will have a profound effect on the adoption of aims and objectives that subsequent policies are intended to achieve.

As we saw in the previous chapter, some definitions treat disability as the result of personal impairment, whereas others locate the causes of disability in the way society is organised. Which of the foregoing approaches ('negative' through to 'rights-based') any society might make will depend therefore first on the kind of definition of disability that prevails at any particular time, second on the nature of understanding of the problems faced by disabled people and the knowledge of what is required to set matters right, and third on the will and resources so to act. Accordingly, we may place flesh on the bones of the policy approaches outlined above in order to describe what governments have actually done or may do in future.

Negative policies: the deliberate annihilation of disabled people

That any state could contemplate the intentional and systematic destruction of its citizens, disabled or not, is a notion abhorrent to the civilised mind. Yet history is littered with such examples. The reader will see in Chapter 6 how the hegemony of German Nazism, its ideology of racial supremacy and the pseudo-science of eugenics led to just such a policy during the Second World War (Lifton, 1986).

Negative policies: the desire to eradicate physiological and cognitive disorders, thus minimising the numbers of children born with impairments

While the active destruction of disabled adults or children, promoted by state policy, is mercifully rare, other disquieting questions have emerged about the status of human fetuses. These questions have become increasingly germane with recent rapid advances in ultrasound scanning, amniocentesis, chorionic villus tests and other procedures formulated by genetic science. The abortion of fetuses has led not only to the passionate enunciation of starkly opposed views, but even to violence. For example, in the United States, anti-abortion activists gunned down medical staff in an attack on a gynaecology clinic (Katz and Bunting, 1993). Those against abortion, such as the Catholic Church, the Society for the Protection of the Unborn Child and British politicians like David Alton and the late Enoch Powell, broadly took the view that human life begins at conception, consequently, the deliberate termination of pregnancy amounts to murder. However, pro-abortionists argue that human life commences, if not at birth, then at some definable point at which the fetus is able to survive independently of the mother. Up to this point – the argument goes – the fetus is to be regarded not as a separate human being but as a part of a woman's own body, and she has the right to choose, the right to exercise 'autonomous control over reproduction' (Berer, 1988; Himmelweit, 1988). Seen from this point of view, abortion amounts to no more than a further method of contraception.

About 170 countries now allow abortions, and each state applies its own more or less restrictive criteria (Coward, 1994). The concern expressed by disabled people is that no matter how cautiously the rules may be drafted in any particular country, a commonly accepted ground for permitting an abortion is medical evidence indicating that a fetus has severe impairments. Beyond the fact itself (of termination of some fetuses solely on the basis of impairment), disabled people argue that such a stance has the consequential effect of devaluing disabled people as human beings. These issues are considered in greater detail in Chapter 8.

Policies aimed at ignoring or denying the existence of problems connected with disability

Beyond these forms of active intervention, some states have left disabled people to their own devices. In China, for example, which has some 10 million disabled people (of whom 4 million are children), physical impairments can often be life threatening. The danger arises less from the intrinsic nature of any particular condition than from the contingent response of the state. In June 1995, China passed a law banning marriages between couples where there was a risk of congenital deformity in their offspring (Rufford, 1995). Some 300 000

Chinese children are born each year with cognitive impairments, and those (especially girls) whose parents abandon them may be left to their fate, ending their lives in what Lightfoot (1995) has called the 'dying rooms' of state orphanages.

More broadly, a *laissez-faire* approach of this kind means that disabled people who have neither resources nor other avenues of support may compete unsuccessfully in a world designed *by* non-disabled people *for* non-disabled people. I return to the position of disabled people in China, and the *laissez-faire* model of policy making, in Chapter 6.

Policies intended to isolate disabled people (from society and from each other), for example through the use of institutions

Yet other societies have sought to isolate disabled people in colonies or institutions. In Britain, long-stay institutions and residential homes have historically been a prominent feature of the state's response to people with severe cognitive and physical impairments. To take just one example, in 1912 the Liberal government of Asquith and Lloyd George brought forward a Mental Deficiency Bill, which, had it been enacted, would have entailed the permanent detention of the 'insane and feeble-minded' in official establishments. The Bill enjoyed broad support from groups such as the Association for the Permanent Care of the Feeble-minded and church luminaries like the then Bishop of Exeter. However, the Bill was opposed by many influential and well-respected (Liberal) humanitarians, perhaps most notably the King Edward VII Professor of English Literature in the University of Cambridge, Sir Arthur Quiller-Couch (Brittain, 1947). The Bill was withdrawn just prior to its third reading. Nevertheless, institutions such as sheltered homes, long-stay wards, psychiatric hospitals and almshouses have loomed large in the lives of disabled people in Britain. Their impact has been to remove disabled people from mundane society and thus to accentuate the difficulties they have faced in seeking to regain their place in the everyday world.

Policies seeking to integrate disabled people but which offer a limited and piecemeal approach to supporting nominated individuals within specified services

Where states have recognised the undesirability and failure of the institutional approach, they have turned instead to policies aimed at integrating disabled people into society. We should note, however, that by 'society' is meant the social and physical environment constructed by and for an essentially non-disabled population. By accepting the medical model of disability, many Western countries have developed disability policies that classify and categorise people according to their impairments. They have then responded on an *ad hoc* basis by supplying specific services, aids or equipment intended to adapt (rehabilitate) disabled people to life in the community.

Policies based on hybrid solutions involving some environmental change and the provision of individual aids and adaptations

Most of those states which proceed on the assumption that there is a need for the kinds of intervention described above have usually also been willing to make some (often piecemeal and minor) changes in the urban environment. With this kind of approach, any response to disability is fragmentary. Typically therefore, measures are lodged in several different pieces of legislation arising from diverse orbits of governmental concern. As a result, policy coordination and implementation are made all the more difficult because several agencies, both statutory and voluntary, may have duties and responsibilities in similar or adjacent policy areas. There are inevitably both hiatuses and clashes of interest in this kind of system.

Policies conceived radically to change the contours of everyday life in order to open a society to all its citizens, including disabled people

In societies that perceive disability as an individual pathology, the response hitherto has been focused largely on specific medical conditions 'presented' by particular individuals. The aim has been to integrate ('empower') disabled people by reducing their differences or degree of deviance from the prevailing social norms. Behaviour modification, 'normalisation' programmes and other techniques have been employed by welfare professionals in attempts to effect changes in their clients. However, societies that have come to regard disability as a result of the configuration of society itself have responded by trying to provide an environment accessible to all and a unified and consistent set of laws to protect the rights of every citizen *irrespective of individual physiolog-*

ical or cognitive condition. These kinds of disability policy locate the need for change in society, rather than in the individual.

From the several examples I have just outlined, the reader may see that the stance adopted by any particular country will have a crucial impact on disabled people. Throughout the chapter, I have suggested that those differences may either enhance or diminish a person's citizenship. So before going any further, we need to be clear about what is meant by *citizenship*.

Citizenship

To be a citizen is to be able to take part in the decisions that create or re-create the contours of a society, and to be able to participate in key functions such as work, leisure, political debate, travel and religious observance. (I say 'be able to' because not all citizens wish to exercise their right to participate in all of these things.) The opposite of citizenship is social exclusion.

In line with this thinking, Barbalet (1988: 1) argues that citizenship is a concept that essentially defines 'those who are, and who are not, members of a common society'. In the contemporary Western democratic context, the status of citizen is predicated on the 'capacity to participate in the exercise of political power through the electoral process' and entails 'legal membership of a political community based on universal suffrage'. Furthermore, a political system of equal citizenship 'is really less than equal if it is part of a society divided by unequal conditions' (Barbalet, 1988: 1–2). This is because inequality of condition hinders the participation of some but provides privileged participation for others. In practice, even if not in theory, there is differential access to the exercise of power and to legal protections.

Marshall (1963) argues that inequalities arise not randomly but as a result of social and, in particular, class structures. Marshall (1950) therefore postulates *citizenship* as a counterweight to inequality and describes it as a multifaceted concept comprising three kinds of right: civil, political and social. Civil and political rights are needed to protect individual freedoms and to secure access to justice. They are also crucial if an individual is to participate in the exercise of power in the governance of his or her own community. Marshall's notion of social rights or 'social citizenship' responds to – indeed, directly attacks – the social inequalities that threaten civil and political citizenship. Marshall explained that by the 'social element' he meant:

the whole range from the right to a modicum of welfare and security to the right to share to the full in the social heritage and to live the life of a civilised being according to the standards prevailing in the society. The institutions most closely connected with it are the education system and the social services. (Marshall, 1950: 10–11)

However, the gaining of social citizenship necessarily involves social change, first because of the direct impact on the extent of inequality, and second (and more indirectly), because of the impact on access to the power or governance of society and its social structures.

We may readily see, then, how this kind of analysis can be applied to the position of disabled people in society and, in particular, to the social model of disability. To the extent that disabled people are unable to participate in the governance and conduct of society, changes are needed to remove the blockades that prevent that involvement. In other words, within any society, universal citizenship can only be acquired and fully sustained if there is an end to discrimination and a guarantee of integration. But the aim is not *sameness*, one approach to all persons irrespective of their personal circumstances. Instead, what is needed is a recognition of, and valuing of, differences between people. The equality sought is that of opportunity and of process, not necessarily of outcome. For Barton (1993: 18), a fundamental ground for the exclusion of disabled people has been 'the definition of their difference from others in mainly negative and offensive terms'.

Clearly, then, the most appropriate test to use in assessing the value of disability policies is to ask how far such policies extend (or perhaps restrict) disabled people's access to citizenship. Do policies, by recognising different requirements and conditions, result in environmental changes and social responses that allow disabled people to go where their fellow citizens go, do (subject to the constraints of impairment) what other citizens do and have the status that their non-disabled contemporaries enjoy? Notwithstanding physiological and cognitive differences, how far may disabled people participate in society on an equal footing, subject to no special, discriminatory rules or practices?

I mention the 'constraints of an impairment' and should perhaps point out what may be obvious: that each human being (disabled or otherwise) has physiological and cognitive limits. Only some of us can run as fast as Olympic athletes, play chess to Grand Master level or learn the whole of *Paradise Lost* by heart. The point, in terms of the foregoing discussion about citizenship, is the source of the incapacity. It is only legitimate if our inability stems from our own inherent limitations rather than from externally imposed restrictions. These may be occasioned by lack of equality of opportunity or as a result of prejudice against a group of citizens based on some perceived condition (such as being black, female or disabled).

In sum, the claim that disabled people are denied citizenship is a claim that they are subject to impediments beyond purely individual (cognitive or physiological) constraints, and that these obstacles are imposed through social inequalities that manifest themselves as discrimination. A main purpose in scrutinising disability policies is to discover whether they remove such discrimination, ignore it altogether or actually enhance it.

It will be important to bear in mind the consequences of the various policy models I have outlined above as, in future chapters, we analyse the development of disability legislation and evaluate the contemporary situation in Britain. The question of citizenship is also crucial in assessing the influence of disabled people over policy formulation, and it will be pivotal in Part III of the book when we assess the impacts and outcomes of policies on disabled people.

While legislation aimed at disabled people (or not aimed at them directly but nevertheless affecting them) holds an important place in determining the extent of their citizenship, so too do material conditions and prevailing political ideologies. High levels of unemployment and cuts in public expenditure on the one hand, and a competitive and individualistic culture on the other, may emphasise inequality and lend weight to discrimination. Some commentators have argued that the position of disabled people, far from having improved, has actually worsened in recent years (Barnes, 1991; Glendinning, 1991).

Finally, in this part of the chapter, it is important to contrast the notion of citizenship, which, as we have seen, concerns the way in which people have rights and can therefore exercise power, with the New Right's more recent elaboration of concepts such as the 'active citizen' and the 'consumer'. By equating citizens with consumers, their exercise of power is limited to a particular set of predefined choices or even merely to the expression of a preference. Consumerism has little to do with taking control. As in supermarkets, so in society at large, consumers may choose between nicely presented, individually wrapped packages of goods and services, but a commercial ethos prevails in questions of cost. No consumer is present in the boardroom where decisions are taken about what to put on the shelves (Winkler, 1987; Winward, 1990). Borsay (1990: 118) argues that, in any case, the consumer is not sovereign when need outruns supply because 'market sensitivity crumbles and "customers" have to accept whatever is available, irrespective of their expectations'.

The interpretation of citizenship will clearly differ according to the government and the model of policy that stands dominant at any given time. Where citizenship is used to mean 'choice', it may offer disabled people no more than different sorts of shackles. Piecemeal service provision decided by professionals in the light of their budgets may not give much, or even any, choice. Where citizenship is used to refer to circumstances of equal civil, political and social stature between the members of a community, it conveys a far more powerful sense in which disabled people have direct control of resources and legal powers sufficient to effect changes in their own lives and in the environment at large.

Using the concept of citizenship, then, it is possible to evaluate the various models of policy set out earlier in the chapter, and it becomes at once apparent that only policies formulated in accord with the final model (social and environmental change) are likely to bring about and protect citizenship. As one moves further and further away from this model, through maximal approaches to care, specific piecemeal responses, the adoption of a *laissez-faire* stance, and ultimately to negative policies, citizenship is enhanced less and less until, finally, it is actively denied by the state.

Conclusion

In this chapter, I have been concerned to set out basic models or approaches to the creation of disability policies and to offer a way of evaluating their outcomes. These models range from the direct exclusion of disabled people from society to attempts at specific forms of inclusion, through to the establishing of total integration, in which disabled people occupy a position equal in all respects to that of non-disabled people and in which they therefore enjoy the rights of citizenship and experience equality of opportunity. I have suggested that we can use these several approaches in order to comprehend the development of disability policy in Britain, and, furthermore, we can apply the tests of civil, political and social rights to determine the extent to which legislation establishes (or restricts) the citizenship of disabled people. It is thus, to the development of disability policy that I now turn.

4

The Development of Disability Policies in Britain

Introduction

This chapter paints the backcloth against which any evaluation of contemporary British disability policies must be set. In the previous chapter, I described several points along a spectrum ranging from extremely negative responses towards disabled people right through to the guaranteeing of their citizenship. In what follows, the reader will see that the British experience has consisted of a general trend, starting with policies intended to isolate disabled people from society and from each other, and moving gradually through a piecemeal service approach towards the 'foothills' of citizenship. The encapsulation of disability within a medical context is of critical importance here because such understandings have been paramount in the formulation and implementation of policy. From Victorian times through to the present day, policies have reflected four successive (but overlapping) kinds of objective, and medicine has provided the main context for the first three of these. The goals of policy have been:

- to effect the containment or segregation of disabled people;
- to provide redress for social exclusion, and especially to compensate disabled people for injuries received in war or at work;
- to provide welfare through social services, ostensibly as an attempt to reintegrate disabled people into society and also as an attempt to 'normalise' or control them;
- to secure rights and citizenship, and, where necessary, reconfigure the social and built environment.

The historical context

How came disabled people to be separated from the ordinary progress of everyday life? One of the most influential explanations has been advanced by Finkelstein (1981), who proposed that, prior to the industrial revolution, disabled people were readily accommodated within the pastoral life of feudal society. However, the advent of machines altered the nature of work itself. Apparatus used in large-scale production was designed for use by 'average' human beings, and physically impaired people thus found themselves progressively excluded from the workforce. Their expulsion resulted in the emergence of segregated institutions and asylums to deal with an emerging 'surplus' population. Given this analysis, it is unsurprising to find that an inventory of pre-1900 legislation shows containment to be a prime purpose.

Containment: a principal aim of Victorian legislation

The earliest rationale, which prevailed almost to the end of the Victorian era, was that of *containment*. A fundamental nineteenth century response to people with physical or cognitive impairments was either to ignore them or to incarcerate them in prisons, asylums and workhouses. The first chink in the wall came through the medium of education. Section 42 of the 1868 Poor Law (Amendment) Act allowed the guardians of any union or parish, with the approval of the Poor Law Board, to send any deaf and dumb or blind child to any school 'fitted for the reception of such child'. However, a Royal Commission on the Blind, Deaf and Dumb, set up in 1885, reported in 1889 that, notwithstanding this permission, there appeared to be an absence of system and compulsion: 'many children have grown up uneducated and the Guardians of the poor have been led too often to look upon such education as a charitable concession rather than a duty'. The Royal Commission made a number of recommendations: that aid from the rates should be used to enable blind adults to learn a trade; that blind men should be helped to acquire tools and raw materials to set up their own businesses (such a scheme already operated in Saxony); that, where necessary, their wages might be supplemented with grants; that, as their poverty did not arise from any fault of their own, 'the workhouse test should be relaxed and outdoor relief be given to them on a liberal scale'; that since there was no difficulty 'in teaching the blind reading, writing and arithmetic... there was no reason why they should not be taught in elementary schools up to a certain age'; and that there should be help for the parents with the costs of such education (*The Times*, 16 July 1889, p. 4).

Following the report of the Royal Commission, parliament passed the Education of Blind and Deaf-Mute Children (Scotland) Act 1890, and similar laws were established for England and Wales in 1893. Both measures enhanced educational opportunities for disabled children:

> If the parent of a blind or deaf-mute child between five and sixteen years of age is from poverty unable to pay for the education of such child... it shall be the duty of the school board of the parish or burgh... to provide out of the school fund... for the efficient elementary education of such child in reading, writing and arithmetic, and for his industrial training.

In 1899, schooling of this kind was extended further to include what were labelled 'defective and epileptic children'. For its time, then, the Royal Commission produced a remarkably humane response and signalled that motives other than containment had come into the reckoning. Chief among these were *philanthropy* and *compensation*.

As the end of the Victorian era approached, disabled people were dealt with in a variety of ways. Those who were itinerant continued to stand in peril of the vagrancy laws and committal to prison. Others, notwithstanding the Royal Commission's findings, continued to fall foul of the Poor Law and were forced to endure the workhouse. The more 'fortunate' received institutionalised philanthropy, as provided in the late 1890s by, for example, Grace Kimmins and her Guild of the Brave Poor Things, or by the Council for the Care of Crippled Children (Bourke, 1996). Finally, under the Idiots Act 1886, those with cognitive illnesses or impairments were crudely labelled 'idiots' (*incompos mentis fatuus et naturaliter idiota*) or 'criminally insane' (*incompos mentis prodigus et furiosus*) and were dealt with under that and several other Lunacy Acts. Between 1837 and 1901, there were no fewer than 26 measures dealing with insanity.

Other Victorian legislation related to disability only in tenuous ways. First, there were several public health acts that sought to improve sanitation and combat contagious diseases like cholera and polio. Second, laws such as the Chaff-cutting Machines (Accidents) Act of 1897 were brought in to regulate the use of dangerous machinery and thus reduce the number of injuries involving mutilation or death. Third, there were Workmen's Compensation Acts in 1897 and 1900 that made employers liable to compensate those of their workers who fell victim to industrial accidents. We may see, then, that until the end of the 1880s, laws concerning disabled people did little other than provide regulations for their incarceration. Even in the final decade of Victoria's reign, help was offered only in very limited contexts: injury at work, elementary education and philanthropy.

If there had been little recognition of disability, the same was not true of medicine *per se*. Surgeons had been granted a Crown charter as early as 1800, and apothecaries, effectively the precursors of GPs today, had their status and qualifications regularised in an Act of 1815 (Jones, 1955). Parliament gave powers to doctors very early on. For example, the County Asylums (Amendment) Act 1815 compelled:

> overseers of the poor to furnish returns of all lunatics and idiots within their parishes to the justices on request, *and to provide a medical certificate for each.* (Jones, 1955: 78, italics added)

By 1857, legislation, as a matter of course, required the medical certification of lunatics, and as the century proceeded, the influence of medicine extended into other domains such as public health, education and the regulation of industry, including the examination of employees wishing to claim compensation for injuries sustained at work.

Compensation is the key theme of the next section in this chapter, but before leaving the notion of containment, there is one further policy area that it is important to consider. Education policies have served to segregate disabled children from their non-disabled counterparts. As early as 1890, the Education of Blind and Deaf-Mute Children (Scotland) Act empowered local school boards to build schools for disabled children. A similar measure was passed for England and Wales in 1893, and by Education Acts of 1914 and 1918, 'mentally defective and epileptic' and 'physically defective' children were also consigned to segregated schooling. Thereafter, the separation of disabled and non-disabled children became a familiar feature of the educational landscape. The Education Act 1921 obliged parents 'to cause [their children] to receive effective elementary instruction... in a certified class or school suitable for the child'. Likewise, s. 57 of the Education Act 1944 conferred powers 'for classifying children suffering from a disability of mind as children unsuitable for education at school'. These powers remained in force until they were eventually repealed in 1970, and, as Lane (1981) records, the Education (Handicapped Children) Act of that year brought a shift of emphasis so that 'mentally handicapped children' (sic) were given the right to education, and health authorities were displaced as the prime service providers to children with 'special educational needs'.

Not until the Education Acts of 1981 and 1993 was the term 'mentally handicapped' replaced by the phrase 'learning difficulty' and some disabled children began to be educated in mainstream schools, but both measures continued to support the notion that there was a need for separate education for the rest, giving rise to a fierce debate about integration (see Chapter 5). It is in the crucial decision about which child is educated where that we may observe the pivotal role of the medical profession.

Compensation: the impact of work and war

The second key type of policy response has been *compensation* or *amelioration,* through the provision of either services or cash allowances. Here too, medicine has been instrumental in regulating access to disablement benefits. The Workmen's Compensation Acts 1897, 1900 and 1906 brought forward a new principle in the treatment of people who became disabled, in this instance by accidents at work. Concern had been growing for some years about the prevalence of industrial injuries, especially in coal mining and the building trade, and in 1907, a Building Accidents Committee (House of Commons, 1908) was set up to conduct an inquiry. Ultimately, the twin ideas of insurance and compensation came together in the National Insurance Act 1911, ground-breaking legislation that introduced a disablement benefit of 5 shillings (25 pence) per week for men and single women, and 3 shillings (15 pence) for married women, but only for those insured under the Act.

Nevertheless, the twentieth century began much as the Victorian age left off, and the advent of the Liberal government in 1906, an administration later renowned for its welfare reforms, initially did little for the promotion of disability legislation. Along with a rather modest Workmen's Compensation Act, there was one measure to reduce the cost of postage for literature for blind people and another to secure education to the age of 16 for disabled ('defective') children in Scotland.

It was with the outbreak of the First World War that the readiness to compensate became a common principle of disability legislation. By the end of the carnage, three-quarters of a million British soldiers were dead, and twice that number had been wounded or gassed (Taylor, 1965). From the French battlefields alone, there returned some 41000 amputees and 272000 men with other serious injuries, of whom a little over 60000 had sustained wounds to the head or eyes (Bourke, 1996).

Towards the close of the First World War, Lloyd George voiced the country's obligation to its fighting forces when he coined the slogan 'Homes fit for heroes'. Walter Long, then President of the Local Government Board declared:

> To let them [our heroes] come home from horrible, water-logged trenches to something little better than a pigsty here would, indeed, be criminal... and a nega-tion of all we have said during the war, that we can never repay those men for what they have done for us. (Quoted in Burnett, 1986: 219)

Between 1914 and 1920, there was legislation to provide war pensions, to compensate those injured, to help those who had been widowed or orphaned, to regulate charities for the wounded, to extend to blind persons over 50 years of age the pension paid to the elderly of 70 and over, and to help disabled ex-servicemen to find work, for example through the Disabled Men (Facilities for Employment) Act 1919. If we may leap ahead to the Second World War, it is possible to discern similar motives at work in the passing of the War Charities Act 1940, the Determination of Needs Act 1941 (which disregarded up to £375 of the war savings of blind people in determining their needs) and the Disabled Persons (Employment) Act 1944.

Bourke (1996) argues that, notwithstanding the recognition that compensation was an appropriate principle for policy, the war actually had a number of detrimental effects for disabled people. The war pension scheme was similar in form to that instituted by the Workmen's Compensation Act 1897 (Sainsbury, 1993). However, disabled civilians found themselves displaced by the priority given to disabled ex-soldiers in the search for work, accommodation and access to health services. According to whether an injury was sustained at work or at war, there was even differentiation in the quality of artifi-cial limb provided (aluminium, more costly than the traditional wooden peg-leg, usually being reserved for the military applicant). Second, divisive public attitudes took hold, to the effect that the war wounded were 'unnaturally abnormal' while disabled civilians were 'naturally abnormal'. Finally, Bourke argues that initial public sympathy soon turned to mean-spiritedness (and even antagonism) in the awarding of war pensions and other help – the shock of seeing so many crippled men soon wore off such that 'limblessness became normalized' – and the husbanding of state finances became yet more acute as the deep and chronic recession of the late 1920s and early 30s increased its grip.

During the interwar years, we may recognise several strands inter-woven in the fabric of disability legislation. First, the Victorian policy of segregation was represented not only in the lunatic asylums, but also in the new industry of orthopaedics. Watson (1930) reports the opening of new orthopaedic hospitals in many of Britain's major cities and the growth of a formidable army of surgeons, nurses and ancillary staff. Watson argued that, after the war ended, the obvious employment for these resources lay in the treatment and care of the civilian population of disabled people.

We may note, in passing, that medical jurisdiction over physical impairment was matched by new perspectives on cognitive conditions. The crude use of the word 'lunacy' gradually gave way to new medical terminology. Legislation now spoke of 'mental deficiency' and 'mental treatment'. Indeed, the Mental Treatment Act 1930 did away with the terms 'lunatic' and 'pauper lunatic' altogether. Interwar legislation also set out in great detail the medical and legal requirements for the committal of persons to mental hospitals. But this was not yet the era of community care, and institutions were still regarded as the prime loca-tion for the care of the 'insane'.

Second, the persistence of the principle of containment or segrega-tion was represented in the provision of 'special education' in certified schools for disabled children, as specified in the Education Acts 1918 (s. 20) and 1921 (ss. 51–69), and for disabled adults in the continuance of the Poor Law. Even as late as 1927, an Amendment Act set out regu-lations concerning the use of boarding houses for disabled people and the poor. However, we also see in the interwar years the perhaps grudging, but nonetheless irreversible, development and extension of compensatory legislation. National Health Insurance Acts were passed in 1920 and 1924, through which, *inter alia*, disability benefits were uprated. There were further extensions to industrial injury legislation in the Workmen's Compensation Acts of 1923 and 1925, and to Unem-ployment Insurance through Acts passed in 1924, 1934 and 1935.

Of all the groups to make headway at this time, perhaps the most successful were blind people. Why was it that this particular group seemed to attract more attention than those with other physiological impairments? In part, the answer may lie in the point I made earlier, that large numbers of men were blinded or visually impaired during the First World War, but there was another factor at play: lobbying by pres-sure groups. The National League of the Blind and Disabled (NLBD) pressed hard to secure legislation such as the Blind Persons Act 1920. In using the innovative idea of 'promotional welfare', the Act reduced the danger of penury by providing a pension to blind people of 50 years or older (Sainsbury, 1995). It also laid duties on local authorities to promote the welfare of blind persons and regulated the creation and workings of charities for blind people. (This more positive approach was later taken up in the National Assistance Act 1948 – see below.) Mike Barrett, former General Secretary of the NLBD, argued that the Act was important because:

> it was the forerunner... of making money available to assist disabled people. This was because local authorities and government then were able to make money available to sustain workshops and to provide workshops. So our aim was to campaign to get better conditions, wages and employment into the workshops during those early years. (Quoted in Campbell and Oliver, 1996: 40)

Other concessions were also gained and built on during the middle years of the century. The waiving of fees for various items was embodied in a number of statutes. Free or reduced-cost licences for wireless telegraphy equipment were secured through the 1926 Wireless Telegraphy (Blind Persons) Act and confirmed in the Wireless Telegraphy Acts of 1949 and 1955. As technology developed, blind people also gained exemption from the payment of purchase tax on radios ('wireless sets') through a clause in the Finance (No. 2) Act 1945. The 1959 Dog Licences Act exempted blind persons from payment.

The Blind Voters Act 1933 included the right to receive the assistance of a relative or friend in exercising the franchise, and later, blind and other disabled persons were allowed to vote by post (Elections and Jurors Act 1945, Representation of the People Act 1948, s. 8(1)c) or by proxy (Representation of the People Act 1983, ss. 21 and 34).

Finally, there were two measures passed in 1938. An Act applying only to Scotland empowered local authorities to 'make such arrangements as they think desirable' to assist in the prevention of blindness and, in particular, for the treatment of persons who were suffering from any disease of, or injury to, the eyes. Second, further lobbying by the NLBD was rewarded by the Blind Persons Act 1938, which reduced the qualifying age for the pension from 50 to 40 and made it the duty of every county or borough council to 'make arrangements for promoting the welfare of blind persons'. The measure specified the provision and maintenance of workshops, hostels and homes. The willingness of governments to provide certain reliefs to blind people, and the initiatives mentioned earlier in this section, are indicative of a broader, gradual but distinct shift in attitude in the years leading up to the Second World War.

In summary, then, we have seen that such disability legislation as existed before the turn of the century was devoted principally to the segregation and containment of disabled people. Primarily in response to mounting industrial injuries at home and the massive numbers wounded in the First World War, there emerged a new motivation, the obligation to compensate, and this was expressed in the form of pension payments, disability and sickness benefits, a growth in health services, and support for social welfare activities. An example of the latter may be found in the Local Government Act 1929, which permitted local authorities to make contributions from the rates to voluntary welfare associations. The growth in size and influence of the health profession, the tightening of regulations concerning the education of disabled children, the facilitation of at least some of the requirements of blind people and the imposition of duties on local authorities to supply certain kinds of services represent the first stirrings of a new approach to disabled people, one which coincided with, and was indeed intrinsic to, the flowering of the welfare state.

Welfare: the growth of social services and social security

As we have seen, the earliest measures relating to disability were intended first to contain and later to compensate. The gradual emergence of health and ancillary services, and the commensurate growth in influence of the staff engaged in such work, brought a new form of intervention in the lives of disabled people: health and welfare services. For Lowe (1993: 261) the project of social work was to:

> provide for extraordinary individual need; and [to be] concerned not with one specialised area of care but with their clients' overall welfare so that, as far as is possible, these clients can adapt to – or at least come to terms with – society at large.

Thane (1982) identifies the Second World War as a major catalyst in the development of health and social services. The war laid bare the inadequacies, and hastened the integration and improvement, of the country's health services. Post-war Britain also saw the growth of several new welfare professions. The first postgraduate generic course for social workers was set up at the London School of Economics in 1954 (Jones, 1991).

Clearly, then, in assessing disability legislation from the Second World War onwards, we may expect to encounter three, rather than just two, interwoven strands: first, the containment and segregation of disabled people certainly continued to happen; second, piecemeal compensatory measures gradually expanded and were woven into a more coherent system of social security; and third, there was a rapid growth and refinement of professional interventions in the lives of disabled people, often through services that were, in the main, isolated from the congress of everyday life. The overriding aim of welfare was to 'rehabilitate' or 'normalise' disabled people, and the new professions claimed that they had the expertise necessary for the job. How, then, were these developments reflected in, and supported by, disability policies of the time?

First, policies were devoted to rehabilitation. By instituting work quotas, training schemes and sheltered workshops, governments tried to make at least some of the disabled population 'employable'. Second, resources were made available through a system of benefits intended to offset the exclusion of disabled people from work and other aspects of social life. Third, policies sought to 'normalise' disabled people, either by altering their physiology through aids, adaptations or surgical interventions, or by putting in place specialised welfare services whose goal it was to adapt disabled individuals to the non-disabled world. Fourth, and to this same end, some (limited) attempts were made to ameliorate environmental difficulties through the use of specific changes and concessions. Let us examine in turn each of these four welfare-orientated approaches: rehabilitation for work; resource provision; the growth of services, aids and adaptations; and the making of minor environmental adjustments.

Rehabilitation

In December 1941, Ernest Bevin set up the interdepartmental Tomlinson Committee on the Rehabilitation and Resettlement of the Disabled. The committee's report was published in 1943 (Cmd 6415) and its proposals provided the framework for the Disabled Persons (Employment) Act 1944 (Thane, 1982). Although owing much to Bevin's initiative, we should note that the Act was passed by a coalition government with a Conservative majority in the House of Commons and that the legislation was backed by all three major political parties (Jones, 1991).

The Act defined a disabled person as 'a person who (on account of injury, disease or congenital deformity), was substantially handicapped in obtaining or keeping employment'. A number of innovative measures were set in train, including the introduction of vocational courses and industrial rehabilitation programmes. At the same time, a register of disabled people was created. The intention was that companies with more than 20 staff had to employ a quota of those on the register. In theory, 3 per cent of the workforce of each qualifying employer was to be made up of registered disabled persons. In the event, however, the quota scheme was widely ignored. About 80 per cent of firms failed to meet their obligations, and exemption permits were granted in huge numbers. Only ten prosecutions were ever brought, none of these within the past 20 years. Government departments were among the worst offenders. In March 1994, the Department of Health employed a mere 68 disabled people, 1.4 per cent of its staff (*Hansard*, 15th March 1994, col. 564), which was similar to the rate for the civil service as a whole (*Hansard*, 11th March 1994, col. 564) The quota was eventually abolished in the Disability Discrimination Act 1995 (s. 61(7)c).

The Act also allowed for the introduction of regulations by which certain jobs could be reserved solely for disabled people, but these tended to be relatively ill-paid occupations such as lift monitor or car park attendant. Together with an amendment Act in 1958, the legislation allowed for the setting up of special sheltered workshops and companies such as Remploy (Blakemore and Drake, 1996).

Resources and financial support

For those who could get no work, the emerging system of state support continued to evolve and accrete new pensions and benefits along the way. Financial support took two forms. First, money was supplied through disablement benefits, which were uprated from time to time. Second, disabled people were allowed certain reliefs. For example, the Pensions and Determination of Needs Act 1943 allowed the first £400 of a blind person's savings to be disregarded for the purpose of calculating the value of his or her capital assets. Again, the National Insurance (Industrial Injuries) Act 1946 permitted the minister to:

> make arrangements to secure the provision and maintenance, free of charge or at a reduced charge, of equipment and appliances for any person who, by reason of the loss of a limb or otherwise, is in need of them as a result of injury or disease

against which he was insured under this Act. (National Insurance (Industrial Injuries) Act 1946, ch. 62, s. 75)

The tradition of compensation for work-related injuries continued, represented, for example, in the Industrial Diseases (Benefit) Act 1954 and the National Insurance (Industrial Injuries) Act 1965. The latter specified conditions for the payment of supplements to disablement pension where there was special hardship, where the victim required constant attention or where the applicant had been rendered 'unemployable' as a result of 'loss of faculty' such that the beneficiary was 'incapable of work and likely to remain permanently so incapable' (ch. 52, s. 13(1)).

But what of those disabled people who had not been injured at work, or indeed who had never been in work, and could therefore count on neither insurance cover nor personal savings? The problem was recognised by William Beveridge (1942) in his report *Social Insurance and Allied Services*. Beveridge argued that a system of social security should meet needs caused by disability, which he defined as 'the inability of a person of working age, through illness or accident, to pursue gainful employment'. To support those who may not have contributed to national insurance, Beveridge proposed the creation of means-tested social assistance. His scheme, embodied in the National Assistance Act 1948, thus established a 'safety net' for those not covered under the contributory arrangements. Initially, some 144 000 disabled people received National Assistance, and by 1965 the figure had doubled (Lowe, 1993).

By the 1970s, we begin to see a proliferation (and fragmentation) of the forms of support. The National Insurance Act 1971 and Social Security Acts of 1973, 1975 and 1977 set out regulations governing invalidity benefit, sickness benefit, attendance allowance, industrial injury benefit, non-contributory invalidity pension, invalid care allowance and mobility allowance. Access to these funds was controlled first by careful definition of the criteria for eligibility, and second, by the use of medical tests on individual applicants to determine their entitlement.

Notwithstanding their diversity, the actual levels of benefit have never been generous, seldom exceeding 20 per cent of the average male wage. Even so, by the 1980s, social security in general was under a Thatcherite cloud, and changes were aimed more at the constraint, rather than the enhancement, of benefits. For example, the Social Security Act 1986 replaced single payments for particular needs or items of equipment with the (cash-limited) social fund. As a result, once a local social security office had spent its allocation under the fund, no grant or loan could be made irrespective of the urgency or severity of the claimant's need.

As the economic and political environment militated increasingly against social security, access to jobs became all the more important, and in 1988 a report by the Social Security Advisory Committee adjured the government to adopt a new strategic direction in relation to disabled people, one which responded positively rather than punitively to their obtaining paid work (Social Security Advisory Committee, 1988). The resulting White Paper (Department of Social Security, 1990) recognised that disabled people encountered fewer opportunities to work and reduced levels of earning at work, and agreed that the framework for disability benefits should be revised. Accordingly, the following year, the disability living allowance (DLA) and disability working allowance (DWA) were introduced. The DLA included a 'care' component and a 'mobility' component.

However, while disabled people were allowed to do more paid work (if they could get it) without affecting their benefits, initial access to benefits was tightened up. The Social Security (Incapacity for Work) Act 1994 replaced sickness and invalidity benefits with a new 'incapacity benefit', the criteria for which were rather more stringent than what had gone before. The government argued that, notwithstanding improvements in health, expenditure on incapacity had been rising year on year, and this could only be due to:

> the incorrect application of entitlement criteria or absenteeism from work and fraud. One particular criticism was that the test [for incapacity]... had only to relate to work which the claimant could reasonably be expected to undertake. This, it was claimed, meant that too much concern was being directed to non-medical criteria. (Cooper and Vernon, 1996: 169)

In the immediate past, then, innovations like the social fund and incapacity benefit have tended to weaken rather than enhance the availability of resources to disabled people.

The growth and professionalisation of 'welfare'

To recapitulate, governments sought to sustain disabled people first through rehabilitation using vocational training, sheltered workshops and other disablement resettlement services, and second, through the evolution of social security. The third main welfare-orientated focus for disability policies was the creation and growth of social services. Social work in the Victorian age had been philanthropic in nature. Individuals like Octavia Hill and C.S. Loch supplied accommodation, alms and 'moral guidance' to the poor, and charitable efforts were coordinated through the Charity Organisation Society, founded in 1869 (Fraser, 1984). But state sponsored social work is a much more recent innovation. Section 29 of the National Assistance Act 1948 gave local authorities:

> power to make arrangements for promoting the welfare of persons... who are blind, deaf or dumb, and other persons who are substantially and permanently handicapped by illness, injury or congenital deformity or such other disabilities as may be prescribed by the Minister.

From somewhat fragmented beginnings, social work developed rapidly in the 1950s and 60s. In the immediate post-war period, child care officers, probation officers and medical and psychiatric social workers received different training and had separate roles in separate service structures (Younghusband, 1947, 1951). Just as the philanthropists had sought to bring about changes in the behaviour and circumstances of individuals, so too the Report of the Working Party on Social Workers (Ministry of Health, 1959, paras. 22 and 23) declared the aim of social work to be:

> to help individuals or families with various problems, and to overcome or lessen these so that they may achieve a better personal, family, or social adjustment... The aim of social workers... is to assist individuals or families with a specific need, a disability or a misfortune.

The report proposed a major expansion in social work and recommended its professionalisation through the creation of a National Institute of Social Work and a new qualification, the National Certificate in Social Work. These proposals were given life in the Health Visitors' and Social Workers' Training Act 1962. It was on the recommendation of the Seebohm Report (1968) that unified social services departments were created under the leadership of directors of social services. Seebohm shared with the working party of 1959 an understanding of disablement as a quality inherent in individuals. For example, although 'many people with major physical handicaps cope well with life... [others] quietly retreat under the burden, defeated and depressed' (Seebohm, 1968, para. 316). Key recommendations of the report – to unify the personal social services and to establish local authority social services committees – were put into effect by the Local Authority Social Services Act 1970 (Younghusband, 1978).

We may see just how quickly social services activities grew by comparing the latest figures for social services staff with the numbers employed at the time of Seebohm (1968) and the earlier position in 1959. The Working Party Report of 1959 recorded the total number of social welfare staff in England, Scotland and Wales at 7828. Although not using precisely the same categories, Seebohm estimated the total number at 113 417, the major expansion being in home helps (from 952 to 30 244) and the staff of residential homes (from 672 to 31 970). By 1995, the whole-time equivalent staffing of social services departments (in England alone) had reached 233 862. Of these, 27 636 specialised in services to 'under-65s with physical disabilities and adults with learning disabilities' (Department of Health, 1996, Table 6.23).

The growth of social services was in part due to the policy of community care, which inevitably placed more emphasis on services such as home helps, home laundry and meals on wheels. But even during the period of fastest growth, dark clouds were already on the horizon for social work. The main pressures came from a worsening economy and a new political dogma, and from disabled people themselves. The fragile economic situation of the 1970s and early 80s ultimately meant that social services departments struggled to provide the community services expected of them. In any case, Margaret Thatcher was determined to bring market principles (and market operators) into the provision of welfare. For example, the Health and Social Services and Social Security Adjudications Act 1983 (Part VII) introduced the principle of charges for local authority services. Second, the Griffiths Report (1988), the Government's own White Paper (Department of Health, 1990) and the subsequent National Health Service and Community Care Act 1990 cleared the way for private sector and voluntary organisations to bid for contracts to supply services that had previously fallen within the mainstream of state responsibility (Gutch, 1989; Kunz *et al.*, 1989; Anderson, 1990).

The result was that social services underwent a purchaser/provider split. The guidance that followed (Department of Health, 1991) gave social services care managers the responsibility of commissioning services on behalf of their clients but within a predefined overall budget. This limitation was important on a number of counts. First, the holder of the purse strings was still the welfare professional rather than the disabled person him- or herself. Second, an insufficiency of funds compelled managers to ration help, even if the need for it had been established through assessment procedures. In a test case in 1997, the Law Lords decided that Gloucestershire Social Services was not compelled to provide services if it could not command the necessary resources (Brindle, 1997; Cooper, 1997a). However, Morris (1997) argues that authorities still have duties to clients if the withdrawal of services would result in an unacceptable quality of life or severe physical risk. Third, insufficient funds precipitated a failure to develop the necessary community support, particularly for people with cognitive impairments, and led to a very small number of high-profile cases involving attacks on members of the public. One consequence of these incidents has been renewed calls to reverse the thrust towards community care envisaged in the 1959 and 1983 Mental Health Acts, and agencies such as SANE have lobbied for an increase in the number of beds in psychiatric institutions and a tightening of supervision through the Mental Health (Patients in the Community) Act 1995 (Bowcott, 1996). Finally, the very notion of social work has been criticised by some disabled people who regard social welfare as an oppressive rather than liberating concept (see the section below on citizenship and rights, and Chapter 11).

Sainsbury (1995) argues that three factors are important in understanding the relationship between personal social services and disabled people that has developed since 1945: first, the fact that local services have always been constrained by the vagaries of centralised policy making; second, that these services have been accorded a weaker position than other demands on resources; and third, that there has been a continual battle over the definition of disability and therefore over the focus and purpose of intervention. In the history of disability policy and practice, whether aimed at containment, compensation or social welfare, the medical or personal tragedy model has clearly had the upper hand. In the fourth and final section of the chapter, however, we may glimpse the seeds of change.

Ad hoc *environmental adjustments*

As we have seen, the focus of both welfare policy and welfare professionals has overwhelmingly remained fixed on disabled individuals. It is difficult to pinpoint the first time that an official document mooted interventions to change or adapt the environment rather than the individual; however, as early as 1951, the Ministry of Health issued a circular (Ministry of Health, 1951) that adjured local authorities to assist wheelchairs users who wished to travel and, in particular, wanted to gain access to churches and leisure facilities. Equally, the Public Service Vehicles (Travel Concessions) Act 1955 (s. 2 (d) and (e)) permitted local authorities to grant concessions to blind persons and 'persons suffering from any disability or injury which, in the opinion of the local authority, seriously impairs their ability to walk'.

Although these initiatives were little more than sporadic attempts at encouraging local authorities to respond, they did constitute some form of acknowledgement that the configuration of the built environment might of itself *disable* people. The Chronically Sick and Disabled Persons Act 1970, and a related Amendment Act 1976, took further modest steps to render the non-disabled world more accessible. Under the 1970 Act, local authorities were required to discover the numbers and needs of disabled persons in their areas and to publish information about whatever services were available. Local authorities were empowered to assist disabled people through practical help in the home, including structural modifications, the delivery of meals and the provision of radio, television and telephone equipment. Help could also be given with recreation, travel and the arranging of holidays. The Act also charged housing authorities to have regard to the special needs of disabled people (ss. 3, 4 and 5) and ordained that buildings open to the public had to make provision 'so far as it is in the circumstances both practicable and reasonable' for disabled people's access to parking, their entry to such buildings and their use of toilets and public conveniences. Similarly, the legislation adjured better access to schools and universities (s. 8), and s. 21 introduced the orange badge scheme that gave disabled people certain privileges for car parking. Although the Act was iconoclastic in its intent, the actual wording was weak, and this limited the amount that could actually be achieved in terms of environmental change (Barnes, 1991).

Further help with travel and transport came in the Social Security (Misc. Provisions) Act 1977, which set out conditions for the payment of mobility allowances, and with the Disabled Persons Act 1981, which imposed on local authorities and others a duty to have regard to the needs of disabled people when undertaking road repairs or other highway work. So, for example, care had to be taken in the siting of lamp-posts, bollards and traffic signs. Further duties were also imposed on those modifying buildings, and entrances to buildings and local authority planning departments had a specific duty to draw attention to the British Standards Institute *Code of Practice for Access for the Disabled to Buildings* (BS5810, 1979).

To recap, the 25 years between 1951 and 1976 saw gradual changes in the law designed to effect particular kinds of environmental change. These fragmentary moves were an acknowledgement that causes of disability might be found outside the individual and his or her impairment.

In part, as a recognition of such material disadvantages, the Housing (Homeless Persons) Act 1977 placed a duty on housing authorities to provide accommodation to homeless disabled people. However, the obligation was later diluted by the Housing Act 1996, which altered the meaning of 'in priority need'. These (albeit limited) environmental adjustments are the policy initiatives that come closest to the aims expressed by disabled people themselves in recent times. However, as we shall see in the next section of the chapter, their concern has been far broader than merely gaining a stake in the design and management of services and the built environment.

Citizenship: the search for rights

In the foregoing three main sections, I have described the overriding principles that have governed disability policies since Victorian times. These were: containment, compensation and the growth of 'welfare' in its various guises. We have seen distinct (but overlapping) approaches to the 'problem' of disabled people: their segregation; the provision of private alms and state benefits to compensate them for exclusion from work; and the imposition of physical and other interventions with the aim of 'rehabilitating' and 'normalising' them. Changes to popular attitudes, and to the social and built environments on the other hand, have been comparatively scanty. What is clear about all three of the approaches so far is that change has been located in the lives of disabled people rather than in the contours of society. My history of disability policy, set out in the foregoing pages, has come pretty well up to date. There is, however, one further, new and important influence on disability policy that has to be considered, one so radical that it has the potential totally to alter the nature of disability policies in the future. Disabled people themselves have found their voice and have laid down a challenge to the received understandings on which policies have hitherto been based. But has any legislation yet responded to their call for rights and citizenship?

We may detect some gradual movement towards disabled people's aspirations. Before leaving office in 1979, the Labour government, under pressure from disabled people's groups, set up the Committee on

Restrictions Against Disabled People (CORAD). The Committee's report, published in 1982, found discrimination to be commonplace and catalogued the lack of access and rights across a range of public institutions. However, the new Conservative government essentially dismissed the report's findings.

The Disabled Persons (Services, Consultation and Representation) Act 1986 did little more than acknowledge that disabled people should be consulted about the services intended to help them. But citizenship required resources, and disabled people lacked work and therefore wages. During the 1970s, they had campaigned hard for a disability income: only this would allow them the normal range of choices available to others. In the event, the fight for a disability income was unsuccessful. Ken and Maggie Davis attribute the failure of the Disability Income Campaign to its falling into the hands of non-disabled lobbyists and failing to gain massive grass-roots support from disabled people themselves (see Campbell and Oliver, 1996: 63), and apart from social security benefits, resources had remained in the hands of the professionals. However, two pieces of legislation were passed in the early 1990s, the Disability Living Allowance and Disability Working Allowance Act 1991 and the 1993 Disability Grants Act, which established the Independent Living Fund, monies payable directly to disabled people themselves rather than through the intermediary filter of service providers.

Other influences have supported pressures for a civil rights approach to disability policy. From the United States came the example of the Americans with Disabilities Act (see Chapter 5), and in the UK in 1994 a private member's bill was introduced – the Civil Rights (Disabled Persons) Bill – which would have created legislation fundamentally to shift the focus of change away from the individual to the social. However, the Government's Disability Discrimination Act 1995 was a pale shadow of the opposition's proposed civil rights measure. Its lack of teeth was demonstrated by the BBC programme *From the Edge* broadcast on the 14th April 1998, which revealed that only 10 out of the 850 disabled applicants were successful in industrial tribunal cases brought under the Act, and only 40 cases have so far been brought regarding goods and services. Indeed, Dobson (1996: 21) argues that some may be worse off than before the advent of the Disability Discrimination Act:

> In what appears to be a singularly ironic twist of fate it looks as if the Disability Discrimination Act will be used as a licence to bar deaf-blind people from jobs

and services... the government's definition of 'reasonableness' as to what
employers should provide for disabled workers is unreasonable to deaf-blind
people.

Where disabled people are prevented from gaining the rights and
resources necessary for full participation in society, the impacts will
affect not only them, but there will also be a knock-on effect on their
relatives and friends, whose support helps to overcome the obstacles in
the social and built environments. As much was acknowledged in the
passing of the Carers (Recognition and Services) Act 1995. The Act
provides carers with the right not to services *per se* but to a 'community care assessment' at the same time as a disabled person's needs are
being assessed. The new law requires that carers' views and their
ability to cope should be taken into account, but for Clements (1996),
the Act is open to criticism for being very limited in scope, for having
terms whose definitions will be the cause of dispute and for having no
additional resources available for implementation.

Although the Disability Discrimination Act was disappointingly
weak, it was important for signalling the headway made by supporters
of the social model of disability and indicated that legislators were
prepared to accept that the lives of disabled people might be affected by
the social and physical environment as well as by cognitive or physiological impairments. The Labour Party manifesto for the 1997 general
election promised disabled people a Disability Rights Commission
comparable to those bodies safeguarding the rights of women and
ethnic minorities, and the promise was repeated in a Department for
Education and Employment press release in October 1997 (304/97).
However, a month later, rumours surfaced that Labour planned to curb
the benefits of at least some disabled people (Bevins, 1997), and as I
write the specific intentions of the government remain unclear. Indeed,
there are pressures antagonistic to the securing of rights for disabled
people. For some opponents, even quite modest proposals aimed at
altering the built environment are claimed to be unacceptably costly
and to smack of 'political correctness' (Harris, 1995). Indeed, the
holders of such opinions were instrumental in defeating the Civil
Rights (Disabled Persons) Bill. We should therefore explore briefly the
views of those antithetical towards disability policies, the origins of
their objections and the credibility of their arguments.

Opponents of disability rights legislation have enunciated three main
kinds of disagreement. First, they have proved reluctant to relinquish a
traditional philanthropic stance and have refused to accept the idea of

disability as a political issue. Second, they have voiced straightforward financial objections, believing that any proposed legislation would cost British industry so much as to render it uncompetitive in the cut-throat markets of the global economy. Third, as part and parcel of a broader antipathy towards interest groups and lobbyists, they have argued that such pressure as has been exerted stems from a vociferous minority who are unrepresentative of the majority of disabled people. In seeking to refute these opinions, disabled activists point out that while impairments may be apolitical, the availability of services and resources, and the general configuration of the built environment, all hang on political decisions made by governments of the day.

Nor are the economic arguments as clear cut as they may first appear. The government's own compliance cost assessment (Department of Health and Social Security, 1994) estimated that implementing the comprehensive civil rights legislation envisaged in Dr Berry's Civil Rights (Disabled Persons) Bill, might require as much as £17 billion in (non-recurring) capital expenditure and a further £1 billion per annum in revenue costs. However, the Rights Now organisation argued that the assessment contained serious flaws and maintained that the cost of implementing the Bill could be some £12 billion less than the official estimates (Rights Now, 1994a). The group also calculated substantial cost benefits (between £2.25 and £5 billion per annum) accruing where disabled people found work and ended their dependence on social security payments (Rights Now, 1994b). Further evidence came from Scott (1994), who demonstrated that the rights-based legislation on which the Berry Bill was modelled, the Americans with Disabilities Act, led to minimal extra costs on American businesses and actually resulted in the opening up of several new market opportunities for those providing goods and services to disabled consumers. Economic worries are therefore, at best, not proven.

As to the third point, that disabled pressure groups are unrepresentative, Campbell and Oliver (1996) reveal that the British Council of Organisations of Disabled People has grown to 108 member groups, with over 400000 disabled members. However, when challenged to name even one group of disabled people that she had consulted on the Civil Rights Bill, one of its chief opponents, Lady Olga Maitland, was unable or unwilling to do so (*Hansard*, 6th May, 1994: cols. 966–7).

The antagonism towards rights-based legislation may be founded primarily in economic considerations, but it also has much to do with broader fears about changes in social relations. In the meantime, however, given their lack of authority and access to positions of power, disabled people face an uphill struggle in many different walks of life. In particular, the political exclusion of disabled people has been catalogued by Fry (1987), who recorded the lower rate of participation by disabled people at general elections, and by Barnes (1991), who documented the absence of disabled people from positions of authority in central and local government.

Blackaby *et al.* (1998) have identified two principal difficulties for disabled people seeking work: first, the initial search for employment itself, and second, the lower earnings compared with those of non-disabled counterparts. Such arguments are confirmed by Barnes (1991), who adds a third element: overt discrimination by employers against disabled people. Martin *et al.* (1989) have discovered that under a third of the two million disabled people in Britain have paid work.

Morris (1988, 1990) has described a broad range of disadvantages faced by disabled people with respect to housing. Between 1980 and 1986, homelessness among physically disabled people almost doubled. Those who have homes are more likely than their non-disabled counterparts to live in poor housing, and few housing authorities have either any clear policy on the adaptation of dwellings or any records concerning the specific requirements of disabled people on their waiting lists. Furthermore, disabled people also experienced detrimental effects because of the Housing Act 1980 (the 'Right to Buy' Act), under which councils were compelled to sell off stock to sitting tenants who wanted to buy their homes. Housing designed for the use of people with 'special needs' was exempt, so by keeping such stock, disabled people found themselves increasingly isolated, excluded from the housing market and unable to benefit from the windfall that other citizens had enjoyed. This differential treatment exacerbated a process that Forrest and Murie (1991) called 'social polarisation'.

Finally, even many of the traditional charities who purport to empower disabled people actually exclude them from committees of management, strategic planning teams and employment as staff (Drake, 1994, 1996b). There is, then, no shortage of examples to show that the current mix of welfare and charity fails to ensure the citizenship of disabled people, not only at the personal level, but also as a section of the population in its own right. The purpose here is simply to emphasise the range and seriousness of the problems that disabled people face and the extent to which they are excluded from prestigious occupations and powerful social institutions. It is not too much to claim that disabled people experience inequality and disadvantage across the board.

Conclusion

Disability policy in Britain has expressed several objectives: the desire to contain, to compensate, to 'care' and, latterly, to achieve citizenship. As we shall see in the next two chapters, this succession of differing motives, aims and purposes has led to a contemporary position in which a patchwork of influences is at play. Different groups, politicians, professional welfare workers, voluntary agencies and disabled people themselves subscribe to differing definitions and principles, and vie for different kinds of disability policy in pursuit of differing purposes. The next chapter reviews the implementation of contemporary British policies at the institutional level, and Chapter 6 then makes a comparative assessment of the contemporary British experience with policy models prevailing elsewhere in the world.

5

Contemporary Disability Policies in Britain

Introduction

In the previous chapter, I argued that different kinds of motive and objective have been at play in the development of disability policies since the Victorian era. The task here is to provide an analysis of policies in Britain today. The four principal approaches towards disabled people that I outlined (containment, compensation, 'welfare' and civil rights) are all present to varying degrees in the contemporary policy montage. This chapter concentrates on evaluating a number of key policy areas:

- health and social services;
- voluntary organisations and charities;
- income maintenance and social security;
- housing;
- education;
- employment;
- transport;
- law and access to justice;
- government and administration.

My first task is to assess the influence of policy over the creation and operation of social institutions, and then to discover how policies are mediated by these organisations. In other words, how are policies inter-
d by the very institutions used to implement them, and what kinds
they produce?

Contemporary disability policies and social institutions

The statutory health and social services

We have seen how, traditionally, in Britain, 'disability' has fallen within the ambit of medicine, and authorities have, to a large extent, focused their interventions in the lives of disabled people through health authorities, social services, 'special needs' housing provision, education and social security policies.

Major policy programmes have been channelled particularly through the health and social services. Although these organs do deliver domestic services (for example, 'home helps'), their main thrust historically has been to develop an increasingly diverse range of segregated projects such as day centres, social clubs, residential homes, workshops and long-stay institutions. There has been an incremental and piecemeal approach to welfare that has enjoyed an (albeit weak) party political consensus. Political agreement has been based on a shared understanding that disabled people were disadvantaged through misfortune, that they were not to blame for their 'conditions' and that a benevolent response was appropriate. These beliefs led to the gradual expansion of state-run services.

At the same time, however, the sheer centrality of the medical model, which portrays disabled people as being 'incapacitated', has been responsible for their significant exclusion from the workforce and everyday social world. Even with the advent of community care policies that sought to end the incarceration of disabled people, for many their exile from the main avenues of an ordinary life – work, education and leisure – continues.

Since 1979, the main thrust of government social welfare policies, and the containment approach, has been guided by two key principles: welfare pluralism and community care. Welfare pluralism is the notion that services should be provided not by the state alone but by a plurality of organisations from different parts of the economic and social landscape. In tandem with this idea, the preference of successive governments has been to move away from institutional settings towards 'care in the community'.

It is important to understand the aims of welfare pluralism and community care because of their potentially direct impact on the lives of disabled people. Glennerster *et al.* (1991) identify the political origins of these policies in the ascendancy of a hard right lobby from 1979 onwards. A strand of radical Conservatism brought into question the role of the state in social welfare and militated for the wide-ranging privatisation of services.

Such moves clearly had implications for local authorities, whose role in the direct provision of services would be diminished, and for central government departments, who had already seen big cuts in their large capital programmes as a result of the collapse of public expenditure in the 1970s. Officials at national and local levels thus sought a new *raison d'être* in the regulation, rather than the direct supply, of welfare services.

However, Glennerster warns us against overestimating the amount of real change that took place during the 1980s. In his view, the results of privatisation were much less dramatic than the ideologues had expected because of low take-up. The provision of public services was a hard and unglamorous task, and, except perhaps for one or two specialised areas, potential suppliers would find profits difficult to carve out. It was unsurprising therefore that the private sector largely steered clear of such opportunities as were on offer. In the event, Glennerster's analysis has proved remarkably accurate, and many of the core tasks of social work have remained within the purview of state agencies. Perhaps the most significant diversification has taken place in the area of residential care. Between 1979 and 1990, the number of places in nursing and retirement homes increased by 165 per cent, from 37000 to 98000, and costs increased from £10 million to £1200 million per annum (Langan and Clarke, 1994).

The main vehicle for the implementation of welfare pluralism was the policy of care in the community. With its continuing squeeze on resources and its desire to rein in public spending, the government launched an across-the-board review of community care policies under the chairmanship of Sir Roy Griffiths. The result was an increasingly favourable climate for private sector initiatives and the articulation of a more residual role for social services: the provider was to become the 'enabler' (Walker, 1989). Griffiths (1988: vii) saw the essential role of the public sector as being:

> to ensure that care is provided. How it is provided is an important, but secondary consideration and local authorities must show that they are getting and providing real value.

As for the users, Griffiths (1988: 6) took the view that public services must decide what packages of care would be best suited to needs, whether provided directly by local authorities themselves or indirectly by others, while 'taking account of the views and wishes of the person to be cared for'. We may note that the phrase 'to take account of' carries much less force than phrases such as 'to act upon' or 'to accord with'. In terms of user participation and involvement, the language employed by Griffiths was even weaker than that in the Disabled Persons (Services, Consultation and Representation) Act (Department of Health and Social Security, 1986), which sought 'to establish further consultative processes and representational rights'. Following the publication of the Griffiths Report, a subsequent White Paper (Department of Health, 1989a) confirmed that the government agreed with Sir Roy's approach and adjured public funding agencies to develop an increasingly contractual relationship with the private sector and with voluntary organisations. Policy guidance (Department of Health, 1990) made it clear that collaboration was expected between all the authorities and agencies that contribute to the care of what were called 'vulnerable people'. Subsequent guidance about the implementation of community care (Department of Health, 1991: 20, 25, 29) made it clear that spending power rested not with the user but with the care managers 'as purchasers on behalf of clients'.

The twin approaches of welfare pluralism and community care have attracted much criticism. First, some have pointed to a dissonance between overt and covert intentions. Beresford and Croft (1984), for example, attacked 'welfare pluralism' as a vague piece of jargon being used to cloak right-wing policies that sought the abnegation of (formerly) state responsibilities. As a corollary of welfare pluralism, the government took advantage of opportunities to reduce in real terms the per capita funding for public social services, and, as a result, community care services relied increasingly on the unpaid help of users' families and friends. It was not until 1995 that the role of unpaid carers was formally recognised in legislation in the shape of the Carers (Recognition and Services) Act.

Government policy on carers has created real tensions; Morris (1993: 16), for example, interprets the emphasis on carers as an obstacle to the citizenship of disabled people. She argues that:

> the words 'disabled people' rarely appear these days in policy documents and discussions without the words 'and their carers' tagged on behind. The meaning which is given to both the concept of 'caring' and of 'informed carer' is a crucial part of disabled people's experience of a lack of autonomy.

While most commentators accepted that there might be advantages in the aim of enhancing choice by encouraging the growth of a multiplicity of service providers, writers such as Trevillian (1988) argued that the philosophy espoused by Griffiths had been generated 'from within the preoccupations of Thatcherism'. As a result, there had been little or no debate about the content of policy, the only questions addressed being those of machinery and resources. This was hardly surprising given the 'credentials of [the Report's] author as a managing director of Sainsburys'.

The Association of Metropolitan Authorities (1990: 8) argued that any genuine enhancement of consumer choice would create a real problem for local authorities in that it would entail increased costs. The Association of Metropolitan Authorities believed that the government would be highly unlikely to regard such additional expenditure as legitimate for social services authorities but would see the extra spending as optional and to be funded not from the revenue support grant but entirely from local taxation through the rates.

A more positive note was struck by the Association of District Councils (1990: 7), which broadly welcomed government policy but emphasised the need for partnership between statutory and voluntary agencies, and suggested, unsurprisingly, that district rather than county councils were best placed to take the lead role. With the advent of unitary authorities, however, this debate became increasingly moribund.

Finally, criticisms were levelled not at the direction of policy but at its implementation. Moves towards the introduction of a purchaser/provider split and the greater involvement of commercial enterprise stimulated the further criticism that competition was an inappropriate device to bring to bear on the provision of care. It would merely serve to foster role myopia among the practitioners: social workers, doctors and housing workers. Quasi-markets and quangos would encourage conflict and decrease the potential for cooperation, would lead to perverse decision making (calculated on economic rather than social grounds) in the rationing of resources, and would lead to a proliferation of administrators and accountants. Indeed, the number of general and senior managers in the English health and social services rose from 4609 in 1989 to 22954 in 1994, an increase of very nearly 500 per cent in 5 years (Department of Health, 1996, Table 6.1). The Department of Health issued guidelines to health authorities about setting out overall objectives but offered little or no help to purchasers about how to meet these aims, and it was left to regional health authorities to try to fill the gaps (Emanuel and Ackroyd, 1996).

Summary

The new politics of welfare, based on the values of the radical Right, placed increasing emphasis on the use of non-statutory forms of care (McCarthy, 1989). These political influences were bolstered by economic imperatives originating in Britain's financial problems of the 1970s and 80s, and in demographic changes that fuelled a hefty rise in the demand for services by a growing population of frail elderly people. Taken together, these pressures stimulated a shift in direction, first from state provision towards private and voluntary care, and second, from care by professional and voluntary sources to care by the community itself. But as Beresford and Croft (1984) have contended, the word 'community' was frequently no more than a euphemism for unpaid female carers. An illustration of this gender imbalance is seen in the membership of the Carers National Association, 72 per cent of whose members are female (Carers National Association, 1992). The first indications are that, while the new Labour government intends to dismantle the internal market and take the competitive edge off GP fund-holding, the government is also taking a pragmatic stance towards service provision in general and is therefore not disposed to return newly privatised social services to the public domain.

The voluntary sector

One consequence of all the changes in the 1980s was the Conservative government's assiduous courting of the voluntary sector, encouraging charities to enter into partnership with state agencies and urging them to take on service contracts. Sheard (1986: 34) noted that the government's overtures were greeted (initially at least) with some alarm. There were those who feared that the voluntary sector was in imminent danger of colonisation. Even so, charities were quick to accept the money and staff made available through various schemes of grant aid and job creation programmes. As Handy (1988: 7) remarked at the time:

> Anyone who offers money for the cause is welcome, and more money is even more welcome. Many voluntary organisations have found themselves becoming the agents of their paymasters, be those paymasters a government department, a local authority or the Manpower Services Commission.

For voluntary organisations, then, the contract culture promised the twin attractions of resources and security. Even the circumspect and cautious Audit Commission (1986: 4) had proclaimed that:

> Provision for cost-effective voluntary organisations must be sufficient to prevent them being starved of funds for reasons unrelated to their potential contribution to the support of clients and those caring for them in the community.

Balkam (undated) argued that groups who had been surviving on jumble sales and the help of volunteers were now provided with purpose-built premises, paid staff and generous running costs. Indeed, the formal voices of the voluntary sector welcomed the changes brought about by the new policies. As Leat *et al.* (1981: 1) remarked at the time, voluntary organisations were:

> showing a new audacity. Not only are they identifying themselves in national debate as a permanent and indispensable part of the welfare scene in this country but they are increasingly claiming the right to help determine the future of welfare provision by participating in its planning.

Thompson (1983) believed it naïve to think that such changes could be divorced from wider political considerations and wondered whether volunteers were becoming 'the Tories' fifth column'. Along similar lines, Stubbings (1985) juxtaposed the increase in volunteering with the diminishing availability of paid work and questioned the voluntary sector's motives in taking money from temporary job creation programmes such as Opportunities for Volunteering, the Volunteer Projects Programme and the Community Enterprise Programme (Stubbings, 1982, 1983, 1984).

Darvill's (1985) concern was as much social as it was political. He argued that the privatisation of the social services and the emergence of a contract culture threatened the nature, if not the very existence, of volunteering. He believed that volunteers would be used both to mask cuts in services and to obscure the longer-term failure to provide real jobs. In short, by accepting government money, the voluntary sector was 'dancing along the lion's teeth' (Darvill, 1987). Bryant (1990: 12) contended that the consumer-based approach of the contract culture threatened the fabric and structure of volunteering in Britain. He foresaw that:

> the introduction of internal markets will result in conflicts between voluntary organisations, and that larger national organisations will be better able to secure contracts than smaller local groups.

In any case, the anticipated increase in choice for users might not materialise where, in the light of stringent funding limits, demand exceeded supply (Borsay, 1990; Rao, 1991).

We may detect two crucial themes here. First, there was the powerlessness experienced by those disabled people caught in the maelstrom of change as voluntary agencies attempted to engage with the new competitive ethos. Second, voluntary groups agonised over the dilemma of needing funds to survive but fearing for the preservation of their independence once they signed on the dotted line. Writing a decade earlier about the American experience, Beck (1970: 147) had reached the conclusion that such a dilemma was in fact, not open to solution:

> Truly voluntary associations are desperately needed for the revitalisation of the democratic process, but they cannot be supported by government funds since governmental funding immediately contaminates their nature and is self-defeating.

Brilliant (1973) identified further potential problems in any attempt to harness the voluntary sector as a provider of mainstream services. First, a proliferation of agencies might impede the development and implementation of a cogent policy for social welfare. Second, as the number of service providers increased, the act of coordination would become ever more complex. Third, as regulations were increasingly formalised, administration could lose its flexibility. Finally, it might be more difficult to ensure the accountability of non-statutory bodies, run in the main by volunteers (Hinton and Hyde, 1982). Leat (1986b, 1986c) asserts that these factors, particularly the growing financial dependency of the voluntary sector on government, brought into sharp focus the nature of the relationship between statutory and voluntary agencies.

During the 1980s, then, successive Conservative governments extended some aspects of their industrial and commercial policies to the area of social welfare (Le Grand and Robinson, 1984). Government support for the voluntary and private sectors was, however, interpreted by some as a possible mechanism for the construction of an alternative, non-statutory, welfare state (Lawrence, 1983). Nevertheless, the Conservatives believed that 'consumers' would enjoy wider choice from a broader array of services delivered by a plurality of agencies.

In sum, it is clear that the recent political agenda of the health and social services has been concerned more with the structure and management of these services, and with the problems of privatisation and the contract culture, than with questions of disabled people's citizenship.

Income maintenance and social security

As with health and social services, so too with social security, the emphasis has rested on structure and cost minimisation. To this end, governments have taken forward market testing of at least the administration of the benefits system, if not the benefits themselves. These matters are of critical importance in as much as contemporary social security policies are the main response to the recognition that disabled people experience widespread exclusion from the workplace. The Green Paper on welfare reform by Frank Field (Department of Social Security, 1998) has recommitted the government to the protection of disabled people's civil rights through the introduction of a Disability Rights Commission and – recognising the extra costs faced by disabled people – has promised the removal of barriers to work (for example, the potential loss of benefit or limits on the amount of work a disabled person may do). However, the Green Paper's lack of detail, Field's resignation in July 1998, and the new Secretary of State's (Alastair Darling) warning of further change to come, leaves doubts about access to social security and about the government's stance on disabled people and work.

For those not in a job, there are a number of benefits designed for differing purposes. Some, like incapacity benefit and the severe disablement allowance, were intended as a core weekly source of money. Others addressed more specific needs. For example, the DLA is intended to meet some costs for personal care and attendance, and some travel or mobility costs. A recent decision by the Law Lords has confirmed that the DLA should not be confined only to activities needed to keep people alive but (according to Lord Slynn) should 'enable a person so far as possible to live a normal life' (Wynn Davies, 1997: 10).

Equally, there are benefits, like the DWA, intended to supplement low incomes earned by disabled people who have been able to find work. There are also other reliefs outside the mainstream social security system. For example, the orange badge scheme allows disabled people to avoid car parking fees, and many will obtain prescriptions and certain kinds of medical equipment without charge; equally, some will pay only a nominal sum for a TV licence. These reliefs recognise the reality that disabled people are seldom wealthy. There has latterly also been acceptance of the desirability that disabled people should have some direct control of resources. The Community Care (Direct Payments) Act 1996 permits local authorities to make payments to disabled people so that they can arrange and pay for their own help rather than having to accept whatever services a local authority happens to provide.

Three recent surveys (Dawson, 1995; Kestenbaum, 1995; Zarb and Nadash, 1995) confirm that disabled people who organise their own personal and domestic assistance enjoy greater satisfaction than those who receive local authority or other direct services. Zarb and Nadash found not only that direct payments could reduce costs, but also, more importantly, that the amount of unmet needs diminished when disabled people controlled their own resources. Dawson (1995) noted particularly beneficial effects where local authority staff had ensured that management training was available to disabled people to help them in their new roles as employers of personal assistants. Less positively, Kestenbaum (1996b) examined the Independent Living Fund and discovered that many local authorities had failed to consult disabled people before formulating their priorities for use of the fund; it was unsurprising therefore that confusion had arisen (initially at least) over the uses to which money might be put, resulting in both underspending and the viring of budgets for other purposes. Brindle (1995) concludes that one key factor appears to be the extent and quality of advice available to disabled people so that they may maximise the value of the funding.

While disabled people themselves have been keen to acquire this kind of control, many fear that the present scheme does not go far enough. In particular, there is some disappointment that they are not allowed to employ relatives as assistants and some concern that levels of payment may not meet the full costs. Local authorities have been permitted, rather than compelled, to introduce direct payment arrangements (Kestenbaum, 1996a; Simpson and Campbell, 1996). Even so, it appears that the degree of compliance is good. Research in 1994 by the British Council of Organisations of Disabled People (BCODP) confirmed that some 90 per cent of authorities were willing to implement such legislation (see Whiteley, 1996), and by the middle of 1996, about 60 authorities were already running *indirect* payments schemes with monies channelled to service users via third parties. Many of those schemes are now switching over to direct payments. For Kestenbaum (1996b: 33), the importance of direct payments is:

> that they begin to enable disabled people to move away from dependence on welfare professionals and make the kind of flexible arrangement that suits their own priorities.

However, some social services departments have been more hesitant, and their reluctance is shared by the Association of Directors of Social Services, which has given only a mixed welcome to the scheme. The main fears seem to be that, first, increased expenditure on direct payments may result in cutbacks to local authority-run services, and second, that direct payments may be a Trojan horse: they may establish a precedent for shifting the responsibility for other kinds of disability benefits across from the Benefits Agency to the local authorities (Hirst, 1996).

In summarising contemporary income maintenance policies for unemployed disabled people, we may identify a number of criticisms commonly made of the *status quo*. First, there is the general point that were equality of opportunity to prevail (especially in the worlds of education, vocational training and work), disabled people might not have to rely on what many of them regard as 'state handouts'. Second, disabled people deplore the fact that the system through which they receive resources is tainted by negative imagery. For example, social security recipients are often portrayed in the tabloid press as 'spongers', 'scroungers' or 'moral defectives'. Third, resources (in the form of cash, equipment, services and various dispensations, discounts or reliefs) are channelled to disabled people through a number of disparate sources rather than through a single structure. Nor are resources available automatically: each element must be applied for separately, often in a time-consuming way. Criticisms are levelled, then, not only more generally regarding the structure and ethos of social security but specifically with respect to the 'shape' of benefits and the amounts paid.

Furthermore, incomes should reflect not the levels of benefit paid to other social security applicants but should more closely reflect the normal levels of salaries attracted in the world of work. This is an important point. The social security system was designed mainly to support people while they were *temporarily* out of a job, and the lower levels of remuneration were in part a reflection of that expectation of temporariness. However, the reality for many disabled people has been that they commonly experience (very) long periods out of work so benefit levels are, for them, inappropriately low. Equally, the low benefit levels are in part intended to deter people from relying on them as a permanent way of life, and this deterrence is also inappropriate for some disabled people, particularly those with very severe impairments who cannot work even in the best-adapted work environments.

A further common criticism of the present structure concerns the operational aspects of social security. Perhaps in order to deter claimants, it is not made easy for them to know how to claim or what to claim. I have already referred to the fragmentary nature of benefits, to means testing and to medical inspections, but there are further obstacles. Benefit offices are unwelcoming, understaffed and usually have long queues and waiting times. A free telephone advice line was withdrawn by the Conservative government in 1996, to be replaced with a 'tip-off' line that invited the public to inform on 'scroungers'. Local offices of the Benefits Agency may not have copies of booklets in appropriate languages and are unlikely to have interpreters for disabled people. It is for the individual claimant to discover his or her entitlements, there is no automatic right to be informed of the help available, and many professionals who might be expected to give advice fail to keep themselves sufficiently abreast of the fast-changing benefit structure.

Overall, then, the disability movement in particular argues for equal access to jobs, thus allowing many to earn a wage rather than having to depend on benefits in lieu as a result of their exclusion from work. If some disabled people's impairments are so very severe that they could not work, so still need state resources, these should be in the form of an income that should be paid as such, and should be contiguous with normal salary levels.

The disability movement argues that wages paid to disabled people should equal those of non-disabled people doing the same work. In reality, disabled people often receive low wages, and this is recognised through the social security system in the form of the DWA. However, the existence of this benefit (and the disablement resettlement schemes at job centres) reflect a view that disabled people are less able than non-disabled people, and can therefore only be expected to get low-level jobs, and that employers will need compensation to take them on. Barnes (1991) aims further criticisms at such schemes on the grounds that Disablement Resettlement Officers' work has hitherto been contradictory: seeking to enforce the (now abolished) quota scheme while aspiring to build up relationships with employers. These circumstances and the understandings that have brought them into being, together with the complexity of the benefit structure, the restriction of access by medical testing and the fragmentary forms of help, lead disabled people to argue that contemporary policy is severely flawed and that its failure accounts in large measure for the extensive and chronic poverty that they experience.

Housing and the built environment

Savage and Warde (1993) argue that the built environment seems impervious to change and that urban dwellers regard the streets and buildings around them with a sense of permanency and immutability. The built environment is configured according to dominant perspectives, first concerning the centrality and promotion of economic utility and the supremacy of the market, and second, concerning the human body, how it is structured, how it moves and operates. The idea of the ambulatory, hearing and seeing human being prevails in traditional urban design. The use of steps and kerbs, and the lack of audio and tactile signs or suitable public transport, has led to the segregation of disabled people, restricting them not merely to certain areas but, for some, to specific institutions. About 422 000 live in communal establishments, a fifth of these residents being below retirement age (Martin *et al.*, 1988). In response to such exclusion, Blomley (1994) has postulated the need for a 'geography of rights'.

In similar vein, Imrie (1996: 167) argues that:

> planning practice is neither neutral nor benign in its effects on communities; planning outcomes have particular distributive consequences which, potentially, exclude some while conferring advantages on others.

He uses the terms 'design apartheid' and 'denial of place' to describe structures and buildings that, for example, force wheelchair users to enter a building via its loading bay or compel them to ring a bell to summon help in order to get in. Imrie also notes ineffective modifications, such as ramps too steep to be used or levelled flooring rendered useless by the presence of steps further along the same corridor. Even where there is a desire to enable disabled people to gain access to society, the prevailing attitude tends to be that the *status quo* should be maintained as far as possible. Finally, in a society in which the market stands pre-eminent, disabled people are cast as 'consumers', and goods such as accessible buildings have to be paid for, but exclusion from employment denies the income needed to meet the costs.

To establish the link between theories of 'spatial imperialism' and the creation of disabling environments in practice, it is necessary to identify the agents involved. These include governments, planners, architects and builders. The approach of successive governments has been based on inviting (voluntary) changes and modifications where necessary rather than introducing legally enforceable rules so that buildings serve all citizens rather than just a dominant majority. This voluntaristic approach is clearly evinced in the ambiguous wording of the Disability Discrimination Act, which requires modifications to be made 'where reasonable'.

Notwithstanding the centrality of access issues to the quality of people's lives, voluntarism permeates the planning system, and local practice differs so widely that access is simply not guaranteed (Royal

Town Planning Institute, 1988). Notwithstanding the creation or desig-
nation of 'access officers' within planning teams and the setting up in
many places of voluntary 'access committees', the issue has not, hitherto, been afforded any high priority by planning departments, and,
lacking powers to compel, they have had to rely substantially on the
consent and cooperation of builders and developers. Indeed, they have
on occasion been afraid to exercise such powers as may exist, first for
fear of losing much-needed investment and new developments in the
area, and second, because planning refusals are likely in any case to be
overruled by central government (Imrie and Wells, 1993).

I have mentioned that the Chronically Sick and Disabled Persons Act
requires developers to provide access where 'practical and reasonable',
and the Disabled Persons Act 1981 urges planning authorities to draw
the attention of developers to a code of practice (BS5810) on access to
buildings for disabled people. Planning policy guidance from the
Department of the Environment (1992) declares that planning authorities may 'seek to negotiate' accessibility, but access cannot be used as a
mandatory condition for planning approval. Finally, part M of the
Building Regulations 1992 also provides some guidance, but the legislation is vitiated by the exclusion of domestic dwellings, older buildings and minor works.

Given all I have said so far, it is unsurprising that a medical model
prevails in questions of access, and most councils treat the issue as one
requiring specific design solutions rather than an entirely new policy
framework. In recent research, Imrie (1996) discovered only three local
authorities that informed their planning policies from the perspective of
the social model of disability. Many were ignorant of the issues, gave
them low priority or felt impotent to act.

Architects are in part responsible for failing to offer designs that
guarantee access for disabled people. Among the possible reasons for
this failure are a prioritisation of the aesthetic over the functional and
the belief common among many architects that all sections of the population have uniform expectations of the environment and its functions
(Matrix, 1984). These expectations remain unchallenged since disabled
people are substantially absent from what is essentially a private and
self-regulating architectural profession. However, Moore and Bloomer
(1977) are hopeful that the fragmentation of discourses and perspectives in postmodern architecture may provide opportunities for new
schools of design more sympathetic to the needs of hitherto disadvantaged groups. This remains to be seen.

Equally, house builders themselves, mainly for fear of the impact on their costs, have militated against the strengthening of access and related legislation. The House Builders Federation has dismissed the problems encountered by disabled people as at once 'not severe' and 'surmountable'. For example, the Federation has asserted that where a disabled person goes on a visit, it is reasonable to expect that he or she would be 'assisted over the threshold by the host' (House Builders Federation, 1995). Finally, in the education of professionals in all these areas, disability remains on the periphery of, or absent from, the curriculum. In sum, social and spatial polarisation has led to the segregation of disabled people in our towns and cities, and to their clustering in residual (usually publicly owned) housing.

Governments have long accepted that many disabled people struggle with houses ill adapted to their needs (Department of the Environment, 1977). In a survey in South Wales, Hunt and Heyes (1980) highlighted several of the problems faced by a majority of disabled occupants. These included wheelchair users coping in houses with stairs, inadequate room and corridor dimensions, and a lack of aids and adaptations.

Laune (1993) has argued that, by identifying special needs provision as the solution to disabled people's housing needs, general house builders have been able to ignore their needs by default. Even then, the rate of building adapted premises has actually fallen in recent years. In 1979, housing associations built 129 wheelchair standard houses – but in 1990 a mere 67. As for local authority provision, the figures are 567 in 1979, declining to just 69 houses in 1990. Even were the number of accessible houses to increase substantially, actual tenure closely reflects income levels, and only 46 per cent of disabled people are owner occupiers (Martin and White, 1988), as against almost 68 per cent of the population at large (Balchin, 1995).

Fiedler (1988) reports that only one in ten housing authorities, one in five health authorities and one in three social services departments provide any accommodation for people with severe impairments, and these are usually warden-assisted sheltered schemes. To put these data in perspective, the total expenditure on housing (the Housing Revenue Account) planned by local authorities in England, Wales and Scotland in 1995/6 amounted to £13 440 million (Chartered Institute of Public Finance Accountants, 1996).

Education

The previous chapter charted the development since Victorian times of a separate system of education for disabled children, away from mainstream schools attended by non-disabled pupils. However, Oliver (1996) identifies the 1944 Education Act as legislation pivotal to the reversal of that trend, replacing the principle of segregation with the aim of integration. At first sight, such a fundamental switch in policy seems to promise much for the education of disabled children, their access to society and their status within it. Furthermore, in recent times there has been, in line with the aim of integration, a reduction in the number of children taught in special schools. In England in 1985, there were 100 hospital schools with 4485 students, and 1429 special schools responsible for 110 262 pupils. A decade later, these figures had fallen to 31 hospital schools with 228 full-time pupils, and 1291 special schools with 95 271 pupils (Department of Health, 1996).

Despite this progress, several obstacles to integration remain. Some local authorities, contrary to the wishes of parents, have blocked the way of disabled children by allocating them to special school places rather then allowing them a mainstream education (Riddell, 1996). Second, even where local authorities have not stepped in, competition between schools has resulted (either tacitly or overtly) in the selection of some pupils and the rejection of others. The annual publication of school league tables over the past few years has forced head teachers carefully to consider what kinds of student they should admit. The more talented its intake, the better a school is likely to perform in these critical tests. The security of teaching posts and the level of funding depend on the retention and expansion of student numbers. Clearly, parents desire to place their children in good schools while avoiding those with poor records of achievement. However, disabled pupils and those designated as having special educational needs find it difficult to be accepted in the first place and are 'among those most at risk of exclusion' (Brodie and Berridge, 1996: 9).

Third, it remains the case that mainstream schools are still largely inaccessible: only 18 per cent of secondary schools and 46 per cent of primary schools consider themselves 'three quarters' accessible (Spastics Society, 1993). Even then, certain facilities, such as libraries and toilets, proved particularly ill designed. In recognising these problems, the incoming Labour government made an early announcement of £3.6 million of supplementary credit approvals for improving access to schools, and the minister (Estelle Morris) agreed that children with special educational needs should be integrated with their peers (Department for Education and Employment, 1997).

Fourth, even where disabled children are accepted into mainstream schools, there is no automatic guarantee that they will therefore enjoy education of the same value as that available to their fellow (non-disabled) students. This question is of fundamental concern to writers such as Barton (1986, 1988, 1989) and Barton and Tomlinson (1981), who have detailed the debilitating effects of teaching practices that target attention and resources on the (apparently) most able in the class while neglecting the less gifted. They also highlight the deleterious consequences of inherently selective education structures that condemn some children to residual provision, and lay bare the academic polarisation that results from contemporary education policies. As Oliver (1991b: 143) contended, even before the introduction of league tables, 'integration in the sense of social inclusion cannot be delivered by politicians or educators, it is a process of struggle that has to be joined'.

Fulcher (1989: 22) has been particularly concerned with the differential ways in which the concept of 'integration' has been interpreted, and in the way that teaching practices mediate policy:

> government policies do not control schools in any direct sense as far as teaching styles and pedagogic practices are concerned, yet these are obviously central to real integration.

From a comparison of integration policies in four countries (the United States, Denmark, the United Kingdom and (Victoria) Australia), Fulcher concluded that, while all four ostensibly had integrative policies, only Denmark had translated that overall aim into integrative teaching practices: the human agent within the institutional setting was critical in determining both policy outcomes and what actually happened to children. Fulcher (1989) argued that, even when children succeeded in gaining admission to mainstream schools, they were marked out and treated less favourably than other students. Slee (1993) contends that there has been 'jealous protection of special educational expertise' such that integration has meant little more than 'new sites for old practices'. The importance of education is especially apparent in assessing disabled people's access to vocational training and to work. Atkinson *et al.* (1981: 236) have argued that, notwithstanding attempts by successive governments to persuade employers to take on disabled workers, at times when youth unemployment is high:

employers can pick the more attractive candidates from the dole queues for even the most menial of tasks, clearly a different approach is required if the handicapped [sic] school leaver is to have any chance of a job at all.

Accordingly, it is to the question of employment policy that I now turn.

Employment

As in other areas of life, so too in employment, the policy approach has sought to contain or compensate. The absence of disabled people from work has much to do with the lack of access to workplaces and the lack of commitment by successive governments (Imrie and Wells, 1993).

A major difficulty is that disability, unlike race or sex, can be relevant to job performance and what to some might seem like discrimination may in reality be recruitment based on legitimate preferences and likely performance. (Department of Employment, 1990: 30)

Equally, a study of employers' attitudes by Morrell (1990) found that 91 per cent believed they would have problems employing disabled staff, two-thirds believed that the kind of work they did was unsuitable for disabled workers, and just over half believed their premises to be unsuitable.

Clearly, then, given resistance by government and employers alike, it is entirely unsurprising that, despite their desire for jobs, disabled people endure rates of unemployment about three times higher than do the population at large (Prescott-Clarke, 1990; Berthoud *et al.*, 1993), and three-quarters of all disabled adults depend on state benefits for their income (Martin and White, 1988). In 1992, the value of benefits equalled just 18 per cent of average earnings (Foley and Pratt, 1994).

Even where disabled people have work, their wages are lower than those of their non-disabled counterparts. Men working full time received on average only three-quarters of the wage earned by non-disabled colleagues doing the same jobs, and disabled women earned only two-thirds of the wage of disabled men (Liberty, 1994).

Containment of disabled people away from the world of 'real' work has been vested in activities such as occupational and industrial therapy, often located in sheltered workshops. Where such work has occurred in a health or social services setting, the efforts of disabled people have been rewarded by 'therapeutic earnings', pitiably small sums of money that no more than mimic the earning of a real wage.

Other work, in reserved occupations or firms such as Remploy, have also brought segregated labour and poor rewards, including poor promotion prospects, low-status jobs and wages some 25 per cent lower than those of their non-disabled counterparts (Berthoud *et al.*, 1993; RADAR, 1993). It was through official recognition of these adverse conditions that the DWA was introduced as a means of supplementing the low income of disabled people in full-time employment (that is, working over 16 hours per week) (Cooper and Vernon, 1996). By the end of January 1995, however, there had been only 5202 awards of the DWA, costing £13 million (Department of Social Security, 1996). It was expected that by now, some 4 years after its introduction, the DWA would reach about 50000 people, but only about 10000 receive the supplement, and, of these, only a few hundreds were enabled to gain work through the availability of the new allowance (Rowlingson and Berthoud, 1996). Harris and Wikeley (1995) and Rowlingson and Berthoud (1994, 1996) blame the low take-up figures on a lack of awareness that the allowance exists, the lack of eligible non-recipients and widespread discrimination by employers. They also point to the obstacles arising from the minimum (16) hours of work rule (a third of applicants being thwarted by this test alone).

In addition, the repeal of the quota scheme means that there is now no legal duty on employers to ensure that disabled people are represented in the workforce. Thornton and Lunt (1995) argue that employment policies have moved from a position of recognising obligations towards disabled people as a group (what I have called compensatory policies) towards a position where legislation refers to disabled people as individuals and puts the onus on them to attempt to gain recompense should they encounter discrimination. Thus, while the 1944 Disabled Persons (Employment) Act was designed (ostensibly at least) to prevent the exclusion from work of a class of citizens, it is now for the individual employee to seek what remedies he or she can in the event of discrimination, and the Disability Discrimination Act plays a significant part in giving further impetus to this shift away from collective obligation towards individual self-reliance.

What, then, of the Disability Discrimination Act 1995? Has it provided a greater chance for disabled people to enjoy equality of opportunity and greater access to work? The peculiar circumstances under which the Act was born, following the public exposure of the Conservative government's questionable methods with regard to the talking out of the Civil Rights (Disabled Persons) Bill, meant that it was a reluctant and much diluted measure, hedged about with qualifications and 'let out' clauses.

The previous Conservative government's accustomed position on employment rights for disabled people was made clear in 1994 in a response to a European Commission paper on social policy:

> The most effective way to promote job opportunities for people with disabilities is to get employers to recognise the abilities of disabled people and the business case for employing them. (Department of Employment, 1994)

While the government favoured persuasion rather than compulsion, the Act did nevertheless make it unlawful (subject to certain exceptions) for employers to discriminate against disabled people, either in applying for work or during employment. The Act covered recruitment, interviewing and selection; training and promotion; benefits, working conditions, terms of employment, redundancies and dismissals. However, in the view of Thornton and Lunt (1995: 6), the exceptions were sufficiently broad that 'there are no measures to ensure that workplaces and working practices are suitable for all disabled people'.

The Equal Opportunities Review (1997) undertook a survey of employers in order to gauge their response to the Disability Discrimination Act. Although 1408 companies were approached, only 218 (15 per cent) replied to the survey, but they did provide work for some 2 000 000 people. In almost all the firms who replied, it was the personnel department that had responsibility for ensuring compliance with the Act, and 87 per cent had a written policy on the employment of disabled people. Only about a third had made policy changes in the light of the Disability Discrimination Act and three-quarters had made no audit of disabled staff. Only about half had provided written guidance for managers, and, again, only half had set up procedures for dealing with requests for adaptations to the working environment.

The Equal Opportunities Review survey indicated that some 62 per cent of the respondents had acquired equipment or made modifications for disabled employees during the previous 12 months, but only a fifth had provided a support worker. Firms were divided evenly between those who believed that the Disability Discrimination Act would cause them difficulties and those who anticipated no adverse effects. Only 2 per cent of employers thought that the implementation of Disability Discrimination Act requirements would prove very expensive; the vast majority either had no idea what the costs might be or believed that they would be modest and reasonable. Significantly, most employers believed that the Disability Discrimination Act would make little difference to their existing policies towards disabled employees. One of the difficulties with interpreting the Equal Opportunities Review survey is, of course, that by definition we cannot know the thinking of the 1200 non-respondents: whether they have an antipathy to surveys or to disabled people. The government's Green Paper on welfare reform has the broad intention of continuing, where appropriate, to support disabled people through benefits but aims to extend opportunities for disabled people who wish to work, although it remains to be seen whether the document heralds any fundamental change of thinking on these issues.

Transport

Barnes (1991) has carefully documented the plethora of barriers faced by disabled people who need to travel. Whether they seek to use trains, buses or taxis, the picture is one of ill-designed vehicles, too few adaptations and a common attitude towards change of 'tomorrow, sometime, never'. On the trains, notwithstanding more recent improvements, 'travelling in the guards van with the baggage is an all too common experience for wheelchair users' (*Which*, 1990). Disabled people who desire to go abroad on holiday also face discrimination. By way of illustration, the *Daily Telegraph* (10th May 1997, p. 11) reported the stranding of disabled passengers at Manchester airport when a captain refused to allow them to board their flight. The pilot argued that he could not fly with more than 10 per cent of passengers suffering from any form of disability. The tour company later made alternative arrangements to fly the passengers out to their holiday, more than 8 hours late.

The Greater London Association for Disabled People (GLAD) undertook a survey of London Transport in 1997. The survey shows that progress in the past decade has been 'piecemeal, tentative and very limited'. The circumstances highlighted in GLAD's previous study in 1986 remain substantially true today. Some 450 000 people have difficulty using public transport; 20 per cent cannot use buses at all. In 1994, only 70 of over 5000 London buses were accessible to wheelchair users (*Hansard*, 11th March 1994, col. 566). In sum, then, these examples highlight the reality that public transport has been designed substantially by and for non-disabled people, and the snail's pace of change reflects the weakness of current policy.

Law and access to justice

In the area of justice, particular criticism has been levelled not so much at the level of statute or civil law itself, nor yet at the judiciary, but rather at the organisation that decides whether to take cases forward to the courts. The Crown Prosecution Service (CPS) is the body in Britain charged with the responsibility of deciding whether, or whether not, to launch a criminal prosecution. Research shows what appears to be discriminatory decision making. For example, abuse (including sexual abuse) of people with learning difficulties goes unpunished in up to half the reported cases because the CPS is cautious in viewing people with learning difficulties as reliable witnesses (Cohen, 1994; Dodd and Owens, 1996). We should, however, acknowledge that the service may be seeking to act humanely in not wishing to expose people with cognitive impairments to the trauma of courtroom interrogation. Communication in court has also been highlighted as problematic; for example, there are fewer than a hundred interpreters for deaf people working in the entire legal system (Council for Advancement of Communication with Deaf People, 1993).

Politics, government and administration

I turn finally to policies concerned with politics, government and administration. In this section of the chapter, I assess the treatment of disabled people with respect to their participation in political processes and in the administration of the state.

Political and electoral processes

During the reign of Charles II (1660–85), Whitlocke wrote his *Notes upon the King's Writ for Choosing Members of Parliament* (13 Car 2, Add. Mss. 4749–54, British Museum). In this document, he excluded from consideration those 'rendered incapable by reason of physical or mental disability' (1 Whitelocke, 461). From that day to this, electoral agents and returning officers have been guided in the light of Whitlocke and similarly minded successors. For example, *Parker's Conduct of Parliamentary Elections* provides three grounds on which a candidate may be deemed unqualified to be elected: (a) incapacity by reason of physical or mental disability; (b) incapacity by reason of circumstances, character or conduct; (c) incapacity by reason of holding certain offices or positions. 'Under class A, fall idiots, lunatics and persons under the age of 21, in all of whom the law supposes a want of mental capacity or discretion' (Wollaston, 1970). Similarly, Schofield (1955: 83) argues 'it is said that deaf and dumb persons are ineligible for Parliament'. Whether the opinion would be upheld today remains an open question.

The legal position of some disabled people who desire to stand as candidates is unproblematic (for example, there is now, and there have been in the past, blind MPs and deaf MPs, and the general election of 1997 saw the election of the wheelchair user Anne Begg as MP for Aberdeen South), but for people with some other kinds of impairment, there remains considerable doubt as to whether their candidacy would be accepted.

What of the franchise itself? Several studies have shown that many disabled people are not eligible to vote simply because they fail to appear on the electoral register (Fry, 1987; Ward, 1987). MIND (1989) discovered that, in 1988, only 329 out of 4349 hospital patients were registered to vote. Barnes (1991) has provided a cogent analysis of the reasons for this, including the failure of managers and staff to register residents in hospitals and other institutions such as private or voluntary homes, or the failure of the 'head of household' to register disabled people living at home. At the same time, those who are eligible to vote may face problems of physical access to polling stations. In the general election of 1992, some 87 per cent of polling stations were inaccessible to wheelchair users (Burns, 1997). In contrast, 94 per cent of polling booths in the United States are accessible to disabled people (Scott, 1994).

Beyond physical access, there are bureaucratic complexities associated with proxy or postal voting, which methods are in any case restricted to certain classes of disabled people (see Barnes, 1991: 208–19). Rather than ensuring automatic eligibility to vote and universal access to locations and methods of voting, legislation – from the Blind Voters Act 1933 to the Representation of the People Act passed half a century later – has tried to produce special solutions or arrangements for people with differing impairments, arrangements which have been at best only partially effective.

Disabled people may wish to lobby their MPs. However, the main entrance to the Commons is inaccessible to wheelchair users, and the Sergeant at Arms refuses entry unless they have made a prior arrangement to see a particular MP (Foley and Pratt, 1994).

Administration

In Britain, the administration of government is carried out at national level by the civil service (and such sections of it as have been privatised) and at local level by local government officers and staff. Disabled people remain underrepresented at management level in the civil service despite a general improvement at other levels. Only 2.8 per cent of employees (13 438) are disabled, and this low figure reflects a lack of commitment at the highest levels. Although the unequal opportunities have been recognised at cabinet office level (see for example Cabinet Office, 1994a, 1994b), some 13 civil service departments remain uncommitted to the programme for action on disability (Development and Equal Opportunities Division, Office of Public Service, 1996a, 1996b). In sum, then, what has become clear in the foregoing pages is that disabled people have been held at arm's length in almost every aspect of government, administration and the political process writ large.

Conclusion

This chapter has been concerned with praxis. That is to say, it has sought to trace the way in which contemporary disability policies (stemming, as they do, from medical model understandings of disability) have created institutions, groups of practitioners and modes of practice, all of which have had a direct bearing on the circumstances of disabled people's lives.

Broadly speaking, although policies have been aimed at supporting disabled people in particular ways, it is clear that, all too often, the way in which they have been drawn up, or the way in which they have been implemented, has actually served to disempower. Even where government has a genuine intention that policy should enhance disabled people's lives, actual practice (and specifically key politicians or practitioners) can thwart those intentions if they perceive their own interests or power to be threatened or if they wish to achieve unconnected political ends. In this latter regard, see, for example, the allegations of inappropriate practice in the sale of council housing levelled against Dame Shirley Porter at Westminster City Council (Walker D., 1996).

Furthermore, institutional structures may themselves disempower. Compare, for example, the use in Britain of 'community care', 'social work' and 'social security' as conduits for disability policy, with the concepts of 'rights', 'access' and 'environmental change' that stand at the heart of United States legislation implemented not through the ambit of welfare but through organs such as the Justice Department and the Office of the Attorney General. Again, even where policies have been intended to enhance the citizenship of disabled people, a lack of proper funding and a lack of enforcement have resulted in extensive failure to achieve such aims, and the result has been that disabled people are grossly underrepresented in public life (George and Wilding, 1984; Foley and Pratt, 1994). The extent of this exclusion becomes clear in the next chapter, where I contrast disability policies in Britain with those in other parts of the world.

6

Contemporary British Policy in the International Context

Introduction

How may we evaluate such progress as has been made in British disability policies? Clearly, one way would be to measure the domestic position against the treatment of disabled people elsewhere using an international (and partly historical) context. Recalling the models of policy enunciated in Chapter 3, it is possible to characterise the situations in a number of countries as being particularly representative of one or other of those models:

- the negative policy model, the denial of human rights: Nazi Germany;
- the *laissez-faire* (or minimalist) model: China;
- the maximal welfare approach to policy making: Sweden;
- a hybrid welfare/civil rights approach to policy making: Australia;
- the rights-based policy model: United States of America;
- the piecemeal approach to policy making: United Kingdom.

Given their unsuitability as exemplars for future action, I intend to deal with the first two categories (exemplified by Nazi Germany and China) only very briefly before comparing and contrasting the final four in some detail.

Negative policies: Nazi Germany and China

Disabled people in Nazi Germany and elsewhere

For the most extreme example of a state enacting policies that not merely denied the citizenship of disabled people but actually cost them their lives, we must go back in history to the Third Reich. Hitler's regime built its policies on the theory of eugenics, which had gained an academic following in Weimar Germany (and elsewhere). Lifton (1986) refers for example to a paper by Karl Binding and Alfred Hoche written in 1920 entitled *Die Freigabe der Vernichtung lebensunwerten Lebens* (The Permission to Destroy Life Unworthy of Life), in which the authors nominated as unworthy:

> the incurably ill… large segments of the mentally ill, the feebleminded, and retarded and deformed children. (Lifton, 1986: 46)

Ideas of 'racial purity' became paramount, and policies were formulated accordingly. In October, 1939 questionnaires were distributed to mental hospitals asking physicians to select 'incurable' patients for whom 'euthanasia' might be appropriate. Of 283 000 returned questionnaires, some 75 000 patients were identified as suitable candidates. A programme of gassing was initiated in the jail at Brandenburg in January 1940, and by September 1941, no fewer than 70 723 had lost their lives (Müller-Hill, 1988). Some disabled people escaped death but were instead victims of a forcible sterilisation programme (Müller-Hill, 1994).

Eigner *et al.* (1994: 7) describe the holocaust as the most extreme example of a state and its institutions using science to convince the general public that 'a dangerous and, in this case, genocidal ideology was justifiable and rational'. As I began writing this book, evidence emerged that other states, while not actually terminating the lives of disabled adults, were nonetheless involved in extensive programmes of sterilisation. In Sweden, the neutering of people with cognitive impairments began in 1935, peaked in 1946 and did not cease until 1976. In all, some 60 000 women were described as 'inferior' or of 'poor or mixed racial quality' and were treated in this way (Haydon, 1997). Equally, in the Swiss canton of Vaud, doctors sterilised 'mentally handicapped' patients against their will under a law of 1928. In 1934, a copy of the statute was requested by Adolf Hitler to serve as a template for his own legislation (Reuters, 1997). Beyond the boundaries of Western Europe, Eigner *et al.* (1994: 6) reported that, until the 1970s, legislation in some parts of Canada and the United States allowed for the sterilisation of cognitively impaired citizens without their consent. In December 1997, the Australian government's human rights agency reported that more than a thousand girls with learning difficulties had been illegally sterilised in the previous 5 years (Associated Press, Sydney, 1997). While we may hope fervently to see nothing of the like again, these events cast a long shadow and compel us to consider the implications, for example, of the ethics involved in the routine termination of severely impaired fetuses and the practice of withholding heart surgery from people with cognitive impairments.

The historical lesson to be drawn reinforces my earlier point that the critical test of any disability policy or law is whether it carries within it the affirmation of disabled people's citizenship or the denial of their humanity. There are, of course, no parallels to be drawn between Hitler's Third Reich and the Germany of today; certainly, disabled people are no longer in danger of their lives. However, progress towards full citizenship has been slow. For example, Schuchardt (1991: 5) quotes this court judgement made in 1980 concerning a claim for damages by a disgruntled holiday maker upset by disabled people in her hotel:

> The mere presence of a group of at least 25 persons suffering from serious mental and physical disabilities constitutes a drawback warranting the reduction of the cost of the holiday. For sensitive persons [sic]... enjoyment can obviously be diminished by the presence of a group of severely disabled people... the seriously disabled should be integrated into normal daily life, but certainly no travel agency can impose this on its other clients. (Judgement of the Civil Division of the Regional Court, Frankfurt-am-Main, 25th February, 1980, No. 24)

It would be unfair to leave the reader with the impression that these negative images represent contemporary attitudes and actualities in Germany. The modern state has tried to take a more enlightened stance and has added antidiscrimination legislation to existing policies (Lunt and Thornton, 1993). More specifically, the German government recognises that about 7.5 per cent of the working-age population is disabled (Haveman, 1984) and has ensured that employment quotas are strongly enforced. There are automatic fines for employers who fail to fulfil quota obligations (Lonsdale, 1990). However, financial support for disabled people has been hampered by the commitment to spending limits imposed by the economic 'stability pact' agreed at Maastricht in pursuit of a single currency, and severe cuts have been made in welfare budgets (Karacs, 1996). Finally, Germany has a thriving disabled people's movement that campaigns domestically and has membership of DPI (Disabled People's International, 1997).

China: a policy of non-support?

A state may not actively kill its disabled citizens but it may, nevertheless, fail to support them, even to the extent of allowing them to die, and some states have left disabled people to their own devices. In China, for example, which has some 10 million disabled people (of whom 4 million are children), physical impairments can often be life threatening. The danger arises less from the intrinsic nature of any particular condition than from the contingent response of the state. In some states, marriage has been restricted where persons have a genetic impairment, and China recently proposed a law first to compel the abortion of fetuses identified as genetically impaired, and second, to make the sterilisation of people with disabilities a precondition for marriage. Indeed, in June 1995, China actually passed a law banning marriages between couples where there was a risk of congenital deformity in their offspring (Rufford, 1995).

Some 300000 Chinese children are born each year with cognitive impairments, and those (especially girls) whose parents abandon them may be left to their fate, ending their lives in what Lightfoot (1995) has called the 'dying rooms' of state orphanages. More broadly, a *laissez-faire* approach of this kind means that disabled people who have neither the resources nor other avenues of support may compete unsuccessfully in a world designed by non-disabled people for non-disabled people.

China's attitude towards disabled people has traditionally been negative. Potts (1989) offers a number of reasons for this, including the economic hardship that follows the birth of a disabled child, the lack of tolerance where people appear to be physically or cognitively different from 'ideal types' such as the 'model worker' or 'model teacher', and the one child per family policy (although families with a disabled child are permitted to have a second baby). Even then, Potts points out that this relaxation of the policy reinforces negative attitudes about disabled people. Both underpinning and consequential to this approach, there is no national social security system or network of personal social services. There are very few mobility aids, and welfare benefits are distributed from the school or workplace. Those who are neither in school nor in work remain with their families, for whom there is no specific state support. The only alternative is that disabled people live in a social welfare institution run by the local Bureau of Civil Affairs. There are therefore no area-based or interdisciplinary services: no social workers, speech therapists, health visitors or educational psychologists (Potts, 1989).

Potts acknowledges some indications of change, including calls for the greater availability of aids and adaptations. A handful of special schools have been opened, but these remain atypical. There are nearly 5 million disabled children in China, but fewer than 6 per cent are enrolled in schools (Boylan, 1991). China's position is by no means unique. Stevens (1997), for example, records that, in developing countries, 98 per cent of disabled people have access to no services or 'rehabilitation', and worldwide there are some 20 million people who need wheelchairs but are without them. In some countries, blind people are permitted neither to vote nor to stand for election, and in poorer countries, 99 per cent of disabled children receive no secondary education.

Before leaving this part of the chapter, I must, in the interests of fairness, draw a distinction between, on the one hand, the pursuit of negative policies as a deliberate action based on beliefs and intentions antagonistic towards disabled people, and on the other hand, negative policies (characterised principally by inaction or neglect) originating in the poor economic circumstances or low per capita income of a population, in the unstable infrastructure of the state or in the underdevelopment of public policy *per se*. In these circumstances, all citizens are likely to experience poverty and the lack of services such as education or health care. So while, in the former example, disabled people are treated differently (indeed inhumanely) by dint of a government's attitudes and policies towards them, in the latter instance, the deprived position of disabled people may be almost identical to that of the wider population at large.

Clearly, the historical examples of Nazi Germany and post-war China constitute particularly negative kinds of disability policy. I now turn, however, to more positive policy formulations, intended to advance the quality of life of disabled people rather than to harm or neglect them.

* * * * *

By comparing the formulation of policies towards disabled people in contemporary Sweden, the United States and Australia, it becomes evident that there are minimal and maximal policy approaches. The reader will see that (although they are built on a much grander scale) present-day Swedish welfare programmes accord more closely with the British Conservative government's (minimalist) concept of targeted help for disabled people. On the other hand, the American and

Australian rights-based approach has clearly informed the (maximal) stance taken by the British Labour Party in the civil rights Bill put forward in 1994.

Contemporary Sweden: a maximal welfare state?

In 1995, the Swedish population stood at 8 830 000 (United Nations, 1997). The Statens Institut för Handikappfrågor i Skolan (SIH) estimates that about 880 000, or 10 per cent, of the population is disabled (Statens Institut för Handikappfrågor i Skolan, 1995), and of these, over half, some 470 000, are members of the Swedish disabled people's movement (Swedish Institute, 1995). At the national level, there are some 40 organisations that represent distinct disability groupings, and there is a network of 2000 local associations nationwide. The national organisations have formed the Swedish Cooperative Body of Organisations of Disabled People (Handikappförbundens samarbetsorgan), an umbrella movement comprising 29 member associations (Swedish Institute, 1995).

The structure of Swedish education for disabled people has similarities with arrangements in Britain. There are special schools for students with impaired vision, hearing or speech and also school programmes for students with severe cognitive impairments. The programmes adhere to the standard curriculum but proceed in a way that focuses on the development of the individual. Special advisors are provided by the National Swedish Agency for Special Education. The Agency recognises that social 'demands, expectations and attitudes' place obstacles in the way of disabled students, but concedes that, although the cogency of this perspective has:

> had a great impact on designing social programs... especially noticeable within the social sector and health and medical sector... unfortunately it has not gotten the same response within education despite that it is there where it should have the most importance. (Statens Institut för Handikappfrågor i Skolan, 1995: 12)

As in Britain, educational disadvantages are clearly detrimental to a person's employment prospects. The Swedish approach to disabled people and work has, until very recently, been compensatory or ameliorative in nature. The Swedish social democratic tradition, which has prevailed for much of the century, has led not only to the development of extensive social welfare services, but also to what Ginsburg (1983) called 'a staggering array' of selective policies designed to overcome unemployment problems faced by specific groups. Because post-war Social Democratic governments have been committed to full employment, there are relatively few people who depend permanently on social security benefits, and many require only temporary help (Gould, 1988). In Sweden, welfare policy is formulated and implemented both by government and by the National Labour Market Board (Arbetsmarknadsstyrelsen, or AMS), whose membership is drawn from government, management and the country's unions and workforce.

The aim of the AMS has been to maintain the highest possible levels of employment, and, in pursuit of that goal, the AMS has followed a strongly corporatist and interventionist approach in industrial policy and in the supervision of the labour market. Regulations concerning conditions of employment, vocational training and other kinds of intervention have been designed to ensure, as far as possible, that disabled people are not excluded from work. Nor are the generous levels of disability pension intended to act as a substitute source of income to replace earnings. Having a job is therefore recognised as a key component in attempts to integrate disabled people into society at large (Gould, 1993).

Although employers have been persuaded to make their workplaces more accessible to disabled people, the fundamental approach of the Swedish system has been to equip people for, and fit them into, jobs. Help of this kind has been made available even where people have needed considerable help in their desire to work. A high level of investment in vocational training has been complemented by the setting up of firms similar to Remploy in the United Kingdom. For example, Samhall is a parent company with about 30 subsidiaries involved in a diverse range of activities, including mechanical engineering, furniture, graphics production, packaging, electronics, clothing, textiles, plastics and horticulture. The company has 800 workplaces in 330 different locations and employs about 32 500 workers, of whom 29 000 are labelled 'occupationally disabled' (Samhall, 1995). The company asserts that:

> employees in Samhall are offered normal terms and conditions of employment, and have the same rights and duties as other employees. They are remunerated according to standard negotiated, contractual agreements rather than receiving a pension. (Samhall, 1995: 7)

Many other strategies are used to maintain high rates of employment and ensure worker protection. These include extensive on-the-job training, grants to encourage recruitment, several job placement schemes, information on new vacancies, detailed guidance and advice on career development, generous mobility allowances and other regional allowances and subsidies (Ginsburg, 1983; Gould, 1993). Where companies get into difficulties, their workers are entitled to receive advance warning of redundancies, and, after losing their jobs, life is made easier through favourable benefit levels. Additionally, Labour Market Institutes provide rehabilitation, training and other work-related measures designed to enhance the employability of those affected by plant closures or recession. Where retraining fails to secure a job, the state also provides grants and subsidised employment. Thus, for example, the number of subsidies to employers taking on disabled people increased from 48 000 in 1979 to 79 000 in 1988 (Gould, 1993).

A further approach is found in the use of 'adjustment groups'. Their task is not only to devise practical ways to help disabled people to get and keep jobs, but also to promote positive attitudes towards them in society at large. Expert advice is available to employers on changes needed to workplaces and working practices, and the adjustment groups also recommend other measures such as the design and layout of buildings and domestic dwellings. In terms of access to buildings, Swedish regulations are far more strongly drawn and much more comprehensive than their British equivalents. Builders must ensure that all new multifamily housing is accessible. Flats that were constructed since 1977 must have no steps at the entrance, and blocks with more than two storeys must have a lift (Imrie, 1996).

Similarly, adjustment groups pay close attention to the modification of transport. Indeed, until all public transport is accessible, disabled people are entitled to monies to allow them to pay for taxis. Following work by the Disability Commission, set up by the government in 1988, many of these several kinds of support – including personal assistance – became a statutory right under the Support and Service Act (LSS), passed in January 1994. In July of the same year, Sweden set up the office of Disability Ombudsman (Handikappombudsmannen) to monitor issues relating to the rights and interests of disabled people. It remains to be seen, however, what impact the Ombudsman may have on the existing legislative framework for disability policy (Sjöberg, 1994; Socialstyrelsen, 1995).

These strategies notwithstanding, disabled people without jobs still face a hard time. There continues to be reluctance among some

Swedish companies to offer work to disabled people. Concerned about profitability, companies who have a free choice continue to opt for non-disabled candidates. This bias is particularly evident during economic recession, but also, according to Gould, even during the good times, disabled people lose out to the mobility and superfluity of non-disabled workers from elsewhere in Sweden and from overseas.

Beyond vocational training and support, health and social welfare services are also seen as public sector responsibilities, and these services are administered by 23 county and 3 metropolitan councils (Swedish Institute, 1996). The swift growth of the Swedish welfare systems has been highlighted by Gould (1988), who traced a dramatic increase in the number of staff from 1960 (when the country employed only 4500 social workers) to 1980, when the figure had reached just over 25000. In the same period, the number of psychologists and related professionals increased from 7000 to 25000. Similarly, Ronnby (1985) observed an increase in the total number of welfare workers from about 35000 in 1960 to over 160000 by 1975.

Personal assistance services are provided through the agency JAG. Although claiming ideological fraternity with the independent living movement, none of the directors is a disabled person.

> Due to their intellectual disabilities, [they] cannot be burdened with the responsibility of being members of the Board of Directors. To risk making the members personally responsible for decisions concerning large amounts of money would be unethical... only a legal guardian can serve on the Board... For the same reason JAG's members are unable to work at the central office. Some of the staff at the central office are parents [sic]. (Tengström, 1996)

The organisation's main role is to train and provide personal assistance to disabled people whose subsequent supervision is undertaken by a person nominated by the disabled person through his or her legal guardian.

One consequence of this 'maximal' and multifaceted welfare approach to state intervention is that, of the country's 8.8 million people, at any one time some 6.7 million are net recipients from the social welfare system. It stands to reason therefore that the voting arithmetic is continually in favour of higher public spending (McRae, 1996). However, how long Sweden will be able to continue with its high level of welfare provision and supportive intervention is now in question. In 1994, unemployment broke the 10 per cent barrier (Savill, 1994). In the same year, total government debt was equal to about 80 per cent of the country's gross domestic product. Thus it came as no surprise when the newly elected Social Democrat Prime Minister,

Ingvar Carlsson, warned that his government would be forced to make deep cuts in welfare spending (Isherwood, 1994).

The relationship between the Swedish state and disabled people has been criticised on a number of counts. For example, Ronnby (1985) has argued that extensive provision serves the interests of modern capitalism because welfare support allows employers more freely to discard people, knowing that they will be 'patched up' by the system. The generous benefit levels ensure that the effects of redundancy will be mitigated in a substantial way. Sjostrom (1984) says of social work that it provides 'janitorial' services. Surplus labour is kept on welfare until the economy recovers and the workforce begins once more to expand. Furthermore, Ronnby argues that it is in the interests of the state to care for disabled people. By doing so, non-disabled family members are left at liberty to go to work. Clearly, then, both Ronnby and Sjostrom portray welfare as a structure designed to support capitalism.

The welfare approach to disability enjoys widespread support across the international community. However, as we will see in Chapter 11, disabled people themselves have fought for equal opportunities in education, employment and social life, and have found their concerns reflected in international standards, for example the International Labour Organisation (ILO) Vocational Rehabilitation and Employment (Disabled Persons) Convention 1983 (No. 159), which requires that appropriate vocational rehabilitation measures be made available to all categories of disabled people; and the ILO Vocational Rehabilitation and Employment (Disabled Persons) Recommendation 1983 (No. 168), which calls for 'research and the possible application of its results to various types of disability in order to further the participation of disabled persons in ordinary working life' (König and Schalock, 1991).

Indeed, Momm and König (1989) describe the adoption of a community-based rehabilitation approach in the UN's World Programme of Action for Disabled People, in the initiatives of the ILO; and in the work of the ILO across Asia and Africa. But while many of these community-based rehabilitation projects have involved the training and reintegration of disabled people, all of them have lacked:

> an essential element to which the United World Programme of Action and particularly organisations of disabled people around the world have drawn attention: rehabilitation efforts need to be complemented by what has been called 'equalisation of opportunities'.

In fact, the essential part of the process falls largely outside the control of specialised rehabilitation programmes since successful integration depends mainly on the attitude of the community and its institutions, and their acceptance of the idea that disabled people should not be marginalised or segregated but offered equal opportunities (Momm and König, 1989: 505–6).

In sum, the welfare approach typified by Swedish disability policies seeks both to compensate disabled people for their exclusion and to locate change ('rehabilitation') primarily at the individual level. Environmental change may also take place (for example, by employers responding to the advice of the adjustment groups), but the notion of rights and citizenship may be less developed than in other policy models. In subsequent sections of the chapter, I draw on examples from disability policies in other states whose principal concern has been to eradicate discrimination and to establish civil rights and equal opportunities for disabled people.

Australia: a hybrid welfare/civil rights approach

In June 1995, Australia had a population of just over 18 million (Shu *et al.*, 1996), of whom some 2 031 900 were disabled people (SCRCSSP, 1997). The country has a central government and eight states or territories that carry out local government functions. The major service providing programme for disabled people is the Commonwealth/State Disability Agreement (CSDA). Under the CSDA, the Commonwealth (national) government is responsible for competitive employment, vocational training and placement or rehabilitation services. These assist individuals to obtain a job or a place in supported employment where it is believed that an individual is unlikely to find work on the open market. State and territory governments are responsible for accommodation support services (for example, group homes, hostels and large institutions) and the provision of care attendants. Community access services are also focused primarily on the individual (as opposed to the disabling environment), their remit being to:

> assist people with a disability to develop or maintain the personal skills necessary to enhance their independence and self-reliance in the community. (SCRCSSP, 1997: 385)

The State and territory governments are also responsible for respite care services and community support services, including counselling, 'early intervention therapy', 'behaviour intervention' [sic] and other therapy services. Total government expenditure for such services exceeded $10 billion in 1994–5, of which $1.2 billion was spent under the CSDA programme (SCRCSSP, 1997: 386).

The welfare programmes of CSDA are clearly informed by a primarily medical understanding of disability. However, in 1992, Australia emulated the United States in enacting civil rights legislation for disabled people (Tucker, 1994). The Australian Act, although growing from different roots, replicated many of the titles (clauses) of the Americans with Disabilities Act (see below) and substantially shared in its philosophy. The Australian measure emphasised the need for civil rights and saw enforcement as a matter of law rather than voluntary concurrence. Even the terminology was similar to the American legislation; for example, employers had to make 'reasonable accommodations' to allow disabled employees to perform the 'essential functions' of a job. Similarly, all facilities available to the public must also be accessible to disabled people. The requirement encompasses services such as banking, insurance, transport, travel and telecommunications. The civil rights-based approach to disability policies is thus expanding beyond the boundaries of the United States and has been adopted in both Australia and Canada.

As I write, the Australian Disability Discrimination Act is being fleshed out with sets of standards against which progress will be measured. For example, in June 1996, Ministers endorsed 'in principle' draft standards for the accessibility of public transport, and by April 1997, draft standards on employment had been produced. Other areas that are being developed include communications, education and the built environment (Australian Disability Discrimination Commissioner, 1997).

In Australia, then, we may recognise a hybrid strategy towards the creation of disability policy. Service provision and civil rights legislation are being promoted in a twin-track approach, and it remains to be seen whether one or other perspective will gain the upper hand. Certainly, groups of disabled people have lobbied for a strengthening of the 'rights' approach, but while they would not wish to see a withdrawal of services, they do argue for a reconfiguration and a shift of control, away from non-disabled professionals towards disabled users (Brown and Ringma, 1989). We may note in passing that a similar desire has also been expressed in Britain (D'Aboville, 1991). However, perhaps the strongest example of the 'civil rights' approach is to be found in the United States, and it is to this country that I now turn.

The United States: a civil rights approach

In July 1995, the population of the United States was 263 814 032 (Central Intelligence Agency, 1997). It is, however, difficult to obtain a precise measure regarding the prevalence of disability. Using data from the American National Health Interview Survey of 1990, LaPlante (1997) estimates the number of Americans with severe impairments ('limited in major activity') to be 22.9 million and puts the number of those with less severe impairments ('limited in non-major activity') at a further 10.9 million, giving a total of 33.8 million disabled people living in households. Census data from 1990 indicate a further 2.3 million disabled Americans living in institutions, advancing the total to just over 36 million. These figures concur with Haveman's (1984) estimate that 14.6 per cent of the American population is disabled. Bradsher (1997), using Bureau of Census data from 1991–92, offers a higher figure of 48.9 million, but the calculations underpinning the Americans with Disabilities Act were based on a somewhat lower figure (itself derived from the extrapolation of a survey carried out in 1979) of 43.8 million.

Before 1973, disabled people in the United States experienced the kind of segregation historically common in Britain, and the special education system concentrated as much on medicine as on pedagogy. However, intensive campaigning by disabled people gained a shift in policy designed to reduce segregation and remove social and environmental barriers, as evinced in the Architectural Barriers Act 1968 and the Reha-bilitation Act 1973 (specifically s. 504 of the latter, which is recognised as the first civil rights legislation covering disabled Americans).

From these limited beginnings emerged the contemporary approach, with its emphasis on securing the rights of disabled people in the United States. Citizenship has been enshrined in the Americans with Disabilities Act 1990. The Act resulted from more than 20 years of powerful lobbying by disabled people and their allies (Anspach, 1979; De Jong, 1979, 1983). Using a broad definition of disability, the Act has accorded extensive rights to disabled people under five main sections, or titles.

Title I outlaws discrimination against disabled people in public and private sector employment. Disabled people who can perform the 'essential functions' of a job are protected by the legislation. Any company employing 15 or more staff is prohibited from discriminating against such candidates and must set in train 'readily achievable' and 'reasonable' accommodations to the workplace to facilitate disabled employees (Blakemore and Drake, 1996). The need for action on employment for disabled people in America has been documented by LaPlante *et al.* (1997), who describe an 'employment gap'. Their data, which relate to 1995, suggest that just over 12 million disabled people are unemployed and only 5.5 million are in work. However, some 723 000 disabled people are actively seeking work, and this figure represents an unemployment rate of 13.4 per cent of all disabled people who wish to work. The rate is more than twice that of unemployment among non-disabled Americans, which stands at 5.6 per cent. LaPlante *et al.* (1997) bring home their point more forcefully by demonstrating that only 27.8 per cent of working-age disabled people have jobs, but 76.3 per cent of working-age non-disabled Americans are in work – an enormous employment gap and a situation that Title I of the Act was intended to redress. From these 1995 figures, it becomes clear that there will be no short-term solution.

Before assessing the next part of the Americans with Disabilities Act, it is important briefly to note that unemployment among disabled Americans is a key factor in explaining the prevalence of poverty among this group of citizens. Thirty per cent of working-age disabled people live below the poverty line. Nearly three-quarters of disabled women who have young children are in poverty. As in Britain, those disabled Americans who have work enjoy wages below the level of their non-disabled counterparts, earning about 63.6 per cent of the norm for non-disabled people (LaPlante *et al.*, 1997).

The second part of the Americans with Disabilities Act dealt with public services and transport. In particular, all activities of local and state governments would have to be conducted in future in such a way as to ensure that disabled people were not discriminated against. Accordingly, public bodies were compelled to make 'reasonable' changes to rules, policies and practices, and had to remove physical barriers, or provide auxiliary aids, in order to ensure that their services were usable by disabled people. The Act covered not only the conduct of government, but also its facilities, services and communications. New public service vehicles had to be accessible, and from 1996, coaches and trains were also included in the requirements (Blakemore and Drake, 1996).

Title III required access for disabled people to educational, recreational and leisure facilities such as schools, cinemas and shops.

Education is a particularly important area. LaPlante *et al.* (1997) argue that employment chances have been blighted by low skills among disabled Americans, and a key reason for this has been lack of vocational training and restricted access to mainstream schools and colleges. Only two-thirds of disabled people graduate from high school (compared with more than four-fifths of non-disabled Americans). The disparities at university and college level are even greater. About 23 per cent of non-disabled people graduate from college, the figure for disabled people being under 10 per cent. Again, although the Americans with Disabilities Act has tackled a major area of discrimination, any impact will only be evident in the medium or long term, rather than in the short term.

Another key part of Title III related to access to public and commercial buildings. The Act recognised that the shape of the built environment was heavily influenced by building codes and guidelines. Under Title III, the United States Department of Justice is authorised to certify that state laws and local building codes meet the requirements of the Americans with Disabilities Act. Code certification therefore:

> allows builders to rely on their local inspection and approval processes, and it ensures that accessibility will be routinely considered in those processes... It eliminates conflicts between local requirements and ADA requirements... [and] certification gives building officials a significant role in enforcing the substance of the ADA. (United States Department of Justice, 1996: 1)

The fourth Title compelled telephone companies, within 3 years, to provide TDD relay (a specialised telecommunications system) for those with hearing impairments. Last, Title V detailed the enforcement structures of the Act and the avenues of redress available to disabled people where employers or service providers failed to comply with the law. The Act is enforced by an Equal Employment Opportunities Commission and by designated state agencies. One of the main strands of argument against the introduction of similar legislation in Britain has been concern about the cost of implementation. Higgens (1992) recorded similar anxieties in America, leading to substantial resistance by businesses and corporations. Even now, some 7 years on, disability rights campaigners in America still detect a backlash against the Americans with Disabilities Act (Disability Activist, 1997).

In the event however, the implementation of the Americans with Disabilities Act has led neither to excessive expenditure or litigation nor to commercial bankruptcies. All but 1 per cent of the workplace modifications made for disabled employees cost less than $5000 (about

£3300) (Scott, 1994). Furthermore, by making businesses more accessible to disabled people, the sales of some goods and services have increased dramatically. Scott quotes the example of a pizza parlour that introduced a TDD telephone system for customers with hearing impairments. The deaf community boosted the sales of the outlet by 80 per cent within a few months of the new equipment being installed. The National Federation of Small Business Owners acknowledged that the Act became a goldmine for them. The economic arguments against the Act were further undermined by the fact that, as President Bush stated in a speech at the White House in July 1990, 'When you add together state, local and private funds, it costs almost $200 billion annually to support Americans with disabilities, in effect to keep them dependent.' In the light of these outcomes, it is unsurprising to discover that, in a recent survey, 80 per cent of large corporations acknowledged the requirements of the Americans with Disabilities Act to be reasonable in balancing the rights of disabled people with the costs of changes to the work environment (O'Day, 1995). Also, as Blakemore and Drake (1996: 154) point out:

> further criticism, that disabled workers were less reliable than non-disabled personnel, was effectively refuted by the results of a survey taken over three decades by DuPont in Washington which found that 97 per cent of disabled workers were average or above average in terms of job safety; 86 per cent were average or above average on attendance; and 90 per cent were average or above average on general job performance. (Scott, 1994: 22)

Conclusion: the United Kingdom's piecemeal approach in context

My prime purpose in this chapter has been to illuminate disability policy in the United Kingdom by setting it within a comparative, international context. It should be said at the outset that Britain is not alone in its piecemeal, welfare-orientated approach. Countries such as Germany and Holland also take forward major welfare programmes aimed at supporting disabled people but in a supplementary, *ad hoc* and often poorly funded way (Daunt, 1991). However, we have seen how Sweden has concentrated heavily on the development of a comprehensive welfare state, the United States on civil rights and Australia on a cogent and properly informed policy-driven cycle of planning. It would be claiming too much to argue that each of these countries was entirely consistent or uniform in its policies, or that disabled people had no criticisms of those regimes – far from it. But as we saw in the previous chapter, the United Kingdom differs from Sweden, Australia and the United States in that it has enunciated no real or coherent strategic policy direction. Indeed, the development of United Kingdom policy has enjoyed little consistency, no enduring overview of aims and methods, and certainly no sustained emphasis on the citizenship of disabled people. In America in particular, disabled people are (at least in theory) armed with an arsenal of legal powers, and the Americans with Disabilities Act has been designed not only to reduce (and ultimately prevent) discrimination against disabled people, but also to bring about changes in society in order to minimise its disabling impacts. In this second part of the book, then, we have seen how the development of British disability policy has proceeded in a substantially haphazard and knee-jerk fashion, and its contemporary profile represents a mixture of strong elements of state welfare, the encouragement of private provision but, as yet, only very limited aspects of a 'rights-based' approach. Having set out the policy environment in which disabled people live, I now turn to the third and final part of the book, which examines the impacts of disability policies on their lives and considers the responses that disabled people have made. Part III begins with an assessment of the ways in which social class may mediate the experience of disability.

PART III

Policy Outcomes and Disabled People's Responses

7

Social Class and Disability

Introduction

In the book so far, I have examined contrasting theories and definitions of disability and described a variety of possible models for disability policy, all of which have been realised at one time or another somewhere in the world. The spectrum of policy models ranges from the extremely negative (the actual annihilation of disabled people) to the very positive (attempts at legislation aimed at guaranteeing their civil rights). I have also described the historical development of disability policies in Britain and have argued that contemporary policies are based on an individualistic (medical) understanding of how disability arises. Accordingly, such policies as have emerged have been designed partly to pacify, and partly to compensate, disabled people for their exclusion from many aspects of mainstream society. Historically, however, such policies have also reinforced their segregation. This isolation may have taken shape in a concrete way, for example through the development of residential homes and asylums, or it may have arisen through more subtle effects of discrimination (intentional or otherwise) so that exclusion has appeared to be a natural effect resulting from personal impairment rather than social ostracism. Either way, such outcomes are challenged with increasing vigour by disabled people today.

In Part II of the book, I evaluated the piecemeal approach to disability policies that has typified the outlook of successive governments in Britain, and I sought to explain the nature of that fragmentation by placing our experience in a broader international context. As we saw in the previous chapter, some countries have provided extensive and coherently planned state support whereas others have emphasised the concept of 'rights', placing the idea of equality of opportunity at the heart of their policies. In the latter case, the focus of state policy has been as much on the need for social and environmental change as on the framework for medical intervention.

The key task in this third and final part of the book is to try to understand the ways in which government policies have made an impact on the lives of disabled people. This is no simple undertaking. As I mooted in Chapter 2, the creation and implementation of policy is not easy to trace. Even where the overall aims of policy have initially been expressed in a pristine and lucid way, these objectives pass through many hands before the results are evident in practice, and the outcomes may be profoundly different from what their authors originally intended. How much more difficult, then, when real policy aims are, from the outset, opaque, contradictory or even covert. There are several points in the policy process at which transmutation may occur. First, goals themselves may be altered, reprioritised or otherwise limited during the very processes of discussion and debate through which government policies traditionally emerge. Second, as policy ideals are hammered into operational practicalities, there often occurs a substitution of the attainable for the desirable. Third, laws and acts are implemented by people who operate within institutions. These organisations have their own cultures and mores, and their employees tend to work from well-worn understandings, customs and traditions. To the extent that people and institutions may exercise discretion, they will implement legislation with enthusiasm or reluctance, observe laws in the spirit or merely in the letter and interpret rules in accordance with local circumstance or general concern. Implementation may thus differ from one area to another. It is hardly surprising, then, that what finally transpires may be some considerable distance from what was first intended. As Bismarck put it, 'politics is the art of the possible'.

Particularly where service provision is concerned, policies are almost always implemented by intermediary organisations or agencies: for example, health policies are put into operation by health authorities and (latterly) health trusts, under whose auspices hospitals and other public medical facilities carry out their work. Within these institutions, there is a variety of staff groupings, each of which has its own profession and traditions of practice. Thus, for any particular area of policy, it may be difficult to specify whether an impact we have discerned has been caused by the policy itself, by the way in which it has been implemented or by the structure within which it was taken forward, or whether an impact arose as a result of the amalgamation of all these factors or even none of them. We must recognise that there are instances where an outcome may be occasioned *irrespective* of any policy in force at the time.

Second, as we saw in the earlier chapters concerned with the machinery of policy making and the particular policy history in Britain, disability policies have not been produced in any heuristic way. Instead, they have emerged at different times, have been created in contexts made up of differing political concerns and professional perspectives, produced by different departments of state, and have been intended to serve different purposes. Little wonder then that there is no sense of cogency to be found in what has gone before and that there are large gaps and significant overlaps.

The third difficulty in trying to assess the impact of policy is a lack of data. Disability (except for the medical investigation of the causes of impairment) remains a scantily researched area even today. The specific information needed precisely to tie outcomes to objectives is often simply not to hand, and we are left to reach tentative, *pro tempore*, conclusions on the balance of such evidence as may be available until more definite findings can be secured. Bearing these caveats in mind, we may turn to the final five substantive chapters of the book. The first four deal in turn with social class, gender, ethnicity and age. The last is devoted to assessing the various responses of disabled people to their experiences in contemporary society and to the impacts that successive policies have had on them.

Social class and disability

In this chapter, I take further the arguments set out in Chapter 5 concerning disabled people and work. In particular, I argue that the class position of disabled people is in large measure determined by – and itself determines – their access to employment. This relationship between social class and the world of work has been, and remains, crucial because, in our society, wealth (and the level of remuneration achieved) is by and large governed by an individual's access first to education, and second, to paid employment. There are other avenues of course: a person may, for example, benefit from an inheritance, win the lottery or the football pools, live off the proceeds of crime or subsist on social security. But in all of these instances there are evident drawbacks: the lack of wealthy benefactors precludes the expectation of a legacy, the chances of a jackpot win are negligible, the risk (or actuality) of imprisonment may deter (or prevent) embarkation on a criminal path to riches, and the low levels of state benefits impede material advancement.

Clearly, then, their disadvantage in gaining work accounts for the fact that half of disabled people in Britain live in penury, and many more are vulnerable to it (Berthoud, 1995). Moreover, a lack of paid work (or restriction to low wages) correlates closely with other deficits associated with a hostile social and physical environment. These include lack of choice in housing, the risk of actual homelessness or an inability to purchase or rent good-quality accommodation, poor diet and susceptibility to ill-health.

Before tracing the detrimental effects on the majority of disabled people of their occupying a disadvantageous class position, it is important to clarify what is meant by 'class' and then explore in more detail policy impacts in four key areas: access to work; poverty and wealth; material and environmental outcomes; and the need for equality of opportunity.

What is 'class'?

There has, as yet, been relatively little research into how social class may mediate the impacts of disability policies on individuals and on how individuals experience disability. Research on the dimension of social class in disability policies therefore represents an important but underdeveloped area of study.

Many of the sociologists who write about 'class' begin by saying how difficult it is to pin the concept down because its meaning has been augmented and stretched over time. In perhaps the most orthodox account, the concept of 'class' is used to analyse the nature of capitalist societies and economies; in particular, 'class' is intended to explain the emergence of social groups who have essentially conflicting interests. At its simplest, we may identify three 'classes': (a) the *bourgeoisie*: those who own the means of production and retain the profits generated by these assets; (b) the *proletariat*: those who work to produce the goods and services (but who do not receive the full value of their labour), hence the creation of profits; and (c) those who have neither the means of production nor work. This group is sometimes called a *lumpenproletariat* or underclass.

In recent years, the usefulness of 'class' as an analytical tool has been the subject of heated debate. In the British context, some writers, like Pakulski and Waters (1996), believe that society has changed fundamentally through significant increases in home ownership, the privatisation of state industries, an expansion of share ownership and, by dint of this expansion, the separation of the actual ownership of companies from their everyday control. As a result (so the argument goes), 'class' is a redundant concept because those who do the work now own the means of production through shares in company schemes or through personal equity plans, or own shares indirectly through their contributions to private pension funds. Furthermore, where citizenship is guaranteed, the notion of 'class boundaries' becomes anachronistic (Ossowski, 1963). For others, 'class' still has a role to play in analysing society, but the concept has to be modernised to take into account new movements and social dynamics (Eder, 1993). A third group argues that, recent changes notwithstanding, it is still the case that only about one-fifth of the population owns any shares at all (Saunders, 1990), and over nine-tenths of Britain's wealth remains in the possession of the richer half of the population (Scase, 1992). Not only this, but the gap between rich and poor widened considerably in the period from 1961 to 1991. Today, the income of one-fifth of the entire population (some 11 million people) falls below half of average earnings. This means that the proportion living on low wages (or no wages at all) has doubled in the past 30 years. At the same time, however, the top 10 per cent of the population now receives 25 per cent of the country's annual income, up from 22 per cent in 1961 (Institute for Fiscal Studies, 1994). While some economists, such as Howard Davies, argue that a widening gap of this magnitude threatens the fabric of society, others, such as Patrick Minford, argue against redressing the balance on the grounds that to do so would harm incentives and profitability (Loney *et al.*, 1992).

Accordingly, 'class' remains a potent tool in describing the distribution of wealth, but, beyond the cataloguing of social and economic 'facts', some sociologists argue that the concept of 'class' has further use in *explaining how* certain patterns of distribution occur in the ways in which they do. More specifically, these scholars contend that privatisation and the separation of ownership and control of the means of production have reinforced, rather than redrawn, the existing patterns of wealth distribution (Scase, 1992).

The importance of this kind of analysis lies in the contention that profits go primarily to owners (shareholders) rather than to workers. To the extent that these are separate groups of people (classes), the result is twofold: there are progressive inequalities in wealth, that is, the gap between rich and poor continues to widen (Institute for Fiscal Studies, 1994), and there is a development of social stratification, groups moving further apart and becoming increasingly distinct and rigid social entities (Crompton, 1993).

Social class and the impact of disability policies

Earlier in the book, drawing *inter alia* on the work of Barnes (1991) and Berthoud (1995), I established that the majority of disabled people are without work and are thus vulnerable to poverty. The majority therefore occupy positions either in the class divorced entirely from work or find themselves among those on the lowest rungs of the employment ladder. How, then, does the class position occupied by the majority of disabled people affect the impact of policies on them? In what follows, this is a key question, and I attempt to answer it by making the fundamental proposition (drawing on theoretical constructs introduced in Chapter 2) that being without work compounds power-lessness. A lack of resources makes it more difficult for disabled people to influence the creation of policy, makes it harder for them to resist any adverse impacts of policy and jeopardises their attempts to secure and maintain their independence. My analysis is in five parts: access to work; poverty and wealth; material and environmental outcomes; education; and equality of opportunity.

Access to work

It is unsurprising that, without equality of opportunity, very many disabled people are (more or less permanently) absent from the world of work: few are employees and even fewer are owners of businesses (Barnes, 1991). In 1986, there were about 6.2 million adult disabled people in Britain – 3.65 million men and 2.55 million women – and there were some 360 000 disabled children. By extrapolation, George (1996) suggests that today the figure for the total number of disabled adults may have reached 6.6 million. Of these, only about one-third of disabled men and even fewer, just 29 per cent, of disabled women have jobs. Compare these percentages to the equivalent measures for the employment of non-disabled adults. About 78 per cent of men are in work, as are 60 per cent of women (Lonsdale, 1990). We must add to this the further caveat that the work available to disabled people tends to be lower paid and of lower status than that available to their non-disabled counterparts, as shown in Table 7.1.

More recent data from Blackaby *et al*. (1998) confirm the discrepancies evinced in Table 7.1 and explain that the great majority of disabled people earn less than their non-disabled counterparts primarily because they occupy jobs demanding fewer skills and qualifications, and have less access to the more professional and well-paid posts. They even earn less when compared with non-disabled people doing similar jobs (Martin and White, 1988). From this overall picture, we may gain an explanation of Berthoud's (1995: 77) findings that 'a very large number [of disabled people] have very little money to live on' and about half of them are destitute.

Table 7.1   Socio-economic status of men and women under pension age according to sex and whether or not disabled (percentage)

Socio-economic group	Disabled		Non-disabled	
	Male	*Female*	*Male*	*Female*
Professional	3	1	8	1
Employer/managerial	15	6	20	8
Intermediate non-manual	9	16	10	20
Junior non-manual	10	28	8	34
Skilled manual and own account non-professional	37	12	37	8
Semi-skilled manual and personal service	19	26	14	23
Unskilled	7	11	4	6

Source: Martin *et al*. (1989) *Disabled Adults: Services Transport and Employment*, Table 7.20, Office for National Statistics, © Crown Copyright, 1998.

How did such a situation arise; how came disabled people to be divorced from work? It was not always so. Bindoff (1950: 120) tells us that, before the advent of capitalism:

> Even those who laboured in industry were not so wholly dependent upon their weekly earnings as the modern wage-earner; not only was much of that industry located in the countryside and its labour part-time or seasonal workers drawn from the rural population, but even the town worker remained both physically and economically near enough to the soil to supplement his earnings by raising crops or livestock.

Finkelstein (1981) concurs with Bindoff's analysis and identifies the industrial revolution as the event that divorced disabled people from work. The advent of machinery designed to be operated only by 'able-bodied' people left disabled people with few ways of coming by their living. Many were thrown on the mercy of the Church or subjected to the cruelty of the workhouse. Oliver's (1991a: 133) analysis concurs with the view that the requirements of large-scale, high-speed manufacturing *dis*-abled people in large numbers. He argues that industrial processes were so configured that, in the great majority of cases, employers preferred to hire, as it were, 'fit and healthy' people, so that consequently:

> disabled people have become an underclass, not because of their perceived or real physical limitations, but because changes in the work system have excluded them from the work process. This exclusion has had profound effects on social relations as well, resulting not just in the marginalization of the disabled within labour markets, but from society as a whole. To put the matter simply, an underclass has been created by society rather than produced by the characteristics of this particular group.

Thus while there are examples of disabled people who have 'made good', who have been successful or who have been able to continue their careers after becoming disabled, others have fared less well. Moreover, the chances of success or failure are weighted according to class position. For example, McLean and Jeffreys (1974) demonstrated in their study of paraplegia and tetraplegia that within 2 or 3 years of becoming disabled, three-quarters of professional workers had resumed their careers or found similar work. But they also found that up to three-quarters of non-professional disabled people were still unemployed 3 years after becoming disabled.

As the figures given in Table 7.1 demonstrate, some individual disabled people are able to buck the trend, even when the dice are loaded against them as prodigiously as McLean and Jeffreys suggest. It has long been recognised that, although there may be 'social stratification' of the classes, the boundaries are not totally impermeable. *Social mobility* is possible, and at least some people do therefore move between classes. The amount of movement, and how easy the transition is to achieve, depends on how open or closed are the boundaries between the classes, how strong the barriers that divide them. The existence of some wealthy and esteemed disabled people shows that the hurdles are not totally insurmountable. At the same time, however, the paucity of their numbers indicates that the thresholds or obstacles in the way are formidable. As I suggested earlier in the chapter, the openness or restrictiveness of class boundaries depends ultimately on the extent to which there exists equality of opportunity.

Clearly, wealthy people who become disabled, or disabled people who are born to wealth (or acquire it later in life), are better able to adapt themselves to the broader social and physical environment than are their less well-off counterparts. For example, in 1995, the Hollywood actor Christopher Reeve sustained extensive injuries in a horse riding accident. Now quadriplegic, he lives life to the full with the help of a team of nurses costing some $400 000 (about £250 000–£300 000) per annum. He continues to work as a film director and has recently signed a book deal worth $2 million (about £1.25 million) (Clark, 1997).

Likewise, those few disabled people who occupy powerful social positions are, *ipso facto,* better placed to bring about environmental changes (the lowering or removal of physical and social barriers) than are the much larger numbers of less well-connected disabled people. For example, the election of a Labour government in 1997 brought a blind MP, David Blunkett, to the position of Secretary of State for Education and Employment, and as previously mentioned, for the first time a wheelchair user, Anne Begg, was elected as MP for Aberdeen South (McGwire, 1997). It remains true, however, that the majority of disabled people have few opportunities to gain the power or resources needed to transcend class boundaries, particularly where these are strongly fortified.

Two questions emerge from what I have said. The first is about the status of work itself, and the second concerns the purpose of the welfare state. We can deal with these issues in the order stated. For Abberley (1996), the question is whether the attempt to transcend class boundaries in pursuit of 'work' is a legitimate goal anyway. Should disabled people aspire to become workers or owners, or is it the concept of 'work' itself that must change: is capitalism, *of itself,* disabling? Abberley (1996: 61) argues that:

> classical social theories give participation in production a crucial importance in social integration; in their Utopias, work is a need, as a source of identity. Such theories imply the progressive abolition of impairment as restrictive on the development of people's full human capacities.

All the main political parties in Britain are agreed that the proper aim of social security policy should be 'a hand up, not a handout', and the new Labour government has set in train a large-scale 'welfare to work' programme. It has also set aside a sum of money to provide vocational training for disabled people (see below). For Abberley, the fundamental question is not 'How should disabled people be helped to attain the goal of work?' but rather 'Why is work central to the ideals to which society as a whole, and governments in particular, aspire?' To put the question another way: what claim to superiority has the capitalist vision of a perfect society over other such conceptualisations, and what legitimacy has it in claiming the right to determine social membership and citizenship? Second, Abberley asks whether there is an alternative way (other than that of struggling towards the Shangri-La of paid employment) through which disabled people might gain their identities, resources, independence and full status in society?

The current configuration of what constitutes 'work' is oppressive. So many of its manifestations exclude at least some people with impairments who are unable to conform to the performance expectations imposed by employers, and Berthoud (1995) demonstrates that the more severe their impairments, the greater the difficulties they are likely to encounter in their search for work, even though they might well match the performance standards demanded in work were it to be differently constituted and defined. However, Abberley is keen to carry his analysis beyond the argument of what does or does not constitute work. He recognises that paid employment (as defined within capitalist, market-orientated societies) carries with it meaning and significance beyond the purely industrial. Quite simply, work is influential in the social and political, as well as economic, spheres. It is so influential, in fact, that it plays a key role in *defining* the individual. On making new acquaintances, one of the first questions one may expect to be asked is 'What do you do for a living?'

In seeking to elaborate a fresh paradigm, Abberley draws on the scepticism towards the pre-eminence of technology frequently found in feminist theory, and he also discerns ethnic differences in the way in which the role of work is now conceptualised and understood. These marginalised groups counterpose an essentially white male account of labour as a 'defining activity' – your work *is* who and what you are – with a view of work as an instrumental activity: a job is what you do to get what you want and need. These counter-hegemonic perspectives can be used to argue that there must be a disengagement of work from the criteria used to fix and understand the prevailing concepts of 'the self' and societal 'Utopia', since it is these same criteria that relegate the social roles and identities of disabled people.

Whether or not we agree with Abberley, it is clear that many disabled people desire equality of opportunity in gaining skills, education and work, and chase promotion in the same way that others do. It is equally clear that the Labour government elected in May 1997 subscribes to the prevailing, traditional view of work. In his first budget, the Chancellor of the Exchequer, Gordon Brown, allocated £200 million from the contingency reserve to provide skills training for disabled people who wished to undergo vocational training or find a job (Cooper, 1997b).

The second question I outlined earlier also relates directly to the status of work and unemployment, and to the ways in which resources are distributed. What is the purpose and nature of the welfare state? Pampel and Williamson (1989: 1) argue that the welfare state plays a crucial (even dominant) role in social class and stratification. They hold that the orthodox account portrays the purpose of social welfare as being to redress the inequalities stemming from class differentials in a market-driven economy. Industrial technology leads to an educated labour force that controls valuable specialised knowledge and demands political power. They further argue that the resulting growth of political democracy allows the masses to combine politically against the élite in competition for resources, and the consequent application of pressure leads to higher welfare spending.

Pampel and Williamson go on to modify their account in the light of newer theories of social fragmentation, and they postulate the existence of a plurality of powerful interests. However, the key point in the orthodox account, and most variants of it, is that the welfare state is a product of contending groups able to summon and use power. By their exclusion from work, disabled people have lacked both the resources and the power to shape not only the specific structures of the welfare state, but also, more importantly, the norms and understandings that prevail in society at large. The failure effectively to influence the social construction of society means that it is configured in ways commensurate with the interests of (non-disabled) others – ways that do not meet disabled people's requirements – and (as demonstrated earlier in the chapter) perhaps the most tangible outcome has been the lack of paid work leading to the prevalence of poverty among disabled people.

A particular example of the fact that disabled people have been unable to shape the welfare state to their own ends appears in Berthoud (1995: 85). He points out that to claim the DWA, a disabled person needs to be in receipt of one of the benefits based on incapacity for work (for example, invalidity benefit, severe disablement allowance or the disability premium on income support) and must be working for at least 16 hours a week. However, in a Kafkaesque twist, the previous Conservative administration decided that, from April 1995, these three benefits that are the passport to the DWA will only be available to individuals whom doctors have certified to be utterly incapable of work. Given its commitment to encouraging disabled people to work should they so desire, it remains to be seen how the Labour government will respond to the paradox thus created.

Poverty and wealth

Clearly, the importance of work lies not only in the esteem that a good job may bring, nor merely in the purpose or shape that it may offer to a person's life, but crucially in making the difference between living a comfortable and active life or living with the burden of poverty. As the Disability Alliance (1991) has cogently argued, for the great majority of disabled people, poverty or near-poverty has been their prevailing companion, and disabled women and people from ethnic minorities in particular are much more likely to receive lower levels of benefit because of indirect discrimination. The Alliance points out that elderly disabled people are directly discriminated against because certain benefits – such as the DLA – cannot be claimed after the age of 65 (although people who had lodged a claim before reaching 65 might receive a lifetime award; see MacErlean, 1997).

The gulf between average wages and the levels of remuneration through state benefits is shown in Table 7.2. Each figure is given at the highest rate for a person under the age of 35 with no dependants. A person receiving the highest rate of incapacity benefit and the highest rates of both components (care and mobility) of the DLA, and the highest age additions to these allowances, plus the average rate of housing benefit (including disability premium), would in 1996/97 have an income of a little over £10 000 net. This compares with the approximate (net) figure for (male) average pay of circa £15 200. Extra costs associated with impairments (for example, higher heating and laundry bills) should also be taken into account, but even the raw figures demonstrate a substantial gap between average male earnings and disability benefits. We may note that, depending on individual circumstances, a person receiving severe disablement allowance may be yet worse off than one who receives incapacity benefit.

Table 7.2   Average wage compared with levels of benefit in 1997

	£ per week	£ per annum
Average male earnings 1996/7		
(gross)	391.60	20 363.20
(net) [circa]	292.30	15 200.00
Benefits (net)		
Severe disablement allowance	50.90	2 646.80
(non-contributory)		
Incapacity benefit	75.60	3 931.20
(long-term, contributory)		
Disability living allowance		
Care	49.50	2 574.00
Mobility	34.60	1 799.20

Sources: (average male earnings) Office for National Statistics, 1996, Table A1.1 (April, 1996); (disability benefit levels) Department of Social Security, 1997 (Benefits Agency Leaflet NI196: *Benefit Rates*). © Crown Copyright, 1998.

Material and environmental outcomes

Before examining different areas in which poor disabled people find themselves at a disadvantage, it is important to make a more general point. Access to work is not merely the key to wealth, but also the key to power in other forms. Professionals such as architects, bank managers, designers, building society managers, planners and so forth make decisions that directly affect people and their environment: the design of buildings, the availability of mortgages, a place at university and all manner of other opportunities sought by the population at large. Their absence from these kinds of position curtails the influence that disabled people can exercise over the social and physical environment to bring about changes they desire.

As a specific example, within the general framework of housing policy, professionals control the supply of housing in the public and private sectors, control mortgage lending, authorise or refuse permission for the building of certain structures in certain ways, and make decisions about enterprise loans and investments. Disabled people are underrepresented in these building and planning professions, and the effects of such absence are clearly detrimental. As Imrie (1996: vii) observes:

'design professionals', architects, planners and building control officers, in the construction of specific spaces and places... literally lock people with disabilities 'out'. In particular, western cities are characterized by a 'design apartheid' where building form and design are inscribed with the values of a society which seeks to project and prioritize the dominant values of the 'able-bodied'.

To take this point further, I referred in Chapter 5 to work by Forrest and Murie (1991), who demonstrated that, since 1979, our cities have become progressively polarised. Owner occupation has become increasingly reserved for the wage earner, public sector rented property ever more the domain of the marginalised groups. For Forrest and Murie, social divisions in the housing market reflect differential bargaining power, and the most significant outcome of the sale of council houses has been a *spatial* one: social segregation and the concentration of different social groups into different areas of the town or city.

If, for economic reasons, private ownership is out of reach, rented accommodation (public or private) is equally difficult to secure. Private landlords provide homes for only 7 per cent of all households (Lund, 1996), and Buckle (1971) found that 15 per cent of local authority tenants and 34 per cent of private tenants had waited in excess of 5 years to gain their homes. More recent data from Balchin (1995) have indicated that the situation has worsened since Buckle's study, both in terms of the time spent on the waiting list and the length of the queue itself, with some 1.5 million households waiting to be allocated council housing.

Furthermore, marginalised groups have consistently occupied the worst housing. A quarter of disabled people live in housing that stands in need of basic amenities such as indoor toilets or lacks appropriately adapted facilities such as stair lifts or baths. About a million disabled people need either substantial housing improvements or actual rehousing (Office of Population, Censuses and Surveys, 1971; Malpass and Murie, 1994). The situation is exacerbated by the unofficial practice of 'red-lining' in which building societies covertly designate entire parts of towns and cities as areas in which they will not provide any mortgage loans. As a result, people with very little money find it hard to obtain advances to buy the least expensive properties because these are situated in areas unattractive to lenders. Furthermore, for those on low incomes who do find a home, improvements to their unfit properties are difficult to finance.

The sale of council houses also meant that councils had fewer properties to house homeless people, and this particularly affected disabled people. Morris (1992) estimates that between 1980 and 1988, the number of disabled people rendered homeless increased by 92 per cent, as against a general increase in homelessness of 57 per cent in the same period.

Even where disabled people occupy homes suited to their needs, access to transport (particularly public transport) remains problematic, and in the context of class, lack of mobility is a feature ancillary to difficulties in gaining work. It follows that the greater the geographical mobility of an individual, the more numerous the potential opportunities for employment.

Education

As revealed in Chapter 5, education policy has resulted either in the actual segregation of disabled (particularly cognitively disabled) people from the mainstream, or from disadvantages arising from various kinds of barrier within the mainstream. Even with a shift away from segregation, contemporary policies, for whatever reasons (structural, attitudinal or practical), result in disabled people receiving a significantly poorer education than their non-disabled counterparts and leaving school with fewer qualifications. They therefore find it more difficult to go into higher education. Indeed, a mere 0.3 per cent of students in higher education are disabled (*Hansard*, 11th March, 1994, col. 523). In so far as it remains critical to future earnings and access to work, education thus plays a key role in determining the class position of disabled people (and their place in the economy).

Equality of opportunity

It has become clear that many of the disadvantages faced by disabled people are systemic and environmental as opposed to personal or medical. It is also clear that, by focusing on the rehabilitation of the individual, policies developed and implemented in Britain have so far done little or nothing to tackle the inequalities of opportunity inherent in an environment determined and built by non-disabled people.

For a more detailed exegesis of equal opportunity policies, I refer the reader to Blakemore and Drake (1996). However, we should note here that equality of opportunity is important to disabled people as a means of combating discrimination and as a tool for transcending and diminishing class barriers.

Early understandings of equality of opportunity stressed the need for positive discrimination, that is, remedial action designed to overcome particular disadvantages faced by specified groups. The employment quota scheme in the 1944 Disabled Persons (Employment) Act was a good example of this kind of approach. However, positive discrimination fails to address the environmental conditions that lead to such disadvantages in the first place, and, as often as not, it can also create resentment among other groups who have not been privileged by special initiatives (Kandola *et al.*, 1995).

A more recent approach has been called 'managing diversity', and the understanding here is that people from different backgrounds have differing skills, talents and knowledge to offer. It therefore benefits any enterprise to equip itself with a varied workforce. The managing diversity approach recognises that, for people to reach their full potential, they must have a fair chance of receiving an education appropriate to them, access to resources they can use to develop their careers and an equitable system of selection when applying for jobs. To ensure equality of opportunity therefore, changes are needed to ensure physical access to education and employment, and to remove prejudice from education systems, selection systems, monitoring and supervisory systems, and other aspects of employment (Kandola *et al.*, 1995). Also, for equality of opportunity to prevail, it is clear that changes must be located in the social and built environments.

Conclusion

I have tried to show in this chapter that the crucial element that renders disabled people susceptible to state intervention is poverty. Wealthy disabled people are able to use their resources to stave off the worst effects and are able to command social esteem. Without sufficient wealth, however, disabled people depend on, and are therefore vulnerable to, social policies, institutions and practices over which they are likely to have little or no control. The great majority of disabled people lack wealth and status. They have fewer opportunities for work and less money than their non-disabled counterparts, and they tend to live in less secure kinds of tenure, often in the less sought-after areas. Without substantial funds, owner occupation is difficult. Lack of access, particularly to further and higher education, prevents (for many) the chance to gain the skills and qualifications necessary to escape poverty and transcend class barriers. Even those who do gain vocational skills and qualifications cannot rely on equality of opportunity but may be thwarted in their careers by discriminatory practices. Clearly, then, the mechanisms that determine the social positions of disabled people and their experience of tangible negative social consequences were (and remain) educational, economic and industrial in origin.

In the following chapters, I trace three particular fault lines of social policy and discuss policy impacts on disabled people according to their gender, ethnicity and age. Then, in Chapter 11, I assess the ways in which disabled people have responded to the situation in which they have found themselves.

8

Gender and Disability

Introduction

This chapter is concerned with two distinct but related topics: gender and genetics. First, I consider the differential impact of disability policies according to the sex of disabled persons. I analyse the concerns of disabled women, then those of disabled men, and finally the position of disabled gay and lesbian couples. I argue that, while the impact of some policies may be felt irrespective of gender, there are other experiences and outcomes more specific to a person's sex. Second, I assess the impact of work in genetics, particularly in the areas of diagnostics and abortion.

How do understandings of disability and the configuration of disability policies affect disabled people according to their gender? If policies are directed towards environmental change and citizenship, then whether a disabled person is male or female will be unlikely to affect policy outcomes. However, where policies focus on seeking to change disabled people, and arise in a piecemeal fashion, disabled men and women may receive differential treatment and experience differing outcomes.

This is, in any case, a sensitive and difficult area of enquiry, first because much policy is overlaid with ethical questions and expectations, and second because (as we saw in Chapter 2) it is profoundly difficult to trace a path from prevailing values and understandings through to the formation of policy, to the setting up of institutions and operations, and finally to the measurement of outcomes or impacts on those affected. What exactly is the nature of these impacts? Perhaps the first point to be made is that experiences are not linear. By this, I mean that policy impacts are likely to be both compound and iterative, and cannot simply be aggregated. Vernon (1996), for example, has argued that it is both inaccurate and unhelpful to talk of disabled women experiencing a 'double disadvantage', or black disabled women facing 'a triple disadvantage'. We may safely say, however, that, in the past, policies have clearly had a fragmentary and isolating effect. Many disabled people have written about the various ways in which they have become marginalised from mainstream society, and such isolation can even be felt in those groups striving hardest for social change and the lifting of oppressive policies and institutions. Perhaps two examples will suffice.

First, a heated argument has developed between two groups who, at face value, one might expect to make common cause: feminists and disabled women. One disagreement concerns the stereotype of woman as carer. Disabled women argue that feminists, by objecting to a caring role, promote the freedoms of non-disabled women at the expense of their disabled sisters. Disabled women propose a counter-position based on the view that all citizens are interdependent and, by providing assistance to each other (both personally and through the actions of the state), they improve the lot of the community as a whole.

The second area of contention arises from twentieth century developments in genetics and obstetrics. Medical technology provides tests to determine whether a fetus is impaired and has developed techniques to abort pregnancies. Feminists argue that, in such matters, it is the 'woman's right to choose' whether or not to use that technology. However, we can only imagine the dilemma faced by disabled women confronted with the question of whether to abort an impaired fetus. Such a decision clearly has implications for their own view of themselves as individuals, and for their beliefs about the status of disabled people in society at large. Rock (1996) asks whether these dilemmas loom quite so large when non-disabled women face the same decisions. I return to questions of genetics later in the chapter.

Differential treatment and impacts of policies on women and men

Be it in health, social services, social security, education, employment or housing, social policies have an impact on disabled people. Some consequences of policy affect disabled people in different ways according to whether they are men or women, and they relate not only to social roles, but also to far more personal aspects of everyday life.

Sexual relations and family life

In an important monograph, Shakespeare *et al.* (1996) examine the question of external impacts on disabled men and women in terms of their sexuality. They begin with the overriding point that social attitudes have frowned on the very notion that disabled people may have sexual identities and desires. If disabled women have not actually been regarded as asexual, some writers have cast doubt on the viability of relationships between disabled and non-disabled people. Greengross (1976), for example, contends that such relationships prompt what she calls the 'cruel and unavoidable' question of why any 'normal' person would 'saddle' [sic] him/herself with someone who would very probably require a lifetime of care.

Throughout the twentieth century, social policies and practices continued to place obstacles in the way of disabled people who wish to recognise and enjoy their sexuality and to establish loving relationships. The hurdles were not only attitudinal (that sex for disabled people was wrong and to be avoided), but also concrete, as seen for example in the provision of no other arrangement than single-sex dormitories in residential care establishments and long-stay hospitals, in the lack of sex education and information to disabled people, in the lack of opportunity to socialise and make friends, in exclusion from leisure settings such as nightclubs and restaurants, and in the lack of funds necessary to pursue courtship and meet the costs of setting up of a more permanent home.

At the same time, however, Shakespeare *et al.* (1996) point out that, perversely, disabled women and men are *more* liable to be the victims of sexual abuse by non-disabled people precisely because of their isolation and powerlessness in institutional (and indeed domestic) residential settings. Their segregation and lack of power render disabled people vulnerable to unscrupulous people who manage to gain work as care staff and thus become involved in intimate personal tasks. The jeopardy is worsened by low rates of detection and the infrequent prosecution of offenders. These findings are by no means unique to Britain. For example, McPherson (1991) records the vulnerability of Canadian women to rape and assault not only in institutions such as psychiatric boarding houses and asylums, but also just as much within the family home. McPherson explains that, although disabled women wish to escape from abusive relationships, it is actually very difficult to leave. They are trapped by their dependence on the abuser and by there being no other options. Canada has few refuges and little or no accessible housing for disabled people. There is, in addition, the contingent threat that, by leaving home, the disabled woman may lose custody of her children.

Equally, in the United States, a report by Seattle Rape Relief (1979, quoted in Lonsdale, 1990) documented 300 incidents of sexual abuse of disabled women and children, of whom 99 per cent were in some way dependent on their abusers. Shakespeare *et al.* (1996) argue that the common result of these two sets of contradictory forces (ascriptions of asexuality and vulnerability to sexual abuse) is internalised oppression: that disabled men and women can develop a negative self-image in sexual terms, and that where they have been subject constantly to the negating of their sexuality, or even to abuse, they may as a consequence be powerless to act as sexual beings in the loving and stable relationships they desire.

Painz (1993) has established that critical advice and information about sexuality, sexual relations, pregnancy and parenting are all too often inadequately provided or missing altogether in the lives of people with cognitive impairments. Indeed, McPherson (1991: 56) points out that disabled women who do forge a long-term relationship are frequently counselled by medical professionals against having children:

> They are told the child would suffer and that they as parents wouldn't be able to cope with emergencies. Even now, physically disabled as well as mentally disabled women run the risk of involuntary sterilisation, usually carried out in conjunction with some other operation.

In sum, then, there is, particularly for disabled women, a dilemma concerning their position within the family. Those disabled women who ally themselves to feminist thinking would, as a result, be keen to contest the roles commonly ascribed to women within the setting of the nuclear family. They would argue that these traditional (and subservient) roles, associated with being a mother, wife or daughter, lead them to regard the patriarchal family as an oppressive institution. Escape from such roles and changes in the concept of 'the family' are therefore much to be desired. However, some disabled women have either not encountered, or have actively rejected, the feminist analysis and take a different view, actually aspiring to these traditional roles, from which they feel they have been debarred on the grounds of their being disabled people. Begum (1992: 75) sums up the dilemma thus:

> As disabled women our experiences of institutions such as the family are significantly influenced by the pressure of conventional gender-role distinctions. We

either make a positive decision for political or personal reasons not to ascribe [sic] to traditional roles, or we fight very hard to conform to the ascriptions which classify us as 'real women'.

Kallianes and Rubenfeld (1997: 205) point to the irony in that the aims:

for which feminists have struggled – for women not to be defined sexually, for their right to roles other than mothers – appear to be the opposite of what disabled women demand... However, rather than differing perspectives they are in fact, two sides of the same coin... Reproductive freedom for disabled women parallels abortion rights: if all women have the right to choose not to bear a child, then all women must have the right to choose to bear children.

Shakespeare (1997: 8) seeks to reconcile (or at least find a way through) these various positions by arguing for consistency, for law that does not discriminate between impaired and non-impaired fetuses. Shakespeare argues that a common time limit should be adopted for all terminations of pregnancy, and the right to abortion prior to such a limit should be protected and be allowed for various reasons including age, economic situation, family circumstances and impairment. For Shakespeare, it is the (adverse) singling out of impairment that is unacceptable, and it is advances in genetic technology that have made such differential treatment possible.

Genetic technologies

In Chapter 6, we saw how certain countries use genetic technology to inform (or even to enforce) decisions about whether, or whether not, particular pregnancies should be terminated or allowed to continue. Even where the state does not compel, it is increasingly common to find similar decisions being taken by prospective parents, decisions based in part on early information about a fetus and partly on their perspective with respect to disability. For the vast majority of non-disabled people, the medical model still prevails in how they think about and understand disability. Information gleaned using genetic technologies is used in extremely persuasive ways: conditions such as Down's syndrome, for example, have been clearly linked to the 'rogue' configuration of particular genes, and many prospective parents, informed that their baby is likely to be severely impaired, choose to terminate the pregnancy. Such a decision is made against prevailing value judgements about the causes of disability, the status of disabled people, the quality of their lives and the amount of support provided by society to parents and disabled people. The outcome, if not the intention, has eugenic overtones. As Kallianes and Rubenfeld (1997: 214) argue, most genetic technologies are concerned with the elimination of 'disability' (that is, impairment) and:

> the promotion and routine use of genetic testing inappropriately exaggerates and emphasizes negative aspects of disability... while ignoring the worth of disabled people's lives.

The same authors identify some of the key implications of the application of genetic science in this way. They propose that society will become less tolerant of, and bring more pressure to bear on, 'irresponsible' women who persist in wishing to bear a disabled baby. This view is supported by Eigner *et al.* (1994), who argue that if disability is viewed as avoidable, the justification for funding support services may be eroded. For example, at a time of financial constraint leading to the rationing of services, health and social welfare professionals may give lower priority to mothers who have decided, notwithstanding prior knowledge, to give birth to a child with an impairment (as an analogy, smokers often find themselves at the bottom of the waiting list for heart treatments), and disabled people may find themselves even more ostracised than is now the case (Johnson, 1990).

Finally, does genetic technology offer women more freedom of choice or merely reinforce medical control? Fletcher (1997: 1, 4–5) reports survey findings from the United Kingdom's National Childbirth Trust indicating that, although some women encountered positive attitudes, others were subject to pressure to undergo antenatal testing and to abort a pregnancy if tests showed 'an increased risk'. One consultant was reported to have said, 'If there's something wrong with the baby, we just get rid of it.' Writing in the context of the United States, Kallianes and Rubenfeld argue that some of the other pressures foreshadowed earlier are already becoming evident in cuts to welfare services, partial access to health and prenatal care, and negative attitudes towards reproductive rights for disabled women.

In the light of what I have said so far, Eigner *et al.* (1994) identify several kinds of risk posed to disabled people by genetic research and procedures. First, they point to a 'geneticization' of human difference. A medical perspective is used to evaluate differences between human beings expressed in terms such as *defect* and *abnormality*. Based on the medical perspective, subsequent social differentiation may be used to justify discrimination and a lack of equal opportunity programmes. There arises therefore not only a threat to choice and self-determination, but also the imposition of particular constraints on disabled people on the basis of genetics. As a further example, I have already cited the sterilisation of disabled people without their knowledge or consent. Finally, Eigner *et al.* argue that the perspective that underpins current research overspills into social and political decision making; for example, the assertion of genetic differences has led in the past to segregated education. Eigner *et al.* (1994: 15) conclude that there is a danger:

> that genetic research and new reproductive technology could frustrate the progress made in achieving rights for people with disabilities by diverting attention away from handicapping social and systemic barriers.

In sum, what all these writers have suggested is that new genetic technologies raise extremely acute political issues. As we saw in Chapter 6, dealing with the international context, there are evident dangers when the state or some other powerful group of people use their power to arrogate to themselves the right to define the meaning of, and standards for, 'normality'. Before leaving the subject, it is appropriate to note the further point that genetic technology has not only enabled medicine to detect the condition of fetuses, but also presages the possibility of intervention to alter the genetic structure of human beings in order to 'rectify' impairments. The implications of this possibility are discussed in Chapter 12, but it is worth making the point here that the danger of these kinds of intervention is that they can reinforce the view that disabled people are 'defective' human beings, somehow not the same as other human beings. Conceptually to divorce disabled people from humanity at large constitutes a major step towards denying their citizenship. This may seem an extravagant claim, but consider, for example, the evidence set out in MacDonald (1997: 4) that babies and young children with Down's syndrome were:

> used as guinea pigs by British doctors in 1960 to test an experimental vaccine for measles... children who were living in institutions for the 'severely subnormal' were subjected to the experiments because the doctors said it was 'useful' having them in hospital where they could watch over them for adverse reactions. One of the children died seven days after being vaccinated from a common side effect of measles, but the doctors described it as coincidental in their report.

The point I am making here is that whether a proposed intervention is intended to make genetic changes or to test vaccines, there are two critical sets of question: first, concerning the validity of assuming that certain states of being are in some way 'abnormal', and second, concerning whether or not individuals have a right to full knowledge and ultimate decision making power over proposed medical interventions. Would the parents of non-disabled babies living at home have allowed doctors to give them an experimental vaccine?

Health and social services: medicine and 'care'

In that the health and social services are the prime institutions for conveying the medical view of disability, it is unsurprising that they are key institutions when we consider policy impacts on individuals. Many disabled writers, both men and women, have expressed deep concern and have recounted painful personal experiences about the way in which medicine stripped them of some key aspects of their self-image, as this disabled woman explains:

> The idea of surgery made me ill, but I grew tired of fighting my parents and Dr P., who, I was told, was a nationally known expert, and at last I agreed to an operation. Dr P. severed the adductor muscle in my right leg... Before surgery, the appearance of my walk was strange and my right leg, in particular, turned in. My walk was fairly steady, though, and with a little exertion I could, when necessary, manage a close to normal clip. I went walking for the joy of it... Nothing good came from the muscle severing, not physically or emotionally... all the surgery did was to weaken my leg. Since the operation my gait has been an unbalanced stagger in slow motion. My anger at what was done to me essentially against my will has never lessened. (Blumberg, 1991: 36–7)

A second set of (primarily medical) influences on the lives of disabled women concerns self-image and the closely related concept of body image. Society, and more specifically men, set great store by the physical appearance of women, and 'ideal' stereotypical images and photographs fill journals, magazines and other media. For disabled women, such stereotypes can have a profoundly negative impact on the way in which they perceive themselves (Morris, 1989). Lonsdale (1990) agrees that sexuality is central to self-image and that physical appearance is equally important. Lonsdale argues that prevailing (non-disabled) notions of beauty, conveyed by newspapers, magazines and other media, have the potential to undermine disabled women's self-image and can render them vulnerable to the attentions of 'men whose motives are exploitative and uncaring' (p. 6). Equally, the medical investigation of disabled women's physiology can have a particularly strong negative force:

> as the doctors poked and studied me endlessly, I learnt more quickly than some non-disabled women that I'm seen as an object... I was made to walk naked... and then lie on a mat while in turn they (5 male student doctors) examined my body, opening and closing my legs, poking and prodding here and there and making comments. I was at the stage when I was developing from a child into a woman... I started to lose my self-respect. (Campling, 1981: 10)

The manner in which health and social services operate gives rise to certain kinds of concern, particularly among disabled women. Lonsdale's (1990) study recorded numerous bad experiences in which disabled women felt that health professionals had treated them in patronising, unhelpful and even punitive ways. Privacy 'very often flies out of the window... [the disabled woman's] body becomes available to other people – to parents, to doctors, to nurses, to physiotherapists, and to groups of medical students on ward rounds' (p. 8). According to Lonsdale, such occasions are liable to cause affront and humiliation and even feelings of violation.

Poverty

As we saw in Chapter 7, disabled women in particular are vulnerable to low incomes either because of chronically low levels of social security or, if they have jobs, because they receive less than their non-disabled counterparts for equivalent kinds of work or are over-represented in low-paid, unskilled manual occupations (Blackaby *et al.*, 1998). Such circumstances have led Glendinning and Miller (1987) to claim that there has been a 'feminisation of poverty'. Clearly, then, disabled women require either access to skills that ensure security in the job market or a state income at a commensurate level.

Employment: bread-winning or bead-threading?

Poverty is a common experience internationally for disabled women. For example, disabled women in rural parts of Asia, Africa, Latin America and the Middle East are denied vocational training because they live in areas without transport services and because family traditions and pressures in any case preclude such activity. Of 55 vocational projects for women in Africa, none had disabled participants, and a survey of disabled women in the Philippines established that only 19 per cent had jobs and that 95 per cent of those who did have work earned less than a third of the sum set by the World Bank as the poverty threshold (Boylan, 1991).

Disabled women in Britain may have fared slightly better than their international counterparts. However, Blaxter (1976) has documented the pressures on disabled women that militate against finding work, and Blackaby *et al.* (1998) have recorded the subordinate position held by women in the British labour market in terms of both occupations and remuneration. Equally, there has been much criticism of the Disablement Resettlement Service based primarily on its orientation. The service appears more sensitive to the desiderata of employers than to the needs of clients (Lonsdale and Walker, 1984). As Blumberg (1991) argues, disabled women need to have 'a lot to offer' to compete with non-disabled candidates and to persuade employers to look beyond both gender and disability.

Education

Lonsdale (1990) proposes that disabled women in Britain are 'invisible' and that their invisibility starts with schooling. Many are taught at home or are sent to special schools. In her critique of special schools, Bookis (1983) points out that pedagogical emphasis commonly rests on practical rather than academic skills, but the evidence suggests that special schools are not wholly successful even in that aim. The same study also discovered that, owing both to the nature of the education received and to the discrimination permeating the world of work, careers advice to school-leavers had little or no utility.

Few disabled women proceeded to higher education, and the few who did usually came from mainstream rather than special schools. Although the picture may now be changing, many universities remain ill equipped to ensure that resources and tuition are available in the formats required by disabled students. Until recently, the University of Swansea was the only higher education institution with a reading centre for blind students, tactile walkways between buildings, specially adapted flats and other accommodation, and designated tutors for disabled students in each department. In sum, then, not only do many disabled people receive an inferior education, but also their segregation during childhood exacerbates the problems they face later in life.

Housing, the built environment and transport

Some 92 per cent of disabled women live in private households, making up 58 per cent of the population of disabled people who live privately. The remaining 8 per cent of disabled women live in communal establishments, where they make up two-thirds of the 'communal living' population. The vast majority of disabled women who live in communal settings are elderly, half exceeding 80 years of age. Although private dwellings offer greater opportunities for independence, both Roberts (1991) and Locker (1983) have argued that the design of housing is far from gender neutral. Since the profession of architecture is male dominated, male concepts of the female role are translated into standard prescriptions for the use of space within domestic dwellings. These can impose unnecessary restrictions and make daily tasks more time-consuming.

Many disabled women, like their non-disabled counterparts, feel unsafe, particularly at night and in the inner city urban environment. Newman (1973), in his theory of defensible space, demonstrates that these feelings are founded in fact. Newman reveals that modern urban planning uses designs and layouts that contain semi-hidden areas that are neither entirely public nor entirely private. These spaces, which he calls 'latent territory', include foyers and stairwells in tower blocks, unsupervised elevators, playgrounds, open spaces (usually of derelict land) and car parking areas. By such places being open to the public, but at the same time partly secluded, they allow assailants to attack their victims in relative safety. That disabled women are not immune to such attacks is well documented (McPherson, 1991).

Given the inaccessibility of public transport, and the relatively low rates of ownership of cars, many disabled people depend on voluntary services such as dial-a-ride schemes for their social mobility. However, many such services operate fixed hours and need to be booked in advance. Spontaneous decisions about going out are hardly possible.

Politics

Just as poverty is an international feature in the lives of disabled women, so too with exclusion from political life. For example, Boylan (1991: x) reports that, at the Nairobi conference that concluded the United Nations Decade of Women, there was not a single disabled woman in any national delegation except that from Australia. Furthermore:

when nearly 100 women with disability [sic], not delegates, assembled daily for a workshop in conjunction with the conference, they assembled outdoors because the facilities provided were inaccessible.

In Britain, the absence of women from political life led to one major party instituting all women short-lists when constituencies wished to select a new candidate to stand for parliament. While there are now more women in the House of Commons, parity with men is still far off, and the number of disabled women is minuscule. A similar bias is to be found at local government level and in the civil service despite some advances for non-disabled women in the 1980s (Chote, 1994).

Responses to the impacts of disability policies

Disabled women

How have disabled women responded to the impingement of policy and practice on their lives? For Begum (1992), there are three cardinal points to be considered in assessing the impact of social norms, policies and institutional structures. These are gender roles, self-image and sexuality. In common with many other disabled writers, Begum argues that contemporary social policies and institutional structures leave disabled women marginalised, not only excluded from many areas of social life, but also potentially isolated from other (non-disabled) women.

In concurring with Begum's assessment, Ellis and Smith (1995) have reported a number of initiatives under the auspices of GLAD designed to reduce that isolation and increase their strength. A prime method has been to bring disabled women together in conferences and meetings at which subjects such as sexuality, reproductive rights, independent living and self-advocacy are discussed. Special meetings are also arranged for black disabled women, older disabled women and disabled lesbians.

Their previous isolation made it difficult for disabled women to be heard not only in the policy making fora but even in those formal settings where their own futures were the topic for discussion. Not only has the development of these new and energetic groups provided disabled women with more positive self-images and greater strength based on collective action, but they have also taken steps to generate a voice in matters of concern to them. While it is still early days, the emergence of disabled women's groups, and their alliances with the broader disability movement, holds out the prospect of a stronger voice offering an effective critique of disability policy formulation and implementation. Strength is also being gained from international links through the European Network of Women with Disabilities, founded in 1986 in Strasbourg. The Network provides a forum for ideas and experiences, helps disabled women to start their own groups in different countries and publishes newsletters and other information (Disweb, 1997).

Disabled men

Hitherto, the chapter has concentrated primarily, but not exclusively, on the impacts of policy on disabled women through its influence over the social and built environment. I have thought it important to provide such an emphasis because the outcomes in at least some policy areas (employment, education, housing and so on) affect women not only as disabled people, but also in specific (and usually disadvantageous) ways *as women*.

Some policies operate across the boundary of gender so have similarly detrimental outcomes for disabled men. If in what follows I appear to treat disabled men's issues less than comprehensively, this is because I want to avoid repeating myself in those areas of intersection already covered in earlier chapters. Accordingly, I concentrate here solely on the issue of *masculinity* and disabled men.

Masculinity

It is perhaps indicative of the 'invisibility' of disabled people in general that the position of disabled men has received little or no consideration in the key sociological texts on this topic. There is no entry for disability or disabled men in major volumes on masculinity by Morgan (1992), Hood (1993), Cornwall and Lindisfarne (1994), Berger *et al.* (1995), Edley and Wetherall (1995), MacAnGhaill (1996) or McLean *et al.* (1996).

The oppressive nature of the (non-disabled) concept of masculinity is revealed by I. Young (1990: 59). He uses the term *cultural imperialism* to describe the experience of oppressed or marginalised groups who find themselves subject to:

> dominant meanings of society [which] render the particular perspectives of one's group irrelevant at the same time as they stereotype one's group and mark it out as the Other.

Morris (1991) argues that just such a process occurs in relation to masculinity, the prevailing conceptualisation of which emphasises physical ability and autonomy. For Morris, the social definition of masculinity is inextricably bound with a celebration of strength and of perfect bodies: to be masculine is not to be vulnerable. Accordingly, Lawrence (1987) argues that, for boys and men, questions of body image are fundamentally concerned with whether their bodies will do certain things. The yardstick for measuring their 'abilities' is the non-disabled male. In recent times, for example, disabled men have sought to demonstrate physical prowess through participation in the emergence on the public stage of disabled people's sporting events, in particular the achievements of disabled athletes in the Paralympic Games.

Thus have disabled men been caught in a dilemma. Some have sought to aspire to, abide by and affirm these 'mainstream' indicators and understandings of masculinity, and they have demonstrated an anxiety to fulfil traditional masculine roles such as becoming a bread-winner, a father and so on. Others have sought to reject traditional definitions of masculinity but in doing so know that they have risked reinforcing the labelling of them as 'deviant'.

In like manner, Bourke (1996: 74) argues that a key ingredient of the male identity is work, and that after the two World Wars, occupational therapy, rehabilitation and vocational training were not only intended to yield productive workers, but were also used as a means of teaching disabled ex-servicemen how:

> to become 'men', shrugging off what was regarded as the feminizing tendencies of disability. Thus, there was a progression of labour in many homes for the disabled [sic] from stitching bags, to work with machinery... By failing to assert a masculine role through bringing in an adequate wage-packet, the disabled man could only be further feminized by the performance of male domestic labour.

While one may take issue with Bourke's argument that emasculation and feminisation are synonymous, the important point here is that policy and institutional responses seek to angle disabled men towards expectations and roles that fall within prevailing (non-disabled) concepts of masculinity.

The various responses of disabled men to the dilemma posed by dominant concepts of masculinity have been summarised by Gerschick and Miller (1993, quoted in Connell, 1995: 54–5). These authors have argued that where masculinity is defined in terms of bodily performance, gender becomes vulnerable when the expected levels of performance cannot be sustained. They set out a typology that lists three kinds of response. In the first, disabled men try even harder to meet prevailing expectations of what it is to be masculine. The second is to reject prevailing expectations, to criticise the predominant stereotypes and to move towards what Gerschick and Miller call 'a counter-sexist politics'. The third is to steer a kind of middle course, accentuating those things (such as independence and control) which may connect the disabled male with prevailing understandings of masculinity but to downplay other aspects (such as physical prowess) that may have been diminished by impairment.

The key issue, then, is one of *identity*. Shakespeare *et al.* (1996) argue that attempts by professionals and welfare services, such as those described by Bourke, to 'rectify' the circumstances of disabled males in line with prevailing notions of masculinity are wholly misconceived.

The alternative (often beyond the apprehension of these same intermediaries) is to recognise the *de facto* validity of the disabled person's status and identity, as a human being, as a citizen and as a disabled man: 'disability is a social identity, not a consequence of physical change' (p. 56). As a result, Barton (1986: 286) has argued that the importance of a positive disabled identity lies in connecting the *personal* and the *political* in order:

> that what has been seen in mainly individual terms, can be viewed as a social predicament and thus a political issue... the task is an immense one – of moving from powerlessness and oppression to self and collective actualisation.

Policies of the kind I have just described, (segregation, institutionalisation and remedial therapy) have provoked some disabled men to strive to 'regain' or 'attain' masculinity as it is commonly defined. However, other disabled men have appeared to be more visibly assertive of their own conceptualisations of masculinity (see Shakespeare *et al.*, 1996: Chapter 3). Indeed, Rock (quoted in Campbell and Oliver, 1996: 73) has argued that the embryonic disability movement was itself a masculine phenomenon and was as such unrepresentative both of women and of people with cognitive impairments. Certainly, men dominated as key players in UPIAS.

Policy impacts have hitherto tended to be focused on the 'men' element, as well as the 'disabled' element of the term 'disabled men'. As a result, some disabled men have experienced the potent emasculating effect of policies intended to achieve the reverse, whether these were concerned with the replacement of real employment with 'make-work' schemes or the substitution of earnings with benefits, and thus the absence (in some areas of policy formulation) of expectations that do apply to non-disabled men, that they will be family bread-winners and so forth. The responses of some disabled men have been aimed at proving masculinity, while others have been concerned to expose and contest the underlying assumptions about the nature of manhood involved in the formulation and application of disability policies.

Policy impacts on gay and lesbian disabled people

Disability policies have a had a number of impacts on gay and lesbian disabled people. Here I refer to matters of sexuality, family and children, isolation and moves for collective action. Ellis and Smith (1995: 181) have argued that:

> disabled lesbians are marginalised, excluded and remain invisible to service providers, the disability movement and generally in society... (They) endure multiple oppression and are among the most oppressed groups within the disability movement and society.

One outcome of their invisibility has been a lack of appropriate services. As Shakespeare *et al.* (1996) have cogently argued, gay and lesbian disabled people have had (and continue to have) a profound battle to establish their right to sexuality and to sexual relations. Bullard and Knight (1981) argue that the needs of lesbian disabled women are ignored by health professionals who concentrate (if at all) on heterosexual matters such as contraception.

Questions of sexuality apart, they face even greater difficulties where their desire is to establish a family. For example, Laurance (1997) highlighted the struggle of a disabled gay couple who enjoyed a long-standing relationship but whose attempts to foster or adopt a child were opposed by doctors, social workers and health managers. The men applied to be foster carers but were rejected by Manchester Social Services on the grounds of disability (one partner had brittle bone disease, the other epilepsy). The two then decided to seek a surrogate mother from a stable lesbian relationship. Their quest was attacked by the director of Family and Youth Concern, who argued that the law should be tightened to exclude gay couples because a child had a right to be born to a man and a woman so that it would have 'a solid base to start from' (Laurance, 1997: 3).

In recent times, gay and lesbian groups have adopted a more visible posture and have received a more sympathetic hearing from government. A 'gay pride' rally in London in July 1997 was addressed by the Minister for National Heritage, Chris Smith, himself gay, who declared the government to be against discrimination on the grounds of sexual orientation. Similar messages were sent by the other major political parties (Knowsley, 1997). However, a recent attempt by the government to lower the age of consent for homosexual relationships has been thwarted by the House of Lords. Disabled people have sought to match the greater visibility of their non-disabled counterparts, for example through the arranging of conferences such as that organised by GLAD mentioned earlier in the chapter, and through the emergence of groups like Gemma, a group for disabled lesbians, and Languid (Lesbians and Gays United in Disability) (Hasler, 1993).

Conclusion

The important focus of this chapter, what has emerged here perhaps more than anywhere else in the book, is that where the formulation of policy and the conduct of practice are centred on the individual rather than the environment, they can have very personal consequences, as well as general social outcomes. Prevailing values and attitudes exert, through the creation of policy, a direct and often intimate sway over disabled people's lives. The institutions and practices spawned by policy in the past have frequently ignored the desires of disabled people, or worse still, opposed them so that their search for self-worth and citizenship has been undermined.

Furthermore, the social beliefs and expectations that underpin policy have driven a wedge between disabled and non-disabled people. To recall just one example, disabled feminists found themselves at odds with non-disabled feminists because state policies on personal care hinged on assumptions that caring for disabled people was essentially an (unpaid) female occupation. By rejecting this idea, feminist writers found themselves (perhaps unwittingly) in conflict with disabled feminist commentators. While both groups could agree with the overall proposition that women needed to break free of the domestic straitjacket, disabled feminists argued that their own independence would be put at risk by any consequent withdrawal of personal care.

The chapter also established that disabled men and women may have different goals in life and thus react in different ways to the existing policy montage. There is, however, some common ground. Both sexes increasingly favour collective responses, and, as we shall see, many thousands support the aims of the disability movement and seek to reject the medical model of disability. In the next chapter, I move on to consider the impacts of, and the responses to, disability policies as they affect disabled people from the minority ethnic communities.

9

Minority Ethnic Communities and Disability

Introduction

As we have seen, policies focused on individual rather than environmental change can exacerbate, rather than obviate, inequalities. I have said that British policy has been based on the medical model of disability, but, more than this, it has also been founded on essentially white and Western understandings of medicine. So, in attempting to identify policy impacts on disabled people from ethnic minority communities in Britain, an author is immediately faced with a number of difficulties. First, although some qualitative material is available, there have been few studies from which to draw conclusions of a more quantitative and universal kind. Such data are so scarce that proponents of the social model of disability have been criticised for failing to analyse the impacts of policy on disabled people from ethnic minority communities (Hill, 1992; Begum *et al.*, 1994). Academic study in this area remains, then, underdeveloped.

Second, it follows from what I have said that scale is also problematic in that there is no accurate figure for the size of the disabled minority ethnic communities in Britain, although their number is known to be relatively small.

Third, there are difficulties in seeking to understand concepts like *race* and *ethnicity*. These terms are neither simple nor synonymous. Blakemore and Boneham (1994) argue that racial judgements are based primarily on physical appearance, for example skin colour or facial features, and they describe racism as a kind of 'biological reductionism', whereas the term 'ethnicity' is more complex, involving at least some of the following attributes: a notion of 'peoplehood'; a distinctive language; the identification of a community with a particular religion, such as Sikhism; and a distinctive culture, which may be expressed in a variety of ways, including social etiquette, dress and diet. In asserting the importance of perception, Blakemore and Boneham argue that definitions of both race and ethnicity are essentially subjective and are based on social conventions.

Finally, in the light of what I have said so far, it is perhaps unsurprising that commentators such as Agar (1990) and Farleigh (1990) have remarked both on the invisibility of black and Asian disabled people in social, economic and political life, and on the lack of specific disability policies and services directed towards them, particularly in the area of social welfare. Millee Hill (quoted in Morris, 1991: 178) has argued that the consequence of this invisibility has been that:

> black disabled people, I have found to my cost, are a discrete and insular minority within a minority. We have been unfairly and unjustly saddled with restrictions and limitations, subjected to a history of purposeful unequal treatment and relegated to a position of political powerlessness and disenfranchisement.

In sum, then, our enterprise is hindered both by a dearth of relevant research and by the lack of any clear definition of the black disabled experience (Atkin and Rollings, 1991) even though race is acknowledged as an important factor in that experience (Nathwani, 1987). Bearing these caveats in mind, I attempt to judge the impacts of existing disability policies on ethnic minority groups and assess their responses to such policies.

The disabled ethnic minority population

People from ethnic minority communities form about 6 per cent of the population of Britain (Balchin, 1995). Atkin and Rollings (1993) estimate that this percentage represents nearly 2.5 million people. Of these, some 43 per cent live in the Greater London area (Office of Population Censuses and Surveys, 1991). It is more difficult, however, to say what proportion of the ethnic minority population may be described as disabled. After taking into account differences in age distribution, the proportion of disabled people in ethnic minority communities (about 10.5 per cent) is roughly the same as the proportion of disabled people found in white communities (Martin *et al.*, 1988). By extrapolation, we may suppose that perhaps a quarter of a million people from ethnic minority communities are likely to be disabled, and, of these, George

(1993) suggests that some 150000 are disabled people from Asian backgrounds. It is interesting to compare these figures with American data from the Bureau of Census for 1991–92 (quoted in Chapter 6), which suggest that the prevalence of disability in the United States may be nearly double that in the United Kingdom. We must be wary, however, first because the British data may be incomplete, second because sampling methods differ, and third because definitions of disability are differently conceived.

Disabled people in Britain do not form a single homogenous group; instead, they are geographically disparate (Young C., 1990) and represent many traditions, cultures and backgrounds (Haskey, 1991). There are also differences according to age, gender and the clustering effect of populations within urban and inner city areas (see, for example, Cameron *et al.*, 1989). George (1993) stresses the importance of the clustering effect by demonstrating that, in Bradford, 33 per cent of Pakistani households and 37 per cent of Bangladeshi households have someone with a long-term illness. These rates are considerably higher than in, for example, the home counties (9 per cent) or even Tyne and Wear (16 per cent).

Equally, research by Modood *et al.* (1997) has highlighted differences in access to employment among different ethnic minorities, with African and Afro-Caribbean communities faring better than Indian groups, and citizens of Pakistani and Bangladeshi origin experiencing greatest disadvantage in their employment prospects. It remains uncertain whether these rankings apply not only to non-disabled, but also to disabled people from these groupings. However, it is clear that black people are more prevalent in manual and unskilled jobs than in professional occupations (Holland and Lewando-Hundt, 1987).

In the absence of more comprehensive national data, we must rely to some extent on local studies that suggest significant levels of particular kinds of physiological impairment among black and Asian groups. These include problems such as rickets, osteomalacia, thalassaemia, sickle cell anaemia and tuberculosis (Bhopal and Donaldson, 1988; Ahmad *et al.*, 1989). Equally, among those of Caribbean and Mediterranean origin, there are records of both sickle cell anaemia and thalassaemia (Keeble, 1984; Francis, 1993). Patel (1990) suggests that about 4 per cent of the ethnic minority community is over retirement age.

The impacts of disability policies

Social welfare and community care policies

The Griffiths Report (1988) recognised the need to acknowledge the multiracial nature of British society, and the resulting Conservative White Paper (1989) took on board this point in its community care proposals, asserting that people from the ethnic minority communities might have 'particular care needs'. At face value, then, the government's approach to service provision was to be based on a recognition that flexibility would be needed in meeting the needs of different groups in the population. However, Atkin and Rollings (1993) argue that policy:

> remains undeveloped and rarely goes beyond bland statements supporting the principles of racial equality while the mechanisms that might achieve race equality, and the principles that underlie them, remain unexplored.

Blakemore and Boneham (1994: 134) concur with this view and record scepticism of the (Conservative) government's approach expressed by some black and Asian observers on the grounds that neither the legislation nor the Griffiths Report paid any real attention to questions of multicultural provision or racial disadvantage.

Without the conversion of such principles into practice, community care policies will not provide a range or quality of services appropriate to, or desired by (much less controlled by), non-white users. Gazdar (1994) therefore contends that there now exists the broad perception among ethnic minority communities that many statutory agencies are neither accessible nor appropriate, and the underuse of services is well documented (see, for example, Atkin *et al.*, 1989). At a recent conference on standards in social care, Gazdar (1997: 7), speaking in her capacity as a member of the Social Services Inspectorate, argued that social services provision to people from ethnic minorities has been dreadful and that:

> local authorities are often reluctant to be seen to be moving resources away from the white community to ethnic minority communities.

Confirmation that policies have been hitherto less than successful may be found in Boneham's (1989) study of older Sikh women, from which she concluded that elderly women from ethnic minority groups are worse off than the indigenous population in terms of both income and the use of social services. Francis (1993) also criticises the track record of social services departments, particularly with respect to services to black disabled women. Francis argues that, as clients, black disabled women have received at best 'token gestures', and she notes their absence in the social work profession. She argues that part of the problem arises from the deployment of personnel and focusing of services according to 'medical model' categories rather than the socially salient factors of race and gender.

Blakemore and Boneham (1994) argue that social services remain inflexible when it comes to acknowledging particular differences between black and white clients. Although having needs in common with everyone else, ethnic minority groups may have more specific requirements connected with rules relating to religious observance, diet, food preparation, aspects of personal assistance and other cultural taboos. They may therefore require a response that differs from the prevailing organisational norms and practices.

However, social services managers have defended their stance by arguing that the development of distinctive responses along racial lines would be tantamount to creating a new kind of apartheid (Blakemore and Boneham, 1994). An answer may clearly lie in the fact that were disabled people from ethnic minority communities to command their own resources, they could then acquire the aid specific both to their needs and their cultural demands without being subject either to segregation or to the colour-blind 'universalist' approach common to many social service providers. Moves to place personal care budgets under the control of service users are therefore likely to be welcomed by black and Asian disabled people.

Apart from the organisation of structures and the focus of interventions, further aspects of community care may be deficient, including, for example, a lack of vital information in appropriate formats and the failure to deliver services in a culturally appropriate way (Baxter *et al.*, 1990; McAvoy and Donaldson, 1990) or actual racism in the structures and operations of social services (Roys, 1988; Williams, 1988). There may also be a failure to recognise that, according to ethnic background, families may be variously constituted, and individual members may have roles and statuses different from those expected or found in other cultures. For example, Shah (1992) discovered many inaccurate assumptions among social workers concerning the role of women in Asian families, and writers such as Atkin *et al.* (1989) and Pearson (1988) have noted the prevalence of the mythical assumption that disabled Asians live within self-supporting families and thus may enjoy greater independence than their white counterparts.

Murray (1992) recorded a lack of services for Asian families with disabled children, including the absence of respite care. Murray's findings have been supported by Wright (1993), who argued that restricted access to services was due to many and varied causes. There were language and communication problems, exacerbated by a lack of interpreters. Professionals generally lacked knowledge concerning cultural and religious imperatives that had to be observed (including, for example, the separation of the sexes in some cultures). There were also specific requirements concerning personal hygiene and social and personal development to be considered (Mapp, 1997).

Ahmad's (1992) critique explains culturally inappropriate social work as having its origins in essentially white values, assumptions and perceptions, resulting in 'some appalling and distressing practices' (p. 1). Ahmad provides two examples. The first was of a young disabled girl who was kept in her nightdress throughout the day because her respite carers did not know how to put on her 'ethnic clothing'. Second, a black elderly man, the only non-white person in a residential home, was labelled 'violent' by the staff because he refused to eat bacon and threw his plate from the table: his religion forbad the consumption of pork. In a report *Double Bind to be Disabled and Asian,* by the Confederation of Indian Organisations, one interviewee summarised the problems by saying that:

> as far as disability is concerned, people (that is, welfare professionals) tend not to want to know about race or racism. In considering provision they do not think they will need to think any more specifically than in terms of disability alone. (Ahmad, 1992: 67)

There have been sporadic initiatives aimed at overcoming cultural inappropriateness in services, but these have almost always been projects led by disabled people themselves from the ethnic communities concerned. Examples include the Bangladeshi Women's Project in Tower Hamlets (Tonkin, 1987), the Torrington Centre Project in Coventry, which serves Asian families who have children with learning difficulties (Cocking and Athwal, 1990), and the Sickle Cell Counselling Centre in Brent (Mapp, 1997). Apart from such projects, many disabled people from ethnic minority communities remain largely dependent on their families for personal support.

Health

A key area of policy in which we may detect differences in the approach to disabled people from white and non-white backgrounds is that of health. First, national health resources and priorities are frequently planned in response to national or regional level pictures of supply and demand. Clearly, where there is a greater incidence of some impairment or condition among a particular minority group, this greater preponderance is unlikely to make any significant impact on national rates for the extent of the condition. As a result, it is entirely conceivable that few, or indeed no, extra resources will be focused on the ethnic minority group in question, notwithstanding the greater significance *for them* of specific kinds of impairment. For example, the prevalence of mobility problems in Afro-Caribbean women was explained by Fenton (1986) in terms of the manual work undertaken by them, which demanded constant standing, lifting and stretching, and produced strained limbs and backs, leading to higher than average rates of hypertension and diabetes. These factors taken together can restrict mobility. However, nothing in what I have said precludes the possibility of local initiatives in response to local needs. For example, a project was started in April 1993 at Hammersmith and Fulham social services to tackle the high incidence of sickle cell anaemia and thalassaemia (Francis, 1993).

Second, diagnoses and responses have been shown not merely to be the result of clinical judgements, but also to be influenced by interpretations of symptoms set within a particular cultural context. For example, scholars have sought to explain why certain mental illnesses have been diagnosed in (or ascribed to) particular ethnic minority groups at higher rates of incidence than in the population as a whole (Cochrane and Bal, 1987; Dunn and Fahy, 1990; Eagles, 1991; Knowles, 1991; Owens *et al.*, 1991). The key question here, of course, is whether diagnoses reflect genuine physiological and cognitive differences between ethnically different groups of people, or whether the diagnoses arise as a result of interpreting a set of 'symptoms' that would be construed in one culture as being pathological but in another as being within the bounds of prevailing norms. Certainly, Mares *et al.* (1985) warn of the danger of 'blaming the victim' in analysing the use of health services by black people, arguing that the promotion of genetic or pathological explanations neglects or obscures the shortcomings of the service providers. In their survey of 100 mental health patients from ethnic minority communities, Wilson and Francis (1997) discovered that 43 per cent had been diagnosed as schizophrenic, whereas in similar studies not targeted at any specific ethnic group, only 14 per cent were diagnosed as schizophrenic and 51 per cent as having depression. Wilson and Francis also noted the ubiquitous use of drug therapy (95 per cent) and a widespread feeling among respondents that they had encountered racial discrimination (58 per cent).

Beyond the differential definitions of disability applied according to ethnicity, there are other differences in, for example: the ease of access to health services; the appropriate delivery of services in line with differing cultural and religious requirements; the variety and appropriateness of treatments and contexts for treatments; and finally, access to help and advice in appropriate cultural and linguistic contexts. The lack of professional staff from ethnic minority backgrounds accentuates these difficulties. Indeed, Esmail and Everington (1993) point to racism as a key factor in explaining the absence of people from ethnic minorities in the higher echelons of the health service.

Finally, Pearson (1986) argues that racial discrimination is 'central in structuring black people's health and experience of the health service'. In line with the general thrust of all these findings, Blakemore and Boneham (1994) analyse racism in three ways: direct racism, such as hostility towards patients; organisational racism, such as inappropriate diets or a lack of translation services; and institutional racism in the formulation of policies and planning that disadvantage certain communities by *default*. McNaught (1988) also provides examples of direct discrimination including inadequate advice, inappropriate treatment, insulting comments to users and 'punitive' care regimes.

In sum, then, health policies writ large may fail to respond to the needs of minority groups, especially where impairments significant to them are less prevalent in the population as whole. Within the operational structures of the health service, members of ethnic minorities, while well represented in the auxiliary and maintenance staffs, are underrepresented at professional and managerial levels. There is evidence that such under-representation arises in part from a reluctance to implement equal opportunities policies (Connelly, 1989) and in part from institutional racism (National Association of Health Authorities, 1988). The absence of ethnic minority staff at policy and managerial levels may explain the lack of culturally appropriate services and the lack of knowledge concerning the requirements of disabled people from the ethnic minorities (Hicks, 1988; Commission for Racial Equality, 1989; Stocking, 1990). Equally, cultural differences between groups may lead to misinterpretations, inaccurate diagnoses or inappropriate responses, as evinced for example in some diagnoses of mental illness in patients from ethnic minorities (Fernando, 1988, 1991; Knowles, 1991; Littlewood, 1992).

Overall, then, while some disabled people from ethnic minority communities have access to projects suited to their needs, this is often due more to local initiatives than to the sensitivity of broader health policies. There are signs that professional training courses are beginning to recognise the importance of antidiscriminatory approaches in the monitoring and delivery of services, but these advances remain embryonic (Blakemore and Boneham, 1994).

Employment and social security

Black and Asian people of all ages are more likely than their white counterparts to have manual or 'working-class' occupations: over 70 per cent of Afro-Caribbeans are in manual jobs compared with 54 per cent of whites (Office of Population Censuses and Surveys, 1991). The risk of unemployment is higher in black communities (Brown, 1984). What is more, language differences, fears of officialdom and lack of information have led to a substantial underclaiming of benefits (Blakemore and Boneham, 1994). In terms of impacts, then, disabled people from ethnic minority groups encounter difficulties similar to those experienced by their non-disabled counterparts, but they do so at a greater intensity and with more profound effects.

Access to welfare benefits has long been an area in which discrimination has occurred. For example, Bourke (1996: 68) records that, after the First World War, state resources were directed to the relatives of those killed, and to disabled soldiers, who could prove themselves to be 'white British'. Those from other ethnic backgrounds – Bourke cites the example of Maltese soldiers and widows – received inferior treatment and lower pensions.

Surveying the contemporary scene, both the Child Poverty Action Group and the National Association of Citizens' Advice Bureaux have documented low take-up, poor administrative practices, poor-quality information and guidance for applicants and the use of residence tests. Gazdar (1994) recorded instances of both overt and covert racism, citing as an example the case of a woman whose application for severe disablement allowance was held up for over 18 months. In all, then, even where disabled people from ethnic minorities are entitled to support, the obstacles in applying for and maintaining such support remain formidable.

Education

I argued in the section on health services that the assessment of phenomena found in one culture using categories of evaluation rooted in a different culture can lead to misinterpretations and inappropriate responses. Booth (1988: 115) describes a prime example concerning the education of disabled children from black communities. He argues that:

> criticisms of segregated special education were closely allied with a critique of the value of IQ tests in working with individual pupils and in propping up the processes of selection. They were also spiced with a growing anger from black people about the way disproportionate numbers of black pupils were sent to special schools for 'the educationally subnormal'.

In concurring with Booth's assessment, Crow (1996: 70) argues that the methods and classification used by the school psychological service have resulted in the placement of a disproportionately high number of black children in segregated units for 'the emotionally and behaviourally disturbed'.

Such evidence as exists suggests that many black disabled children face difficulty in gaining an education that will fit them for independence in later life. However, a lack of specific and appropriate data make it hard to quantify the degree to which disabled children from ethnic minority communities are disadvantaged. A study is needed to discover how well (or badly) the education system responds to the needs of black disabled children, the way in which decisions are taken that are crucial to their education, the reasons for differential success rates (if such there be) between black and white disabled children, and an understanding of outcomes: how well equipped are black disabled children to live independently and to gain work once their education is complete? Finally, what aspects of the system need to change for improvement to occur?

Housing

Several studies have indicated that disabled people from ethnic minority communities have considerable housing problems. Ginsburg

(1992) has enunciated three kinds of institutional racism in this area of activity: the poor quality of housing allocated to members of ethnic minority communities; local policies designed to differentiate between, and treat differently, white and black applicants; and social polarisation in the allocation of properties.

The housing occupied by black and Asian families tends to be of poorer quality than that of their white counterparts, with a large proportion living in high-rise or deck-access flats containing fewer and smaller rooms. There is also greater likelihood of overcrowding (Brown, 1984). Smith (1989) has carefully documented the segregation of white, black and Asian communities by some local authorities through their use of housing allocation and exchange policies. Smith's evidence that members of ethnic minority communities often occupy the poorest-quality housing is supported both by Harrison (1995), who updates Smith's findings, and by Balchin (1995), who adds that black people (particularly black women) face a longer time on the waiting lists than do their white counterparts. Consequently, Bhalla and Blakemore (1981) found that a quarter of Asian families and a third of Afro-Caribbeans wished to move house because of the poor conditions in which they lived. Furthermore, Cole and Furbey (1994: 142) noted a reluctance among housing authorities to establish 'racial monitoring in allocation, effective staff training programmes, standard assessment procedures or effective liaison with ethnic minority communities'.

Although discrimination against black and Asian citizens in the allocation of council housing continues, Harrison (1995) has argued that a fear of racial unrest has prompted governments to seek to incorporate them into the 'most beneficial' parts of the welfare state. However, urban policies designed to overcome racism have been fragmented, specific initiatives have been short lived or ill prepared, and overall aims have occasionally been at cross-purposes. For example, the desire for integration, and therefore the dispersal of black communities, has often run contrary to the desire for separatism, for security from racial attack, and thus the desire for identity and proximity as a community. More importantly for our concern here, disabled people from the ethnic minority communities have remained all but invisible in the creation and implementation of housing policies insofar as they refer to black and Asian communities at all. Harrison (1995: 128) points to the emergence of a black, non-disabled, voluntary movement directed to housing issues, but even here the evidence forces him to the conclusion that:

the state's 'clients' among black communities will tend to be small scale bodies with far less leverage. While there is an element of tokenism on the part of an official agency, or where resources are tightly restricted, there can be a strong element of dependency on the part of small black-run organisations, with ever present fears of being funded for failure.

In addition to discrimination in the state sector, black and Asian people have also faced unequal treatment in the private sector, particularly at the hands of mortgage companies and estate agents (Ward, 1982).

The housing experiences of black disabled people have, as far as I can tell, not been recorded. Most housing research studies and policy texts deal with racism and disability as separate topics and treat disability as, *de facto,* a white phenomenon. Clearly, the question that stands uppermost here is: if non-disabled people from ethnic minority communities face discrimination in their search for housing, how much more difficult must it be for disabled people from these same communities?

Summary

As we have seen, in many policy areas, disabled people from ethnic minority groups may be affected not only by individual, but also by institutional racism. Like Ginsburg (in his analysis of housing tenure), Atkin and Rollings (1993) also argue that this takes one of three forms: first, policies have hitherto promoted services based on the profile of the majority (white) grouping (for example, by providing only English food at a day centre); second, policies have been based on stereotypical assumptions (for example, that care for black disabled people takes place within the family rather than needing services); and third, rules that apply to all actually privilege some and disadvantage others (for example, that applicants for council housing must have lived in an area for several years).

A view frequently voiced is that black and Asian disabled people suffer a double discrimination, arising first as a result of disablement, and second because of their status as members of minority ethnic groups. As I indicated in a previous chapter, however, not all scholars agree with this 'arithmetical' approach, which merely adds various kinds of disadvantage together. With respect to ethnicity, Stuart (1992) and Carby (1982) have argued that what occurs is a special situation, a unique experience in which black people are confronted by 'simultaneous oppressions'. Stuart (1992) argues that 'marginalisation' is the key and identifies three particular effects: damage to an individual's social identity and status, disadvantages arising from resource discrimination, and isolation within both family and community. The upshot is that black disabled people stand at the margins of both the ethnic minority group and the disabled community, and, as a result, they are rendered invisible, having neither social role nor distinct public image.

In this chapter so far, I have documented the potential disadvantages faced by disabled people from ethnic minority communities. At the same time, however, we must acknowledge that black and Asian disabled people may enjoy one advantage not yet available to their white counterparts, namely such protection from discrimination as may be afforded by the Commission for Racial Equality and rights granted under the Race Relations Act 1976.

Even so, there remain limits to the extent to which the law offers redress.

The response of black and Asian disabled people

> The oppression that black disabled people endure is... unique, it is necessary to construct a distinct and separate black disabled identity. (Stuart, 1992: 94)

The major response of black and Asian disabled people has mirrored that of other disabled people in that they have founded their own agencies and pressure groups in order to lobby for change. Michael Jeewa of the Asian People with Disabilities Alliance has long argued that while the (predominantly white) disability movement cannot abrogate its responsibilities towards disabled people from ethnic minority communities, it is nevertheless incumbent on them to organise their own groups in order to fight for their own distinct objectives. In accord with Jeewa's view, the late 1980s saw the creation of the Association of Blind Asians and the Asian Disabled People's Alliance, both formed in London, and in 1990 the Black and Ethnic Disabled People's Group came into being (Hasler, 1993). Clearly, however, the call for, and emergence of, a voice for black and Asian disabled people has been only a very recent phenomenon, and many black and Asian groups have, inevitably perhaps, faced the difficulties of limited funding (Jarrett, 1990) and limited influence (Ball, 1988; Farleigh, 1990). Many have been insufficiently developed and ill equipped to bid for contracts from local authorities, and the loss of various avenues of grant aid such as the Urban Programme has been of particular significance (Taylor, 1995).

In part, the setting up of their own groups by disabled people from minority ethnic communities was not only recognition that they needed a voice in order to challenge the disadvantages inherent in contemporary social policies, but also an acknowledgement that their aspirations were ill served by the (mainly white) traditional voluntary organisations (Field and Jackson, 1989), few of whom have made any significant changes in order to include disabled people from ethnic minority communities (Dungate, 1984; Sedley, 1989).

By initiating their own groups, at least some disabled people from the ethnic minorities have recognised that the constraints they face are social rather than personal, and they have gathered together to promote their own perspectives and demands. Such developments have been particularly important in the same way (and for the much the same reasons) that the emergence of the broader disability movement was important (see Chapter 11), but, as Atkin and Rollings (1993) make clear, the black voluntary sector faces three major problems. First, as I have already indicated, it commands only very limited and insecure resources (Jarrett, 1990; Mitchell, 1990; Phaure, 1991). Second, its relationship with the statutory sector is based on a profoundly unequal distribution of power (Bishop *et al.*, 1992), and third, its presence encourages the assumption among statutory agencies that they are in some way absolved from reconfiguring their services to make them ethnically and racially appropriate (Dourado, 1991).

The growing politicisation of disability issues among black disabled people has been encouraged by the earlier recognition of other kinds of related oppression. For example, Davis (1993: 289) noted that Disabled People Against Apartheid was set up to express solidarity with black people in the days of South African apartheid. It remains to be seen, however, what external impacts the black and Asian disability organisations may achieve in addition to the very real contribution they make to the self-esteem, self-confidence and liberating growth of their own members.

Conclusion

This chapter has assessed (insofar as is possible) the impacts of British disability policies on disabled people from ethnic minority groups. The picture is far from complete: there are few data on the access and experiences of black disabled children in education, particularly in higher education. We are also insufficiently informed about the barriers both to employment and to social security benefits faced by disabled people from ethnic minority communities. It is clear, however, that disabled people encounter problems arising not only from society's responses to their impairments, but also from society's responses to their race. As Stuart (1992) has pointed out, race has a fundamental impact in structuring the experience of disability.

The chapter has also discussed the responses of black and Asian disabled people to the impacts of disability policies. Their experiences of exclusion, not only from society at large, but also in large measure from what may be described as the 'white disability movement', has led them either to remain quiescent (and therefore invisible) or to take a collective approach in response to what they see as an oppressive environment.

Using the models developed earlier in the book, we may recognise how an exercise of power by a predominantly white, non-disabled society has led to policies that have detrimental effects for black disabled people. Such policies are aimed essentially at white disabled people and consequently serve the black population poorly. Here again, we may see that policies designed to protect citizenship, rather than to palliate excluded individuals, might be more successful in reducing the adverse social and personal effects described in this chapter.

10

Age and Disability Policies

Introduction

In this chapter, I consider the impact of contemporary social policies on older disabled people. My main argument is that policy responses that concentrate on interventions at the individual level can fail to meet the social and environmental concerns that disabled elderly people express. To highlight this mismatch, I take data from an action research project in South Wales with which I was involved in the early 1990s, and use other material drawn more broadly. I discuss some of the key problems that disabled older people encounter, including the habit of policy makers to conflate their needs with those of the wider (non-disabled) population of older people. Finally, I analyse some of the responses that older people have made to policy issues.

The population of older disabled people

In 1991, there were just in excess of 10 million people in Britain over the age of 60, but the United Kingdom is ageing, and at the beginning of the new millennium, the number of those 85 years and older will make up about 11 per cent of the elderly population. There is also a gender imbalance. Men tend to die younger than women, so the great majority of very elderly people are female. Of all those over 75, there are five women for every two men. This disparity is significant because nearly two-thirds of very elderly people are disabled. In numerical terms, there are about 1.5 million disabled women and roughly 630 000 disabled men aged 75 or over (Office of Population Censuses and Surveys, 1986, 1991, 1993).

These trends foreshadow extra demands not only for personal assistance, but also for changes to the built environment. Impairments tend to be much more prevalent among the older population groups. While only one-fifth of those aged between 16 and 44 have longstanding illnesses, three-quarters of the over-75s have chronic conditions (Office of Population Censuses and Surveys, 1986). Very old people also experience increased difficulty with personal tasks. About a third of those over 85 are unable to climb stairs unaided, 65 per cent are unable to cut their toenails, and 34 per cent are unable to wash or shower without help (Hunt, 1978). At the same time, because so many elderly people (especially disabled elderly people) rely on supplementary benefits, they are in no position to 'buy in' the extra services they need and find it hard to meet the extra costs they face (Graham, 1992).

Zarb (1993) argues that older disabled people form a growing, but heterogeneous, group and that it is only within recent times that the implications of such a group have been recognised by policy makers. He further contends (p. 187) that 'next to nothing is known about the experience of ageing with a long-term disability'.

Policies and their outcomes

While there have been studies concerned with the distribution of income, housing, access to services and the experiences of older groups according to class, gender and race, these have taken a more general approach rather than looking specifically at the circumstances of disabled elderly people (Phillipson and Walker, 1986; Arber and Ginn, 1991). In the absence of more universal studies, one of the key ways in which researchers have sought to understand the impact of policies on older disabled people is through 'biographical careers'. It has been commonly found that prior experience of disability will shape people's perceptions of ageing (Oliver *et al.*, 1988; Zarb *et al.*, 1990; Zarb and Oliver, 1991, 1992; Zarb, 1993). In their work, Zarb and Oliver develop the idea of a 'disability/ageing career', which comprises a 'series of physical, emotional and social processes' punctuated by what they call 'triggering events'. Ill-health, retirement and bereavement are all examples of such events and can increase the need for support. These events may be mediated by circumstances such as the avail-ability of immediate help, for example through the family, but impacts will also be reduced or exacerbated by broader policy, for example through levels of pension, access to personal help services and the configuration of the built environment.

Recent studies of policy impacts on older people in highly deprived areas have revealed some of the prime disabling environmental factors at play. Between 1990 and 1993, I was involved in two projects from the industrial valleys of South Wales, and their results support Zarb's conclusions concerning the specific difficulties encountered by older disabled people and the environmental origins of the problems they face. The two Welsh projects sought the views of older users of health, social and voluntary services, and their findings are revealing not only with respect to the impacts of welfare policies, but also with regard to older people's own concerns, which, as we will see, do not particularly coincide with those of policy makers and practitioners. I should state at the outset that not all the respondents in these projects were disabled, but the areas surveyed did contain a high rate of disablement or chronic illness in the older population.

In the Afan Valley, an area just north of Port Talbot, the views of 393 out of some 1850 older people were recorded, and in Merthyr and Cynon, over 600 from a population of some 24 000 older people were consulted (Mid Glamorgan Association of Voluntary Organisations, 1991; Upper Afan Valley Elderly People's Project, 1993). Older people were asked for their opinions about the services they received and about other matters of concern to them. In order to ensure that a cross-section of opinion was assembled, project staff visited as many locations as possible and spoke with older people in a variety of settings. Notwithstanding the large number of respondents, the enormity of the task and scarcity of time and staff resources led the Mid Glamorgan scheme to caution that:

> It was in part a limitation of the Project that the sample may or may not be representative of the views of older people. However the Project staff consulted well over six hundred older people in various settings including OAP clubs, church groups, day centres, residential homes and their own homes. In consulting older people project staff made every effort to enable them to express, without prompting, their own views and opinions concerning services for older people. They were also encouraged to talk freely about what they felt could or should be provided to improve the quality of life, either for themselves, or other older people. (Mid Glamorgan Association of Voluntary Organisations, 1993: 4)

The concerns of older disabled people

In both valleys, the views of older disabled and non-disabled people coincided to a considerable extent, and their prime concerns rested with

the fabric of their communities and with their own abilities to participate in the ebb and flow of everyday life rather than expressing any
desire for greater 'welfare' interventions. They therefore expressed
little appetite for the kinds of projects that create surrogate communities, for example through the provision of day centres, social clubs and
other specialist services often sponsored by social welfare agencies.
The major worries and preoccupations centred on subjects critical to
the quality of life. These included for example: the need for more crime
prevention; the desire to see work to halt any further deterioration in
the environment, especially that caused by vandalism; urgent action to
repair unsuitable or poor housing; measures to overcome access problems in public places and buildings (particularly pharmacies); access to
leisure facilities and shops; better transport and communication; and a
reversal of the reduction in domestic support services such as home
helps.

Crime prevention and safety

One of the main hindrances to participation in everyday life was an
acute fear of crime. The perception of a more violent society made
many elderly people frightened to leave their homes. A common worry
concerned the activities of the young, described by one respondent as
'thugs who hang around in bus shelters'. As a result, many older people
from a variety of estates and communities wanted to see more police on
patrol, and their anxieties about violence and crime accorded closely
with research by Hough and Mayhew (1984) and Albrow (1982), who
found that up to half of elderly people are afraid to go out at some time
during the day.   .

Disabling environmental effects and inadequate public transport

Other disincentives to engagement in 'ordinary' life were less dramatic
but perhaps more tangible. Simple things like the lack of buses were
sufficient to prevent participation in the community. There were few
adapted vehicles available and only a restricted supply of parking facilities for disabled people. Car ownership by elderly people in parts of
the valleys was as low as 3 cars per 100 households. This was crucial
because little or no public transport was adapted to the needs of
disabled elderly people. The paucity of service was a recurrent theme,

in terms of not merely frequency, but also of the restriction of bus routes, which tended to follow the valley floor. Some complained of poor public transport, inconvenient routes, infrequent services and buses failing to keep to their specified times or not running in the evenings. The vehicles themselves were thought 'badly designed', and public transport was too expensive. Age Concern's (1972: 19) earlier and larger study yielded similar outcomes, reporting that bus services in particular were prone to being cut in the winter months, leaving some users completely cut off.

Even if older disabled people in the two valleys could travel by bus, routes were by no means comprehensive, and there were other static impediments with which they had to contend. Obstacles included the lack of wheelchair ramps in town centres and poor access to many public buildings. Wheelchair users in particular had difficulty in nego-tiating kerbs, and there were few handrails in public places. Again, these findings are supported in the outcomes of previous research. Age Concern (1972: 19) argued that 'public conveniences, libraries, town halls and so on should be [made] more easily accessible to wheelchair people [sic] by provision of ramps'.

The cost of living also attracted adverse comment. For example, tele-vision licences were thought too expensive, and the rating system for water and the council tax was deemed unfair. Lack of adequate income was a major theme, older people strongly advocating the need for an increase in pensions. Age Concern (1972: 24–5) reported similar finan-cial concerns.

Inadequacies in health care and other support systems

There were also problems with the very systems intended for their support. In many valley areas, there was neither a chemist (pharmacy) nor a doctor's surgery in the local community. As a result, people had to travel some distance to collect their prescriptions. Owen (1977) has confirmed that the number of pharmacies declined dramatically between 1955 and 1976 from 15 302 to 10 900. Other medical restric-tions were also found irksome. Equipment such as small oxygen cylin-ders could not be obtained on prescription, and older people expressed a wish for items such as hearing aid batteries to be available from health centres. It was also frustrating that the tasks that elderly people need help with were precisely those which home helps were not allowed to undertake. Some also reported that GPs were apt to complain when they were called out at night.

Problems caused by unsuitable housing

Amid a more general lack of housing suitable for disabled elderly people, the two surveys uncovered difficulties in obtaining housing transfers from terraced properties to smaller bungalows. Generally, such transfers have become far more difficult in recent years because of the prodigious sale of council properties resulting from the 'Right to Buy' Act. The findings also pointed to poor levels of amenity within dwellings: many respondents had houses with no inside toilet. Here again, the earlier Age Concern (1972: 23) study highlighted that the same problems occurred more generally.

The fabric of the local environment

Many elderly people lamented the decline of the physical environment around them. The inadequacy of certain facilities caused distress. Many older people noted the lack of usable toilets in town centre, and the few that were available were unsatisfactory or even 'dreadful'. Visual amenity was also important to a generation who took particular pride in the valleys. Many lamented that the streets were no longer cleaned properly, the pavements need attention, street lights failed to work, there were too few litter bins and what there were required more regular emptying, there was a lack of public seating, and stray dogs were a problem. It was noticeable that contrary to social policies that focused on the individual, older people themselves looked outwards out of concern for their communities.

The lack of public facilities

Disabled or not, older people in the valleys complained of a lack of many facilities ordinarily found in other communities. In particular, the scarcity of public telephones caused deep anxiety because, as one respondent put it, 'telephones are a lifeline for elderly people'. The crucial emphasis on the availability of the telephone was also recorded in work by Wenger (1990: 1) who argued that:

Access to private cars and telephones... can be an important mitigating factor in the maintenance of independence in the context of declining physical abilities in old age.

Others wanted to see the development of community facilities such as women's clubs, cafés, fish and chip shops, hairdressers, general stores and post offices, cinemas, snooker halls, leisure centres and swimming pools. The plea was for the restoration of vibrancy to declining communities.

Summary

To recapitulate, what is especially noticeable about all these concerns is that they do not coincide with the traditional focus of welfare providers. By and large, traditional voluntary agencies offer services that palliate or ameliorate 'impaired' individuals. But time and again, older people identified the need for remedial action in the fabric and design of the community itself.

The picture as it emerged was initially perplexing for the staff involved in the research, steeped as they were in the perspectives and methods of traditional welfare. They had hoped that the data would indicate what kinds of new voluntary initiative should be developed. From the outset, there had stood in their minds an inventory of the usual kinds of traditional voluntary undertaking such as day centres, luncheon clubs, personal care schemes, respite care, minibuses and so forth. It was simply to be a matter of identifying what was needed where. However, the respondents in the two surveys had revealed a wholly different agenda, one not readily amenable to the discrete, service-orientated approach of voluntary organisations.

The disturbing mismatch between the expectations of the voluntary agencies and the actual outlook of the interviewees forced the project workers (and the charities to which they reported) fundamentally to re-think the purposes of their schemes. Rather than creating new (welfare-orientated) developments to respond to particular ailments, incapacities and impairments, the projects had instead to try to find ways of pursuing the environmental changes that the elderly, and elderly disabled people, had demanded.

The findings from the two Welsh schemes echo Zarb's contention that resources cannot be viewed separately from the meanings and values attached to them by the individual. (For example, such words as 'allowance', 'charity' and 'workhouse' still coalesce in the minds of very elderly persons, leading to their reluctance to claim benefits.) Race, gender and culture will also have an impact on how disabled older people respond to the policies, practices and environments that surround them. However, not only environment, but also personal circumstances and the effects of impairment play a part in the life circumstances of older disabled people, and it is here in particular that Zarb's work is important to the present discussion.

Zarb (1991a, 1991b) reports that many of his respondents disclosed feelings of premature physical ageing, attributed to impairment, and described such deterioration as if it were the 'onset of a second disability'. These developments ran parallel with a perceived down-turn in satisfaction with quality of life, and, as a consequence, there was a diminution in emotional well-being. Zarb also detected some degree of resignation and a prospect of mortality voiced by his inter-viewees, who found it increasingly hard to maintain their independence as they grew older. This fact in particular – the threatened loss of control – became, for many, a matter of great anxiety. It is here perhaps that we may see how crucial the configuration of the social and built environment, and the efficacy of disability policies, may be in ensuring sufficient resources to protect the citizenship and independence of older disabled people.

Zarb concurs in the view that material resources may perform an important role in mitigating many of the above effects, and he found the availability of appropriate help to be particularly crucial. The present structure of support, reliant as it is on institutional 'care' for very elderly people, fails to meet these criteria of citizenship and independence. Equally, research by the Carers National Association (1992) discovered that, far from receiving aid themselves, many older disabled women were actively involved in supporting other family members.

Older people with cognitive impairments

Walker *et al.* (1996) argue that people with learning difficulties are now living into old age, and whereas they may previously have been accom-modated in long-stay institutions, they are now housed in the commu-nity. They have not, however, secured the full rights and resources commonly enjoyed by non-disabled older people. In their research, Walker *et al.* (1995, 1996) discovered age discriminatory practices in the implementation of care policies and service provision. Care workers had low expectations:

> Even though older people with learning difficulties are likely to have greater competence than their younger counterparts, care workers were half as likely to say that older people were capable of developing new skills compared to younger people. (Walker, 1996: 25)

Nor did workers consider outside activities, such as social clubs, to have equal value regardless of age. Residential accommodation was thought more appropriate for older people than younger. Walker's research demonstrates starkly the point made elsewhere in the book that, because disability policies focus on individuals, practitioners have it in their power to limit or restrict a disabled person's access to the rights and opportunities enjoyed by non-disabled people. Were the focus to be on the social and physical environment, the key questions would be: what prevents older people with cognitive impairments from using ordinary social facilities, and how may these facilities be made accessible? Instead, care workers in Walker's study made judgements about the 'fitness' or 'suitability' of particular clients to use certain social facilities.

Responses of older people

MacFarlane (1995) has recognised the danger of segregating older disabled people from their younger counterparts, thus re-creating the enclaves that have been built up by charities and social welfare professionals using the traditional divisions established by medicine. Nevertheless, MacFarlane argues that older disabled people aspire to autonomy over their lives, and the example of collective strength and progress evinced by the Disability Movement could be replicated by older disabled people to their advantage.

Abrams and O'Brien (1981), however, have identified several reasons why, unlike their younger counterparts, it is less likely that older people will organise themselves into unified political pressure groups. They point first to the fact that older disabled people are as diverse a population as may be found in the country at large. Equally, many older people will not see themselves as old and will avoid membership of organisations for 'the elderly'. On the other hand, some will disengage from public activity because of ill-health. Yet others may be unconscious of their lack of power or may simply be unwilling to act.

Midwinter (1992: 23) has also expressed doubts about the feasibility of political pressure: 'the scope for this form of political togetherness is limited... it is unlikely that grey power has any chance of succeeding in the foreseeable future'. Land and Rose (1985) note the quiescence of older women after a lifetime of 'compulsory altruism', and Ginn (1993) argues that 'grey power' in the sense used by those whom she calls 'conflictual ageists' is a myth. Ginn contends that elderly people are not a homogenous group and do not vote for policies that benefit them at the expense of younger people.

These doubts and constraints notwithstanding, the focus on social change has been at the heart of the development in recent times of coalitions of older people who *have* taken an overtly political stance. For example, Dourado (1990: 16) records the 'emergence of a number of groups determined to use the newly-discovered demographic muscle of elderly people to lobby for change'. He asserts that membership of such a group can counter feelings of powerlessness, the aim being 'to re-categorise elderly people out of the exclusive remit of charity and social services'. Among the nascent organisations, Dourado (1990) points to the political and protest-based work of the Pensioners' Protection Party, and Ginn (1993) credits the Association of Retired Persons with 125000 members in 1991, the Pensioners Rights Campaign with 30000 members in 1993, and the National Pensioners Convention (linked to the Trade Union Movement) with 1500000 members. These bodies echo developments in the United States, such as the American Association of Retired Persons, regarded as one of the largest and most powerful organisations in the USA, having 32 million members, and the 80000 members of the Gray Panthers founded by Maggie Kuhn in 1970. If there are class differences to be found in the emphases and make-up of these groups, the common stance is outward looking, towards a full role in mainstream life rather than the development of specialist services. There is, however, a potential dilemma for disabled older people: should they align themselves with pressure groups of disabled people or activists promoting older people? Added to the potential of political pressure, Lawrance and Blackhurst (1989) have also pointed to the economic potential of older people to effect change in their roles as consumers, although wealth may be limited principally to the non-disabled elderly.

Dossett Davies (1987) reported other, more locally based groups in Britain, such as the Pensioners Declaration of Intent Action Group

(Oxfordshire). Despite the cumbersome title, the existence of the group indicated a tenor of thinking towards the construction of a political lobby. The group was taken seriously by local government officers and councillors who were willing to meet and take heed of the group's demands. The nature of these groups is such that there has been a move away from younger 'able-bodied' people doing things for elderly people. Instead, older people themselves are acting together to bring about changes in the general fabric of the community. The key battle concerns resources. If older people in the valleys commanded greater resources, they could exert more influence in their locality. Examples of such empowerment have been traced in the United States by Weaver (1976), Anderson and Anderson (1978), Williamson (1982), and Button and Rosenbaum (1990).

Older people and policy making

In recent years, both policy makers and welfare providers have become increasingly keen to secure the participation of older people in the development of projects and services (Abrams, 1978, 1980; Albrow, 1982; Wenger, 1990; Wenger and Shahtahmasebi, 1990; Thompson, 1992). Similar involvement has been sought among disabled people (Pagel, 1988) and the users of mental health services (Chamberlin, 1977; Levy *et al.*, 1986). A major reason for the upsurge of interest in consumer consultation has been the stress recently laid by governments on user involvement in the planning and management of services in both the statutory and voluntary sectors. In order to understand some of the difficulties in the relationship between government policies and actual outcomes for elderly disabled people, the next section describes a local (Welsh) initiative intended to facilitate user participation in service planning.

Case study: Welsh Office social policy

Because the incidence of chronic illness and impairment has been extremely high among older people in the industrial valleys of South Wales, the Welsh Office has had a more active policy profile than government elsewhere in the United Kingdom and it has actively courted the participation and involvement of users in the planning and development of services.

In November 1985, the Welsh Office convened 'a symposium on services for the elderly' (Welsh Office, 1985a) and at about the same time published a strategy document, *A Good Old Age: An Initiative on the Care of the Elderly in Wales* (Welsh Office, 1985b). The goals were clearly stated:

> The aim is to retain elderly people in the community, living whenever possible in their individual homes. The primary objective is to promote and maintain the independence of elderly people, and secondarily to minimise their dependence. (Welsh Office, 1985b)

In 1987, the Welsh Office established a scheme of grant aid to foster the development of innovative community-based services. During the four financial years that scheme monies were available (from 1987/88 to 1990/91), some 54 experimental projects were funded at an estimated cost of £18 million (Robinson and Wenger, 1992).

At the same time that the initiative went ahead, the Welsh Office gave further advice, not simply on the configuration of services, but also about the philosophy of care that should prevail. In its rhetoric at least, the Welsh Office increasingly supported the concept of consumer participation. When, in 1990, it produced guidance on the construction and implementation of social care plans, the Welsh Office adjured local authorities to:

> promote opportunities for elderly people and their carers to contribute to the design of services and to ensure that they are able to contribute to local policy and operational planning. (Welsh Office, 1990a, appendix A: 6)

These aims were repeated in other draft guidance on assessment and case management (Welsh Office, 1990b: 5). This public commitment to consumer participation was clearly stronger than that pursued in Britain as a whole where, for example, Wagner's (1988) recommendations on residential care for elderly people made no reference to participation in planning or management.

The Welsh Office was also anxious (or, at any rate, wished to be seen to be concerned) to halt the economic and demographic decline of the Valleys. To this end, it produced *The Valleys: A Programme for the People* (Welsh Office, 1988), designed to regenerate the valleys by reducing unemployment, stimulating inward investment, and enhancing the social and environmental fabric.

The need for such intervention was starkly demonstrated by Rees and Rees (1980), who used a range of indices to show that the valleys suffered from multiple deprivation. Equally, Howe (1963) and Moyes (1981) recorded high rates of male mortality in the local coalfields, and Howe (1986) and Richards (1987) listed coronary heart disease and bronchitis as major causes of death. Similarly, Thomas (1988: 19) argued that:

> The most adverse health conditions were closely related to low social status in combination with aspects of material deprivation such as low levels of car ownership, high rates of unemployment and low levels of educational achievement.

Further data (Mid Glamorgan Health Authority, 1985) revealed that the valleys had the highest percentage of houses lacking in basic amenities anywhere in England or Wales and that unfit dwellings tended to be occupied by elderly and unemployed people. In the worst-affected areas, nearly a third of pensioner households had no indoor toilet, and almost three-quarters of pensioners had no car. Nearly 40 per cent of pensioners suffered from chronic ill-health. Against this backdrop, the Welsh Office looked with particular favour on proposals for projects designed to promote the participation of older people as a fundamental part of their plans for developing new services in the valleys. The Elderly Initiative Projects shared a number of aims. First, each aimed to create and sustain effective links between voluntary and statutory welfare agencies. This was necessary because the local voluntary infrastructure was underdeveloped and would remain so for some time. Second, each was intended to cultivate opportunities for the participation of older people, to identify their problems and needs, and to bring together organisations representing the interests of older people as consumers. Third, each had the key task of establishing the conditions necessary for the emergence of a powerful lobby or voice not just *for*, but also *of* older people. Finally, each project was required to document the existing range of services, identify gaps and create new initiatives.

Projects were governed by committees whose members were drawn from the social services, the local health authorities and the voluntary sector, and from representatives of older people's groups. Each project employed one or two development workers and an information officer, and each planned to undertake two phases of action. In the first year, the main job was to sample the views of as many older people as possible living in the relevant geographical areas (and it is from two of these projects that the data I used earlier in the chapter have been drawn). Thereafter, the findings would be analysed to inform new developments in which older people would have major supervisory roles. The projects tried to involve older people in service planning, management and delivery in a variety of ways:

- through mass canvassing and the collation of older people's views;
- through large-scale meetings for older people and service providers;
- by the election of older people to serve on joint care planning committees;
- through the publication and dissemination of the views of older people;
- by the use of existing networks of older people's groups to facilitate communication between them and service providers;
- by improving contacts between older people's groups to allow for the emergence of a 'lobby';
- by the provision of more information about existing services and planning processes;
- by the careful structuring of the management of new initiatives.

As Thompson (1992) highlighted, all too rarely have the views of elderly people been regarded as legitimate sources for academic research. In welfare planning, very few studies have been conducted that investigate the *Weltanschauung* or world view of older people and their experiences of the services upon which they often depend. What is interesting about the Welsh Office initiatives is that they constitute a recognition of the mismatch between the perspectives on life taken by older people and the orientation of service providers. They also seek consultation, but only in terms of the predefined agenda of providing 'welfare' rather than the more revolutionary aim of enhancing citizenship.

Even so, the kinds of data gathered by the projects served as a counterweight to the great majority of studies of age and ageing, which identify older people simply as subjects for intervention. Hitherto research has concentrated on topics such as care needs, chronic diseases and impairments, the development of models for dementia management and so on. Now, more data are available about the social priorities of elderly and elderly disabled people, and, more importantly, the response of older people to policies and practices has begun to find a voice through the creation of their own pressure groups and lobbies.

Conclusion

This chapter has been concerned with policies towards, and the responses of, older disabled people. It has emerged that there exists what we may call a 'policy break'. By this, I mean that, in many areas of policy, the stance of governments is different according to the age group of disabled people concerned. For example, within social security policy, the DWA and the severe disablement allowance may be claimed only by those under the age of 66. There is a clear contrast to be seen in policies towards younger and older disabled people. Older people tend to be regarded as part of the pensioner population at large, and are treated as such.

Older disabled people also fare less well in terms of voluntary sector governance. The traditional charities tend to be led by younger, non-disabled people, and change may be extremely difficult to accomplish. Welfare pluralism and the 'contract culture' have brought intense pressure towards professionalisation. Some agencies (especially those dedicated to fund raising) have little direct contact with elderly people as clients. It may be that changes in the nature of voluntary action require older people themselves to exercise power if they are to ensure that voluntary agencies adopt goals that they themselves would support. To mount an effective challenge, they would need access to the data and expertise routinely available to service managers and their staff. Laing (1993) argues that the empowerment of older people can be enhanced by the direct consumer funding of care services, but Conservative governments have hitherto proved reluctant to allow people over 65 the same access to cash gained by young disabled people through the Independent Living Fund and its successor. Certainly, where older people command resources, they are able to confront many of the circumstances that gave rise to concern in the surveys reported here.

A lobby for the provision of ramps, telephones and buses is in reality a call for free access to the ordinary facilities of everyday life. As we saw, elderly people were little interested in the development of (potentially) segregated and isolating services, be they residential homes, day care centres or minibuses covered in disabling imagery. However, decisions about social and environmental change are, in essence, *political*. This is true whether the subject is the provision of subsidised public transport, the setting of pension levels, the formulation of housing policy or the funding of health services.

For charities, however, movement away from the provision of specialised services towards campaigning of a more political nature is problematic. They are reluctant to involve themselves in politics, first because political action puts charitable status at risk (Drake, 1996a). Second, the funding programmes of successive Conservative governments have clearly been based on the contract culture and a market orientation. *Service delivery* remains the order of the day (Fielding and Gutch, 1989; Gutch, 1989; Kunz *et al.*, 1989; Anderson, 1990; Mabbott, 1992). These pressures (towards user participation on the one hand and towards the free market on the other) are contradictory, and they are strong enough to threaten a fragmentation of the voluntary sector (Drake and Owens, 1992).

Nevertheless, the implications for policy makers are clear. First, the achievement of genuine consumer participation in service development would almost certainly shift the emphasis of voluntary (and, for that matter, professional) action away from service provision towards environmental change. Second, older people's own groups have a legitimate claim for funding, even where their goals run contrary to government policy.

Three areas stand out in which support for older disabled people would be most effective: an increase in the level of resources available from the state; legislation to secure citizenship; and the intervention of the state to transform local environments in order to make them more accessible. In terms of the models of policy discussed in earlier chapters, we may see that the momentum here is away from the individualistic 'medical model' approach towards citizenship and environmental change. This analysis concurs with that made by Barnes (1991), who argued for antidiscrimination legislation similar to that which exists for women and for members of ethnic minorities. From this perspective, policy makers and service providers alike must seek to change the fabric of social institutions (including their own) and must value the subjective perceptions of the older population as well as the quantitative analyses of service planners.

11

Disabled People and the Policy Process

Introduction

A clear picture has emerged of the diverse ways in which governments have exerted a direct impact on the lives of disabled people. These impacts have arisen sometimes through specific policies and action, but are sometimes (just as importantly) a result of deliberate inaction. Informed by medical understandings, British disability policies have been narrow in scope, largely uncoordinated in implementation and fragmentary in effect. They have focused on attempts to reconcile disabled individuals to an essentially alien world rather than reconstructing that world to meet the needs of all citizens irrespective of their cognitive and physical conditions. As a result, until very recently, a civil rights orientation has been substantially absent from legislation. Law makers and service professionals remain the key players in the creation of policy, in the development of institutions and in the implementation and monitoring of practice. The voice of disabled people has seldom, in any effective sense, been heard.

Perhaps the advent of a Labour government in 1997 brought some encouraging signs of change. The ministers responsible (Andrew Smith and Alan Howarth) met a number of disabled people's groups and noted their concerns about the need for civil rights legislation and how it might be achieved (BCODP, 1997). More recently, however, worries have been voiced about government intentions with respect to the structure and levels of disability benefits (Bevins, 1997), and these concerns have not been entirely dispelled by the recent Green Paper on welfare reform (Department of Social Security, 1998), to which I referred in Chapter 5. Notwithstanding the government's stated commitment to civil rights for disabled people and the removal of barriers to work, the Green Paper's lack of detail, and promise of further benefit reviews, means that it has not entirely assuaged disabled people's doubts about changes (restrictions?) to benefits.

In the light of this history of exclusion, my purpose in this chapter is threefold: to review the causes of disabled people's absence from the policy making processes; to discuss the effectiveness of the remedies that have been tried; and to assess the importance of the growing disability movement in Britain.

Causes of exclusion

My prime focus here is the relationship between disabled people and the creation of policy. I have already identified a number of factors that may account for their exclusion from policy making processes, and it will be useful to recapitulate these. They fall into three categories: the exercise of power, the prevailing perception of a helper–helped relationship and the structure of the policy making process itself. First, the almost total absence of disabled people from the echelons of government and administration has meant that decision making powers have rested almost entirely with non-disabled people. These powers have enabled the 'able-bodied' not only to define disability, but also to determine the nature of the state's response to it.

As a result of the pre-eminence of the medical model, what has emerged is a helper–helped relationship in which disabled people have been regarded as the passive recipients of welfare (Finkelstein, 1981). Accordingly, it has for decades seemed natural for disabled people to be missing from the fora in which policy and service management have been crafted.

Even when these perceptions began to change, the first step was not to do with policy but with practice. Providers wanted disabled people to participate in the refinement of welfare services. Also, the participation desired was *not* to occur via the employment of disabled people as managers or planners but in their supplying 'feedback' about the services provided to them. The agenda was predetermined. Views were sought *not* about the basic question of whether welfare services and state benefits were an appropriate response to disability (the assumption was always that they were) but instead about how existing service projects might be improved.

The proof of the pudding lay in the fact that, despite the quest for user involvement, the traditional structures of policy making and service management remained intact, and disabled people still found it difficult to gain a foothold. For example, during the 1980s, the Welsh Office made what was for the time a brave attempt to introduce disabled persons' voices into planning processes. A strategy document in 1983 argued that users of services should be represented in social services planning teams:

> mentally handicapped people [sic] and their families must play a full part in decisions which are intended to help them. (Welsh Office, 1983: 1)

However, 4 years later, during a review of progress, the Welsh Office concluded that:

> there has been little direct involvement in planning services by mentally handicapped people [sic] and planning teams are encouraged to seek means for them to participate. (Welsh Office, 1987: 9)

> the participation of mentally handicapped people, [sic] parents, carers and voluntary organisations in the planning and implementation of services is fundamental to the initiative. (Welsh Office, 1987: 19)

In 1989, however, a survey by the Social Services Inspectorate revealed that involvement remained an elusive goal. In an analysis of six planning meetings, although users:

> made up 24 per cent of those present, they made just 3 per cent of the contributions recorded in the minutes. By contrast, representatives of the statutory sector made up 42 per cent of those present but 65 per cent of the contributions identified in the minutes... there is more evidence of presence than there is of participation. (Welsh Office, 1989: 16)

Even with access to policy making bodies (albeit at local level), disabled people faced the pre-existing power structures constructed prior to their arrival. In my own research (Drake, 1992b: 237), one interviewee, 'Elaine', confided:

> The power relationships... are actually incredible and it's very difficult for somebody to go and sit on a panel with [name of professionals] who they know sees them as being an incapable person, as somebody who needs to be told what to do... so power is the crux of it all.

Without suggesting any malign intent on the part of the professionals involved, we may see several obstacles to their being able to share their power. First, after years of training and the constant mutual reinforcement of the 'welfare' perspective, professionals may find it hard to question, let alone set aside, the value of their 'expertise'.Yet, writers like Begum (1995: 2) point to the constant failures of the welfare approach:

> In the experience of disabled people, services are inflexible and fragmented, bedevilled by confusion over what is health and what is social care. They are also very variable and depend substantially on where you live and who does your assessment. Services tend to be paternalistic, philanthropic, disempowering and inequitable. The welfare state has turned disabled people into passive citizens. Community care services are themselves disabling, segregating people and withdrawing their right to control over their own lives.

Second, policy makers often work on the assumption that all participants share the same kind of attitude about structures, procedures, programmes, budget setting and administration. Target setting occurs not in the personal terms that users might recognise but in more bureaucratic units of measurement. Again, in my own research, a disabled interviewee, 'Philip', spoke for many respondents when he recalled:

> I feel I was not particularly, erm, wanted on committees even though I probably would have played a more active part than most. Perhaps, I think, that was the reason why I wasn't wanted in committees. I've had documents sent to me which [were] weighty to say the least, even if they are not written in, er, using specific jargon they are heavy documents and they tend to be heavy with statistics as well. This can be used for two reasons. This is how they operate, but they can also be used as camouflage for decisions which have been made which might prove unpopular. (Drake, 1992b: 199, 221)

Finally, there are terminological barriers. If the reader will permit a brief personal anecdote, I was once a voluntary sector representative on a government health planning committee given the task of setting 'health gain' targets for services to older people. I had struggled with unfamiliar acronyms and abbreviations for three meetings when, at one point, the courteous and most solicitous chairman turned to me and asked 'are you familiar with the term DNA?' I brightened immediately and, keen to display my knowledge, replied, 'Oh yes, deoxyribonucleic acid'. 'The basic building block of genes', I added, just to show off. He looked apologetic and murmured, 'Well, yes, but here it just means "Did Not Attend"'.

There is a gulf between policy makers and disabled people, summarised by 'Elaine' in these terms:

The sort of old contract, if you like, was [that] we're the... helpful, competent, able people, you give up everything to us, you're the needy ones and we'll, sort of, do it for you. So it involves quite a shift in that contract and *status quo* for jobs like mine to be successful, and for users themselves that are involved in that, it's quite a subversive movement in a way – it's going to subvert the *status quo*, which hinges on power, and the [name] are a very powerful body who actually don't like a lot of the stuff that's going on. (Drake, 1992b: 235)

'Elaine' goes to the heart of the matter. For disabled people to exercise power over social policies and institutional practices, politicians and professionals must relinquish it – this, for all manner of reasons, they are loath to do.

Possible remedies: from exclusion to inclusion

As we have seen, disabled people have contested the prevailing (medical model) definition of disability and have counterposed a social model predicated on confronting the disabling effects of society. Second, and stemming directly from their contrary perspective, they have sought changes in the social, political and economic environment. The consequences of this challenge have been, first and foremost, to identify 'silences' in existing legislation, silences that permit the continuation of widespread discriminatory attitudes and practices. Second, disabled activists have brought into question the purpose and pattern of state and voluntary 'welfare' provision. Third, they have focused attention on the exclusion of disabled people from society, and last, they have brought to bear a formidable challenge not only to the prevailing shape of disability policies, but also to the very mechanisms involved in their creation.

The relationship between disabled and non-disabled people in the creation of policy and practice could, in theory, take a variety of different forms. First, we can imagine a situation in which disabled people are at the heart of policy making and are thus able to exercise power and authority. If these circumstances prevailed, disabled people would be able not only to create policy for themselves, but also to command the resources necessary to implement their decisions. A second possibility would involve genuine power-sharing between disabled and non-disabled people. Here there would exist real involvement, and policies would emerge as a result of decisions made jointly around the planning tables. In a third scenario (one that currently prevails in many places), disabled people are 'represented' by others, usually non-disabled people. My own research (Drake, 1994), for example, has demonstrated the extent to which disabled people lack authority in those traditional British charities hitherto relied upon by government to act as conduits of disabled people's views. Just under a half of these charities have no disabled people at all on their management committees, and in a further 20 per cent of them, under a quarter of the seats on the management committee are occupied by disabled people. Even where they are in control of agencies, groups led by disabled people receive far less funding than the traditional charities. In my study, out of 46 groups with a turnover in excess of £50000, only three were governed by disabled people, the rest having non-disabled people in charge. Indeed, the extent to which the traditional charities are now big business is exemplified in the income figures for the top 500, who commanded funds amounting to £3532 million in 1995/96 (Charities Aid Foundation, 1997; Institute for Fiscal Studies, 1997). In all, the British voluntary sector employs some 11 million people and has a turnover of £16000 million (Cameron, 1997).

The overall situation, then, is one in which disabled people frequently lack direct participation in decision making processes and find their voice usurped by a relatively wealthy charity sector led primarily by salaried, non-disabled, professional staff. Brandon (1988: 27) is unequivocal on this issue when he says:

> My own view... is that their senior staff are really voluntary society civil servants [who] rapidly get out of touch, for example with life inside the rundown council housing estates and the mental handicap hospitals. As they get more powerful, they get more out of touch. Life looks different from the inside of a BMW.

While advocacy and representation by non-disabled people may, on occasion, achieve improvements in the circumstances of disabled people, there are, of course, no guarantees that they will, and the views and desires of disabled people can be filtered, distorted or vitiated. As Adams (1990: 120) concedes, advocacy can be fudged and:

> the anger of consumers or their dissatisfaction with existing services [can be] defused through protracted negotiation or some other bureaucratic process... The anger of [disabled people] may be translated into respectable language, their style proceduralised and their language sanitised.

Some of the traditional charities, often called on by the statutory services as 'representatives' of disabled people, have acknowledged that:

organisations which consider that consumer representation is a part of their function need to ask whether or not this is bourne [sic] out by their membership, the way in which they consult with service users and the proportion of a particular group of users they maintain contact with. (Social Care Network, 1990)

A fourth kind of connection between disabled people and the policy process might involve not even representation by others in the decision making fora but merely being consulted from time to time by those in power. Such consultation may be a genuine exercise in which authorities take seriously the views they receive, or, more cynically, they may simply be intended as a sop in an attempt to offset potential protest. Finally, disabled people may have no relationship with the policy making structures at all, so be no more than passive targets or recipients of policy outcomes, ignorant of the processes and decisions that led to them. Such quiescence may arise either as a result of false consciousness, as mooted by Gramsci (1971), Lukes (1974) and Gaventa (1980), or from what Rosen (1996) has called 'voluntary servitude'.

Rosen's arguments stem from Reich's (1975: 53) observation that:

What has to be explained is not the fact that the man who is hungry steals, or the fact that the man who is exploited strikes, but why the majority of those who are hungry *don't* steal and why the majority of those who are exploited *don't* strike.

In the present context, we may ask: why have disabled people accepted the oppression of the medical or 'personal tragedy' model and its consequences for so long? Rosen accepts that the Lukesian notion of 'false consciousness' (the idea that a subordinate group has internalised or taken for its own, norms, values and beliefs that serve the interests of a dominant group) may provide an answer, but he has such doubt as to want to seek alternatives.

Rosen (1996: 260) first reminds us of the argument that, although a dominant or élite group may have control over the means of coercion:

the disparity of numbers between rulers and ruled is such that, should the ruled choose to act against their oppressors, they could not but prevail. Hence, since it is in their interests so to act, the failure of those who are unjustly ruled to overthrow their rulers must be explained as a form of false consciousness. But what this argument fails to take into account is the problem of collective action – the possible discrepancy that there may be between what is rational for the individual and what is rational for a group of individuals.

Rosen illustrates his argument using the scenario of a gunman with several hostages. If all the hostages were to attack simultaneously, they would prevail, but there may be some casualties. The calculation at the group level is clear: all is to be gained in attacking the gunman *en masse*, but for each individual hostage, there is some uncertainty that the others would actually rush forward at a given signal, and even if they did, the danger of being shot in the ensuing mêlée changes the balance of the calculation. There is what Rosen calls a *coordination* problem.

Leaving aside for a moment the fact that disabled people do not form the majority assumed by Rosen (who, to be fair, was writing in a different context), it remains the case that many disabled people, for their own reasons, have not sought to engage in political battle and have not joined the disability movement. For disabled activists, this situation constitutes a *coordination* problem in Rosen's terms. Why might this be? First, there are practical reasons: disabled people may not have heard of the movement or may, for some reason, be unable to connect with it. Second, as I argued in Chapter 2, Lukes's (1974) idea of false consciousness explains how the personal tragedy or medical model may be not only accepted, but also vehemently supported by a disabled person contrary to his or her own real interests. As Freire (1972: 25) has pointed out:

> how can the oppressed, as divided, unauthentic beings, participate in developing the pedagogy of their liberation?... As long they live in the duality where 'to be' is 'to be like', and 'to be like' is 'to be like the oppressor', this contribution is impossible.

But Rosen is suggesting a third reason, that unless and until a critical mass is reached, at which point success is guaranteed (enough hostages decide to attack the gunman to overpower him), individuals may decide to 'have what they hold'. Furthermore, the possibility of 'free riders', others who do not contribute but who nevertheless share the spoils of any success, may also drastically affect the calculation of whether to act against oppression. To clarify this point: to make a stand often involves risk, the risk of losing what you already have. In my own research (Drake, 1992b: 230), I came across disabled people unwilling to voice genuine grievances for fear of upsetting the powers-that-be, thus endangering their access to the services on which they depended. Because they knew very few (or no) other service recipients, they could not act in a collective way; accordingly, 'Pippa' confided:

I think that because people are using a service they're afraid to criticise it, especially if you're not getting out and you're reliant on a certain service, I think you may be too frightened to criticise.

Likewise, 'Paul' told me:

There's a lot of, erm, some fear of [users] that if professionals are involved in meetings then there'll be repercussions for them, so there's that fear side of it.

Clearly, then, it may be that disabled people who neither control nor are consulted about the policies that shape the environment in which they live their lives, nevertheless fail to rebel against what other (perhaps more politicised) disabled people regard as a grossly unjust and intolerable situation.

I have been describing a range of possible connections between disabled people and the policy making process. Arnstein (1969) pictures these qualitatively different potential relationships as forming a 'ladder of citizen participation', and it was, at least in part, the recognition that disabled people may occupy only the lowest rungs of the ladder (or not be on it at all) that led to the growth of activism through the disability movement. I turn now to the strategies that some disabled people have employed in order to acquire influence over the policy making process, and I discuss what has been a key dilemma for them: whether policy changes might best be pursued through participation and negotiation or through opposition in the form of direct action. The chapter concludes with an evaluation of the position that disabled people have reached in their quest to influence the making of policies that have such a profound impact on their lives.

Methods adopted in seeking to influence policy

Very few disabled people have ever been present in positions of authority in the national level fora where policies are made, and no more than a few have succeeded in gaining important positions in local politics. However, although they have had to employ more distant and indirect methods, it is important to give due weight to the contribution that the disability movement has made in changing the thinking of governments, bringing injustice to light and forcing a radical alteration of the policy agenda.

The growth of self-representation through the disability movement

First, there have been substantial advances in self-organisation and representation, principally through the British Council of Organisations of Disabled People (BCODP) and through coalitions of disabled people around the country. It falls outside the scope of the book to provide a detailed history of the disability movement. Readers may find an excellent analysis by Campbell and Oliver (1996), and there are also accounts by Pagel (1988) and Driedger (1989). The aim here is to point to the growth of organisations *of* (rather than *for*) disabled people and therefore to the making of much stronger and direct representations on their own behalf.

Pagel (1988) notes that disabled people had formed themselves into what would now be called 'pressure groups' even in the forbidding circumstances of the nineteenth century. For example, the British Deaf Association was founded in 1890, and the National League of the Blind registered as a trade union in 1899. Davis (1993) notes the catalytic effect of the Second World War, with the creation of the Disabled Drivers Association (1948) and the National Federation of the Blind (1949). Perhaps the modern era of disability action began in the 1960s with the Disability Income Group (1965) and the Disabled Professionals Association (1968), and then the Spinal Injuries Association, which came into being during the 1970s. Beyond all these, particular importance must be attached to the emergence of a more radical group of disabled people: the Union of Physically Impaired Against Segregation (UPIAS), whose members, witnessing the inertness and inappropriateness of the traditional voluntary sector during the International Year of Disabled People in 1981, were instrumental in the creation of the British Council of Organisations of Disabled People. This new national body was founded with an initial 10 member groups. By 1993, there were 80 (Davis, 1993), and by 1996, the organisation had expanded to over 110 member groups representing some 400 000 disabled people (Campbell and Oliver, 1996).

While some sought partnerships with local authorities to create new kinds of project, such as Centres for Independent Living (CILs), others took a more direct line of action in pursuit of change. These radical groups initially had the image of being propelled by younger, white men with physical impairments. There were, however, initiatives by other disabled people. For example, People First was set up by those with cognitive impairments. Groups of mental health service users and ex-users came into being under the name Survivors Speak Out. Disabled women's groups and black and Asian groups also emerged.

At the same time, it is fair to say that the disability movement has struggled to be inclusive, and Campbell and Oliver (1996) recognise feelings of exclusion from the movement expressed by disabled women, people with cognitive impairments, people from ethnic minority communities and gay and lesbian disabled people. To speak with the authority of a united voice (particularly so that it may counter the 'official' position achieved by the traditional charities as negotiators with government), the movement had to find ways of including these marginalised groups, and a recent step has been the formation of a BCODP women's group. The group produces its own newsletter, *Amazons*. Some of the local member groups of BCODP have taken similar steps; for example, the Greater London Association (GLAD) issues a national newsletter (*Boadicea*) for disabled women and women allies.

Participation in local politics and service planning

Second, notwithstanding the difficulties and failures described earlier in the chapter, there has been increasing participation and involvement in local political and institutional fora, including the gaining of access to the planning teams of health and social services (Beresford and Croft, 1989, 1993; Croft and Beresford, 1990). There has also been some success in redirecting the focus of these agencies, for example through the advent of CILs, of which I will say more below.

Disabled people have also tried to become much more involved in local authority planning, which, as we saw in Chapter 5, has (with honourable exceptions) done little to change the existing contours of the built environment. Thus disabled people have developed the Campaign for Accessible Transport and the Campaign Against Patronage, but there has been less success hitherto in influencing groups such as local Access Committees, many of which (in common with the traditional voluntary sector as a whole) remain dominated by non-disabled people (Drake, 1992a, 1994, 1996b). For the most part, Access Committees have focused on specific remedies to particular situations rather than militating for broader change at the policy level, very few disabled people are represented on planning committees, and there is, in any case, no guarantee that a local authority will heed the advice of its local Committee (Barnes, 1991).

Campaigns at local level and projects by CILs

Third, disabled people have adopted a pragmatic approach in their
attempts to influence policy formulation and implementation. By
campaigning at local level, it has been possible to influence the way in
which policies (particularly service-orientated policies) have been
realised. Pagel (1988) records an encouraging response:

> Local Government has assisted the development of the disabled people's move-
> ment in much the same way as the federal Government helped in the United
> States. While, obviously, not having the power to introduce national legislation,
> local authorities have still managed to involve disabled people in the local deci-
> sion-making process, attempted to tackle the appalling inequalities which are to
> be found in the areas of employment, as well as providing funding for organisa-
> tions controlled by disabled people.

Clearly, then, disabled people have become increasingly active not
only in policy debates, but also in producing self-governed groups and
projects such as CILs, which have proved a cogent and powerful alternative to the traditional gamut of projects like day centres and social
clubs. Davis (1990) has described the achievements of one such
scheme, created by the Derbyshire Coalition of Disabled People
(DCDP).

The organisation was founded in 1981 with the aim of achieving full
participation and equality for all disabled people. With support from
Derbyshire County Council, a joint working group was established, and
by 1983, a CIL had been created. From the outset, local disabled
members of DCDP gained strength from contact with other CILs and
the broader disability movement, which was, itself, still in its early
stages. The purpose of the CIL was to promote independent living, and
the methods included ensuring the provision of skills training, adequate
personal support and seeking to ensure that disabled people were able
to make decisions autonomously about their lives. The Centre sought to
operate a number of services, including the following: a county-wide
register of care attendants; housing services (from design to direct
labour); accessible transport; commercially viable workshops; information and advice; aids, adaptations and other equipment; and a 'halfway
house' to help people to leave institutions.

The Centre made a difference to the lives of disabled people, but
the group also produced a further, and perhaps more far-reaching,
impact on social work ethos and practice, including the phasing out of
segregated institutions. However, Davis accepts that, because CILs

act locally, advances across the country as a whole will be uneven and will depend on whether a CIL exists in a particular region, how strong it is and how receptive the local political authorities and social services are. Davis also points out that, notwithstanding the changes brought about by the CIL in Derbyshire, the power of veto over public funds, and the weight of mainstream provision, remained within the purview of the county council, and this assessment lends weight to the contention that the progress of disabled people towards full citizenship will ultimately depend on their ability to command political power. I turn therefore to campaigning by disabled people at national level.

Campaigns at national level

The fourth way in which disabled people have sought to affect disability policies and practices has been the potent and coordinated lobbying of decision makers at national level over a range of key issues. In 1985, for example, the Voluntary Organisations for Anti-Discrimination Legislation Committee (VOADL) was founded in order to combine the efforts of disabled people's own groups and agencies led by non-disabled people. The umbrella pressure group was later renamed Rights Now. The BCODP also lobbies hard on the same issues and worked with Barnes (1991) to produce a detailed analysis, using the government's own data, of the widespread discrimination faced by disabled people.

Protests, demonstrations and direct action

The civil rights leader Martin Luther King once said that a riot is, at bottom, the language of the unheard. While disabled people have yet to riot, they have nevertheless engaged in forms of direct action specifically formulated to highlight the ways in which society excludes them. Through groups such as the Direct Action Network, Campaign for Accessible Transport and the Campaign Against Patronage, disabled people have used disruption, demonstration and defiance as the tools to make visible the discrimination with which they are routinely confronted (Crow, 1990; Hasler, 1993). Actions under this heading included demonstrations in London, Cardiff and other major cities during which disabled people handcuffed themselves to buses as a graphic way of highlighting their lack of access to public transport. In early April 1997, over 150 disabled people took part in 3 days of demonstrations to campaign for accessible public transport. They occupied the national offices of the bus industry at the Confederation of Passenger Transport and blocked buses in a number of major thoroughfares. A second group handcuffed themselves to a tube train on the London Underground for over an hour (Direct Action Network, 1997).

In previous years, groups have blockaded television charity fund raising events such as the ITV Telethon in order to convey their opposition to the demeaning nature of charity. Such actions also emphasise that the differentiation and exclusion of disabled people is social, rather than personal, in origin. Shakespeare (1993) reports that the police have found it difficult to deal with wheelchair users; for example, at Horseferry Road Magistrates Court, London, charges against several protesters were dropped because the building was inaccessible to disabled people.

Obstacles in seeking to influence policy

In achieving such progress as has been made, disabled people have had many barriers to overcome. First, it has taken time to achieve momentum for the wider recognition that disability is a political issue. Second, it has been necessary to bridge the divisions between groups of disabled people, artificially separated from each other by medicine and charities on the basis of differing types of impairment. They remain fragmented today, although less so now than ever before. Third, traditional charities have commandeered the resources and negotiating spaces that disabled people want for themselves. Fourth, and as a result of the foregoing, disabled people have, until recently, enjoyed little political clout.

Recognition of the issues as political

Shakespeare (1993) argues that whatever power the disability movement has been able to apply stems from the fact that it recognises itself to be a *political* force. Shakespeare compares the relative tardiness in reaching this point with, for example, the experience of disabled people in the United States. Disability action in America emerged in a context rather different from that in the United Kingdom. Americans have a:

> different tradition of protest and social reform.... The absence of a developed welfare state; the strong emphasis on individual rights, expressed in a written constitution; the fullest development of the free market and competitive values; the virtual absence of collectivism and the organised labour movement, are all important factors in explaining the different developments of disabled people's politics.

Shakespeare also recognises the examples set by the black civil rights movement and the women's movement, and the influence of the Vietnam veterans. Given this background, disabled people's campaigns focused naturally on gaining access to society and to social rights.

Fragmentation

In Britain, disabled people have been divided along lines imposed by medical definitions of physical and cognitive conditions, accordingly:

> disability is less of a unitary concept than race or gender: the experiences of people with visual impairment, restricted growth or spinal injury will differ markedly, and factors such as the onset of the condition will also influence the experience, as well as the obvious dimensions of race, class and gender. It is important not to ignore differences between impairments, despite the tendency of writers to gloss over difference in favour of the totalising and unifying role of oppression. Clearly all disabled people face a common exclusion, prejudice and discrimination, and the vast majority share a condition of poverty. But beyond this, there are variations. Can I, as a person with restricted growth, effectively speak for or write about someone with cerebral palsy or visual impairment? I can identify with the basic social experience, but the details can be no clearer to me than they would be to anyone else, disabled or not. If a non-disabled person cannot describe or represent my experience, then can I describe or represent the experience of someone with a different impairment? (Shakespeare, 1993: 255)

Based on his research on the political awareness of blind Asians, Priestly (1995) concurs with French's (1993) argument that impairments themselves have a fragmenting effect. Priestly contends that attempts by disabled people to build a collective voice are hindered because there are many of them (perhaps still the majority) who remain unacquainted with the social model of disability, continue to identify the impairment, rather than society, as the prime source of inhibition and view their own interests and circumstances as being both special and different. The disability movement must therefore discover how to come to grips with the problem outlined above by Shakespeare.

Given the extent of its power, medicine has succeeded in dividing disabled people one from another according to their particular cognitive or physical impairments, thus hindering the ease with which disabled people could come together to pursue common (political) cause. Elsewhere, I have noted the alacrity of the traditional charities to replicate such fragmentation, even to the extent that their nomenclature is based on medical diagnoses and definitions (Drake and Owens, 1992; Drake, 1996a).

Usurpation of resources and voice

In enacting the Disability Discrimination Act 1995, the Conservative government refused disabled people's calls for a Commission similar to that safeguarding the rights of members of ethnic minority communities under the Race Relations Act 1976. Instead, the government imposed a council 'to advise the minister'. In doing so, it followed the well-trodden path of relying for advice on non-disabled people from traditional charities.

At the time of writing, disabled people from the disability movement refuse to serve on the council as a matter of principle. The established charities, however, anxious to preserve their monopolies either by assimilating or by vigorously opposing new groups seeking to work with the same constituency of disabled people, have been less reluctant to work with the Advisory Council. Government support goes substantially to these privileged but unrepresentative groups and is either denied outright or granted exiguously to groups *of* disabled people (Sutherland, 1981; Oliver, 1990; Wilson, 1990; Drake and Owens, 1992; Drake, 1994).

In addition to problems of representation, Cawson (1982) has argued that social pressure groups do not have any great socio-economic leverage. This weakness he ascribes to the fact that members of such groups are usually economically unproductive and so are not among those whose cooperation is needed by government for political survival or economic success.

Successes

Notwithstanding the variety of obstacles outlined in the previous section of the chapter, it has become clear that, in the face of discrimination, in situations in which disabled people have found social policies to have negative rather than positive effects, a common response has been that of disabled people coming together. They have gained strength from each other and have, as a consequence, developed a more powerful and effective voice.

As a result, disabled people have enjoyed victories. Sometimes they have achieved only small modifications to policy, but they have also forced major changes. There is certainly greater recognition of the justice of their claims, and there have been some advances in legislation and more constructive interpretations of existing law, as this cross-section of recent successes indicates:

- Gaining an acknowledgement that disabled people are entitled to a social life. On 21st May 1997 the Law Lords accepted that disabled people were entitled to the DLA not only for essential matters, but also to support their social and leisure activities. The specific case involved a deaf woman, Rebecca Halliday, who claimed that she was entitled to the higher rate of DLA in order to pay for a sign-language interpreter to help her lead a normal life (Wynn Davies, 1997).
- Pushing back the boundaries of *de facto* no-go areas in the job market. For example, in May 1997 BSM employed Ken Brown as its first disabled driving instructor (*Daily Telegraph*, 10th May 1997, p. 16).
- The vigorous pursuit of consumer rights and the claim to equal treatment as customers. In April 1997, a blind and partially deaf customer, Patricia Parsons, threatened to take the National Westminster Bank to court, alleging that she was served far less efficiently than other customers and that the inferior treatment amounted to discrimination as defined by the Disability Discrimination Act (Sandler, 1997).

Conclusion

How much have disabled people advanced in their battle to influence the policy making processes? It is not easy to judge, but we may reach some tentative conclusions. Full citizenship embodied in the kinds of civil rights enjoyed by others in society still seems some distance away. There have been, however, significant successes. Disabled people have a substantially higher political profile than even 10 years ago. The focus of change is being drawn away from the individual towards the social and environmental. In particular, there has been some success in making disability policy a political issue.

Disabled people are increasingly engaging with the processes of government and management, and they are building formidable expertise in advocacy and campaigning. We have seen the flowering of BCODP and the assertion of pride across the disabled community. In official circles, the question of civil rights may not yet have entirely supplanted the mantra of 'care', but citizenship now stands alongside welfare as a major policy concern. The reader will recall that, in Chapter 3, I outlined a range of potential policy approaches from the profoundly negative to the positive assertion of citizenship. Rather like Sisyphus who, with many a setback, heaved a great stone up the side of a mountain, the Disability Movement is pushing with all its might to move British policy up towards the civil rights end of the spectrum. In the final chapter, my tasks are to put into perspective the changes that have occurred and to assess the prospects for disabled people in the future.

12

Conclusions

Introduction

This book has been concerned with understanding disability policies in the United Kingdom. I have argued that, right up to the present day, a 'personal tragedy' or medical model has prevailed. From this perspective, people are disabled by their impairments; consequently, they are unable to participate fully in society, fail to get jobs, cannot use public transport and so on. Such 'inabilities' have resulted in the development of specific responses. These have included social security benefits to compensate for a lack of wages, and a health and social services structure designed to rehabilitate disabled people as nearly as possible into 'normal' life. These interventions have been described with terms like 'remedial therapy', 'behaviour modification' and 'vocational training'. Where disabled people have been thought too impaired for adaptation, a common option has been containment in segregated institutions. Regimes have been developed to fill the days of severely impaired people with occupational therapy, diversion therapy and other manifestations of 'care'. The personal tragedy model plays a major role in subjecting disabled people to policies and practices that segregate and exclude. In sum, the rights afforded to other citizens are frequently denied to people with impairments: in work, in education, in housing, in leisure and in law. It seems that, for years, disabled people have been breasting waves in a sea of policies as likely to drown as to support them.

I do not think that we can infer from this that social workers, medical practitioners and politicians are bad people or that disabled people might, as a matter of principle, prefer to ride out bad viral infections rather than accept antibiotics from a GP. Nor do I cast all philanthropists and charity workers as self-seeking power merchants with no genuine feelings of concern and affection. Nor need we suspect (perhaps with one or two exceptions!) the motives of governments and

...sters down the years. Although there have been cases of ...eakable abuse and intentional discrimination against disabled people by malign individuals and groups, the matter here is not one of personal malevolence but of how citizens understand society and their place in it.

In everything we do, there is a compelling urge to regard our activities as somehow natural. Whether we do something well, or cannot do it at all, our first inclination is to explain our abilities and inabilities in personal terms. 'I'm not using the bus these days *because of the arthritis in my leg.*' 'My mother can't read the small print *because her eyes are bad.*' Perhaps one of the greatest obstacles facing proponents of the social model of disability is the difficulty in getting people to accept that there is not one group of 'normal' citizens and other groups who are 'abnormal'. Human beings come in all shapes and sizes, operate in different ways, possess different aptitudes and also cope with differing inabilities. People may recognise these differences at an intellectual level, but they still have great trouble in applying that knowledge to everyday life. It is really very hard to imagine the world as it may appear to others: 'Though I'm fit and have no trouble, these buses are so badly designed that elderly and disabled people and those with prams and pushchairs couldn't possibly use them; there have to be better designs than this'; 'This print is absurdly small so, although I can read it, many could not – the document will have to be redesigned'; 'I have no trouble getting into the telephone box, but the door is far too narrow for people who use wheelchairs.'

As Chapter 7 explained, there are many barriers to overcome for those who seek to promote this relatively new way of thinking, especially to getting it accepted as a way of formulating not just disability policies, but also all aspects of social living and the built environment. First, in a society driven by profit, the powers-that-be always have an eye to costs. The antagonism towards the Civil Rights (Disabled Persons) Bill (1994) was perhaps in large measure prompted by fear of the costs to industry, to managers being compelled to employ what they (unreasonably) feared might be less able or less flexible workers, and to the possible impact on public spending and the public sector borrowing requirement.

Second, in addition to the prevalence of the medical model, we have seen how the complexity of government has its own impact on the nature of disability policies in Britain. Policies are seldom conceived straightforwardly, and those which do see the light of day are delivered as a result of the multifarious interactions of many different pressures and interest groups. Yet disabled people have rarely been major players

in the production of policy; they have
process. However, as we saw in the prev
affairs may at last be changing.

For the rest of this concluding chapter, tw
development of disability policy hitherto mu
kind of overall perspective. Second, we need
possible, the future prospects for the social mod _____ for
disabled people themselves in their search for ec _____ opportunity
and citizenship. How optimistic may we be about the founding principles and likely effectiveness of future disability legislation? The
answer to that question clearly depends on a number of factors: the
political landscape; the negotiating strength of disabled people's groups
and the extent of their access to the conduits of power; the readiness (or
degree of resistance) in social institutions to accede to change; and
finally, the pace of change itself. First, however, the policy outcomes
discussed earlier in the book must be brought into sharper focus.

Outcomes in perspective

At the beginning of the book, we saw how some less technologically
advanced nations with few welfare resources at their disposal left
disabled children and adults very much to fend for themselves. For
many, the outcome could be grim, even fatal. But we also saw how
little room for complacency there was in even the most 'advanced'
Western states. Many unsatisfactory 'solutions' to disability had been
tried. Disabled people were corralled into institutions and, once there,
kept hidden from view. Medicine had promoted the idea of disability as
'abnormality', and disabled people were often the subjects of surgical
interventions designed to twist and turn them back into the 'right'
social, physical and psychological shapes. The understanding that
disabled people are citizens, and are therefore entitled to the same
rights, privileges and responsibilities as others, came only slowly to
more general recognition. Even then, it has been through the efforts of
disabled people themselves that much of the change has come about.

The institutional approaches to disability may have brought some
benefits, not least when the alternative might be actual abandonment,
leading ultimately to death. However, in those chapters dealing with
outcomes for particular groups according to their age, race or gender,
there emerged stark evidence of many undesirable effects resulting
from the 'personal tragedy' approach. First, by being incarcerated in

ns or trapped in their own homes, disabled people were
ed both from society and from each other. Second, the physical
ct of institutionalising disabled people served to reinforce a common
expectation that they were chronically dependent human beings. This
meant that many were excluded from the world of work and were
therefore liable to penury. Third, by the configuration of the environment, its buildings and transport systems, disabled people were further
constrained in their life chances. In particular, a lack of access to
education restricted their opportunities for career development. More
recently, governments have come to accept the legitimacy of a rights-
based approach. What is holding them back now seems to be questions
of cost rather than cognizance.

Prospects

By the year 2031, there will be some 8.2 million disabled adults in
Britain, an increase of 34 per cent since 1986 (Foley and Pratt, 1994).
Between now and then, disability policies may (in theory at least) take
any of the directions highlighted in the spectrum of policy models set
out in Chapter 3. These range from policies that actively deny disabled
people their citizenship through to measures intended to guarantee it.

There are at least five key factors that may help to shape future
policy in Britain. First, there is an indirect but potent influence exerted
by international developments, particularly the adoption of civil rights
legislation in countries such as America, Canada and Australia. Second,
and more directly, Britain must respond to policies developed by the
European Union. Third, there are ramifications in the shifting landscape of domestic politics. Fourth, we must acknowledge the
increasing influence of disabled people in public and political life, and
finally, policies will continue to be influenced by science through work
in areas such as genetics, computing and technology. Clearly, not all of
these influences take us in the same policy direction. Genetic science
springs from, and thus subscribes to, the medical model, whereas the
others fall within the ambit of a political perspective.

Supranational initiatives

The United Nations

Disability policies in other parts of the world may have a key role to play in future developments in Britain. Their influence may take at least two forms. First, they may exert pressure simply through the example they set. The reader may recall that Dr Roger Berry's Civil Rights (Disabled Persons) Bill used as its template the Americans with Disabilities Act. Second, the influence of policies elsewhere can be more formal and direct, channelled through international organisations such as the United Nations and the treaties and laws of the European Union, to which Britain is party.

Between 1990 and 1993, the United Nations elaborated their Standard Rules on the Equalisation of Opportunities for Disabled People. The Standard Rules include a preamble, 22 rules covering all aspects of social life, and a monitoring system. There are separate rules covering education, employment, income maintenance, social security, family life and personal integrity, and the recognition of the right of organisations of disabled people to act as representatives. Rule 6, on education, recognises the principle of equality of educational opportunity for disabled people in integrated and accessible settings. Rule 7 concentrates on the removal of the social and physical barriers that stand in the way of disabled people in their search for employment. The international elaboration of a set of Standard Rules to guarantee the rights of disabled people is a step forward; however, the United Nations acknowledges that there still remains the harder task of gaining worldwide agreement and implementation (Lindqvist, 1995).

The European Union

A commitment towards civil rights for disabled people is also growing within the European Union. However, because the organisation developed from economic rather than social origins, the framework for introducing social legislation has remained weak, and so far it has only proved possible to take forward social initiatives where they could be located in broader economic contexts. For example, the pursuit of social redevelopment schemes has occurred *as part and parcel* of employment regeneration projects. Howitt (1995: 53–4) therefore contends that disabled people are 'invisible' in European law and there is:

no reference to non-discrimination on the grounds of disability within the Treaties of the European Union... disabled people do not have full rights of citizenship which are granted to non disabled EU citizens.

Accordingly, one of the principles laid down in the Social Chapter of the Maastricht treaty was that there should be 'improved social and professional integration for disabled people'. The treaty also led to a draft directive (OJ C 15/18, 21st January 1992) on the removal of the physical and organisational barriers that disabled people encounter when they seek to travel to and from work. To date, however, the directive has not been implemented. A White Paper produced by the European Commission, *European Social Policy – A Way Forward for the Union*, argues that the omission of antidiscrimination clauses for disabled people is increasingly difficult to justify, and when the treaties are next revised, the European Union must make specific commitments to the principle of equal treatment (Howitt, 1995).

Although the legislative framework is unsatisfactory, there are community programmes to assist disabled people. These include Horizon, which seeks to integrate them into the labour market, TIDE which is concerned with new technology, and Helios, which concentrated on information exchange and 'good practice' (European Commission, 1996). However, in part because of the unsatisfactory legal base, the Helios programme has been criticised by Howitt (1995) for its very limited focus on information exchange and by Hurst (1995) for its having been controlled by governments and the major traditional charities in such a way that the programme was severely restricted both in focus and in impact. The Department of Health has confirmed that it is 'not yet clear what kind of action, if indeed anything, is going to succeed it' (Webb, 1996: 1).

In July 1996, the European Commission adopted a communication (European Commission Communication COM(96) 406 final) that supported a rights-based, equal opportunities approach. The document recognises that societies are organised principally for 'average' persons, but some 10 per cent of the citizens of the European Union are disabled. The communication concedes that many of these may be excluded from rights and opportunities enjoyed by their fellows. Unemployment is two to three times higher and also more sustained among disabled people. The Communication proposes a draft resolution which accepts that seeking to accommodate people to their impairments has failed, and integration into the mainstream is the proper aim. It remains to be seen, however, whether member states will be willing to make the environmental and social changes necessary to achieve mainstream integration. Imrie (1996) notes that the emphasis hitherto has been on what he calls 'socio-technical' solutions to access problems rather than the thorough-going dismantling of disabling policies and environments. Similarly, Hurst (1995) expresses doubt because both the Council of Europe and the European Union have traditionally focused social policy on rehabil-itation rather than rights, and disabled people are included neither in the Treaty of Rome nor in that of Maastricht.

Notwithstanding the limitations outlined above, the tenor of both the United Nations and the European Union with respect to disability poli-cies has been to accentuate the need for equality of opportunity and civil rights, and in March 1997, the European Commission adopted a proposal from Padraig Flynn, the Commissioner for Social Affairs, to set aside 10.8 million ECU from the 1997 budget to support equal opportunity initiatives for disabled people (GMCODP, 1997). To what extent does the government of the United Kingdom share this outlook?

Domestic politics in the United Kingdom

In its election manifesto, the Labour government promised:

> to seek to end unjustifiable discrimination wherever it exists. For example, we support comprehensive, enforceable civil rights for disabled people against discrimination in society or at work. (Labour Party, 1997)

Disappointingly, no disability rights legislation was announced in the Queen's Speech relating to the first 18 months of the new parliament. However, as I have indicated, ministers have followed up the manifesto with promises to replace the Disability Advisory Council established under the Disability Discrimination Act (1995) with a Disability Commission set up more along the lines of the Equal Opportunities Commission, a body that might exercise a broader remit and be given more teeth in its efforts to combat discrimination against disabled people (Department for Education and Employment Circular 304/97). Whether these moves signal an intention to produce further anti-discrimination legislation remains uncertain.

Generally speaking, the omens auger well. For example, the person in the government whose duties are most directly concerned with disabled people (Andrew Smith MP) now has the title not of Minister for the Disabled, but instead Minister for Employment and Disability

Rights, and he resides neither in the Health, nor in Social Security, but in the Department for Education and Employment, whose Secretary of State (David Blunkett) is himself a disabled person. A request for confirmation of the government's commitment to enact civil rights legislation before the end of the parliament, put to Tony Blair during Prime Minister's questions on 11th June 1997, brought the reply:

> We are of course committed to making sure that those who are disabled get proper civil rights. We have made that clear all the way through... It is precisely because we believe that disabled people have a good and genuine role in our society that we are committed to the rights my hon. Friend describes. (BCODP, 1997)

Science

Influences over the general direction of disability policies are, however, neither as homogenous nor as clear cut as the above social and political initiatives would suggest. While international and domestic politicians have declared themselves in favour of civil rights for disabled people, the advancement of science has complicated the picture considerably.

First, the reader will recall in particular the dilemma concerning the abortion of impaired fetuses. For those who believe that life begins only at the point at which the baby is born (or can exist independent of the mother), an early abortion amounts to no more than a method of contraception. But for those who believe that life begins at conception, abortion represents at minimum a denial of civil liberties, and at worst a serious crime.

Second, medicine is seeking to apply new advances and techniques in genetics (such as the Human Genome Project and the successful cloning of animals) to the identification and manipulation of human genes in order to combat impairments. For many years, the screening out of impaired fetuses has been promoted in the antenatal services of many developed countries, including Britain. However, scientists have more recently identified 'defective' genes that cause impairments or diseases such as cystic fibrosis. The aim is presumably either to screen out these genes or to develop treatments to replace them. Some disabled people, especially those born with an impairment rather than acquiring it later in life, reject the assumptions on which this kind of medical research is founded. Instead, they assert their pride in, and the validity of, disabled people as full citizens.

However, there are other disabled people, perhaps some of those who acquired impairments later in life having earlier been 'non-disabled', who may welcome medical intervention as a way of ridding themselves of what they regard as troublesome and unwelcome impairments. This bifurcation of views may cause heated debate in the disabled population as a whole. Clearly, then, while some disabled people may welcome gene therapy and the discovery of 'cures', others, especially some in the disability movement, take a less positive view. For them, being disabled does not constitute being in a 'defective' condition, and medical interventions of this kind would thus be unwelcome, not only for the body-altering propensity of surgery, but because of the underlying message that there is something 'wrong' about a person and that medicine is able to put it right. The crux of the matter here is that those disabled people who take this viewpoint do so on the basis that being a disabled person is an authentic state of being, just like being a tall person, a big person or a young person. In sum, there is fierce argument over whether the influence of science will be beneficial or detrimental. Some express fears that both abortion law and recent advances in genetic manipulation place disabled people under threat.

A second possible direction for policy (the first being to attempt the progressive eradication of impairments) might be the refinement of traditional welfare. This would include attempts to provide better services and increasingly sophisticated (technological) equipment and adaptations. Here we may think particularly of computer equipment and subcutaneous implants designed to make limbs work 'normally'. Roulstone (1993) acknowledges that modern technology may be helpful to disabled people and may expand their potential for gaining jobs, but, from his own research, Roulstone contends that modern technology has not reduced, in nature or amount, the prejudice and discrimination faced by disabled people at work. Stereotyping and misconceptions are likely to persist (Silo, 1991), and, although available, the necessary communication equipment and technology may even go deliberately unused by non-disabled counterparts (Disability, Handicap and Society, 1993).

The increasing influence of disabled people

So far, I have argued that the prospects for future policy may rest on the interaction of three significant forces: a social and political momentum for civil rights; a (contrasting) scientific ability to alter human genes and therefore human beings towards some medically defined norm; and a vested interest in the 'caring professions' that argues for the continuation of traditional services based on the perception of disabled people as recipients within a helper–helped relationship.

Perhaps it remains most probable that future policy may be composed of an amalgam of many approaches: some advance in civil rights, a continuation of genetic and technological research, and a survival of specialised health and social services. There is, however, one more crucial factor that I have not yet taken into account. With each passing day, disabled people are becoming more visible and more powerful in society. Their determination, and the growing strength of the disability movement, can provide crucial momentum for the civil rights campaign. Equally, their penetration of planning processes and the hierarchies of political authority may well increase the amount of control they can exercise over the direction and purposes of policy. Notwithstanding the power and prestige of medicine, disabled people continue to engage that profession in arguments about the definition of disability and the values and understandings that underpin medical interventions.

Perhaps future quality of life and the attainment of citizenship will hinge on the amount of control that disabled people are able to enjoy. Will they have sufficient autonomy to allow them an unencumbered choice between valuing their impairments as an integral part of their own identities or opting instead to undergo certain medical procedures to effect bodily changes? At present, the problem is that such a choice cannot be made freely: the price of valuing one's impairment as part of oneself is the attitudinal prejudices and environmental barriers that society throws up in response. Far easier, then, to succumb to the 'attractions' of 'normalisation' (Chappell, 1992)?

Conclusion

The history of disability policies in the United Kingdom has been hitherto less than noble. But in the penumbra of a new millennium, we may hope to see the creation of policies that not only assert the citizenship of disabled people, but also embrace the need for change in society at large, change guided by the endorsement of every individual's worth. Nor is the motive necessarily one of unalloyed magnanimity, for if history has taught us anything at all, it is that whenever we deny the humanity of other people, we, by that very act, desecrate our own.

Bibliography

Abberley, P. (1996) 'Work, utopia and impairment' in Barton, L. (ed.) *Disability and Society: Emerging Issues and Insights* (London: Longman).

Abrams, M. (1978) *Beyond Three Score and Ten, A First Report on a Survey of the Elderly* (Mitcham: Age Concern).

Abrams, M. (1980) *Beyond Three Score and Ten, A Second Report on a Survey of the Elderly* (Mitcham: Age Concern).

Abrams, M. and O'Brien, J. (1981) *Political Attitudes and Ageing in Britain* (Mitcham: Age Concern).

Adams, R. (1990) *Self Help, Social Work and Empowerment* (London: Macmillan).

Agar, M. (1990) 'Invisible and in the dark', *Community Care*, **821**: 28–9.

Age Concern (1972) *Age Concern on Health: Comments of 600 Old People on the Health and Welfare Services Available to Them* (London: Age Concern).

Ahmad, B. (1992) *Black Perspectives in Social Work* (Birmingham: Venture Press).

Ahmad, W., Kernohan, E. and Baker, M. (1989) 'Health of British Asians: a research review', *Community Medicine*, **11**: 49–56.

Albrow, M. (1982) *The Fears of the Elderly in Cardiff in 1982*, Social Research Unit Working Paper No. 12 (Cardiff: University College Cardiff).

Anderson, B. (1990) *Contracts and the Contract Culture* (London: Age Concern).

Anderson, W.A. and Anderson, N.D. (1978) 'The politics of age exclusion', *Gerentologist*, **18**: 6–12.

Anspach, R. (1979) 'From stigma to identity politics', *Social Science and Medicine*, **134**: 765–73.

Arber, S. and Ginn, J. (1991) *Gender and Later Life* (London, Sage).

Arnstein, S. (1969) 'A ladder of citizen participation', *American Institute of Planners Journal*, **35**(4): 216–24.

Association of District Councils (1990) *Summary of ADCs Evidence on Community Care: Meeting with the House of Commons Social Services Committee* (Association of District Councils).

Association of Metropolitan Authorities (1990) *Community Care: Submission to the Social Services Select Committee of the House of Commons* (Association of Metropolitan Authorities).

Atkin, K. and Rollings, J. (1993) *Community Care in a Multi-Racial Britain: A Critical Review of the Literature* (London: HMSO).

Atkin, K., Cameron, E., Badger, F. and Evers, E. (1989) 'Asian elders' knowledge and future use of community social and health services', *New Community*, **15**(2): 439–46.

Atkin, K. and Rollings, J. (1991) *Informal Care and Black Communities* (York: Social Policy Research Unit, University of York).

Atkinson, P., Shone, D. and Rees, T. (1981) 'Labouring to learn? Industrial training for slow learners' in Barton, L. and Tomlinson, S. (eds) *Special Education: Policy, Practices and Social Issues* (London: Harper & Row).

Audit Commission (1986) *Making a Reality of Community Care* (London: HMSO).

Australian Disability Discrimination Commissioner (1997) *Disability Discrimination Commissioner Project Report* (Sydney: Human Rights and Equal Opportunity Commission). Internet address http://www.peg.apc.org/~dice/rights/hreoc.html

Bachrach, P. and Baratz, M. (1970) *Power and Poverty: Theory and Practice* (Oxford: Oxford University Press).

Bairstow, P., Cochrane, R. and Hur, J. (1993) *Evaluation of Conductive Education for Children with Cerebral Palsy, Final Report* (in 2 Parts), (London: HMSO).

Balchin, P. (1995) *Housing Policy*, 3rd edn (London: Routledge).

Balkam, S. (undated) 'The Management Committee Myth', *Management Issues*, **2**: 12–13.

Ball, H. (1988) 'The limits of influence: ethnic minorities and the Partnership Programme', *New Community*, **15**(1): 7–22.

Barbalet, J.M. (1988) *Citizenship* (Milton Keynes: Open University Press).

Barnes, C. (1991) *Disabled People in Britain and Discrimination: A Case for Anti-Discrimination Legislation* (London: Hurst).

Barton, L. (1986) 'The politics of special educational needs', *Disability, Handicap and Society*, **1**(3): 273–90.

Barton, L. (1988) *The Politics of Special Educational Needs* (London: Falmer Press).

Barton, L. (1989) *Integration: Myth or Reality?* (London: Falmer Press).

Barton, L. (1993) 'The struggle for citizenship: the case of disabled people', *Disability, Handicap and Society*, **8**(3): 235–48.

Barton, L. and Tomlinson, S. (1981) *Special Education: Policy, Practices and Social Issues* (London: Harper & Row).

Baxter, C., Kamaljit, P., Ward, L. and Zenobia, N. (1990) *Double Discrimination* (London: King's Fund and Commission for Racial Equality).

BCODP (British Council of Organisations of Disabled People) (1997) 'Cause for optimism?', *BCODP Update*, **21** (June): 1.

Beardshaw, V. (1989) 'Conductive education: a rejoinder', *Disability, Handicap and Society*, **4**(3): 297–9.

Beck, B. (1970) 'The voluntary social welfare agency: a reassessment', *Social Services Review*, **44**(2): 147–54.

Begum, N. (1992) 'Disabled women and the feminist agenda', *Feminist Review*, **40**: 70–84.

Begum, N. (1995) *Community Care: A Question of Rights – Disabled People's Perspective* (London: King's Fund Centre and NISW). Internet address: http://www.nisw.org.uk/debate/debate.htm

Begum, N., Hill, M. and Stevens, A. (1994) *Reflections: Views of Black Disabled People on their Lives and Community Care* (London: CCETSW).

Benton, T. (1981) 'Objective interests and the sociology of power', *Sociology*, **15**: 161–84.

Berer, M. (1988) 'Whatever happened to "a woman's right to choose"?', *Feminist Review*, **29**: 24–37.

Beresford, P. and Croft, S. (1984) 'Welfare pluralism: the new face of fabianism', *Critical Social Policy*, **9**: 19–39.

Beresford, P. and Croft, S. (1989) 'User involvement, citizenship and social policy', *Critical Social Policy*, **26**: 5–18.

Beresford, P. and Croft, S. (1993) *Citizen Involvement* (London: Macmillan).

Berger, M., Wallis, D. and Watson, S. (1995) *Constructing Masculinity* (London: Routledge).

Berger, P. and Luckmann, T. (1967) *The Social Construction of Reality* (London: Allen Lane and Penguin Press).

Berthoud, R. (1995) 'Social security, poverty and disabled people' in Zarb, G. (ed.) *Removing Disabling Barriers* (London: Policy Studies Institute).

Berthoud, R., Lakey, J. and Mckay, S. (1993) *The Economic Problems of Disabled People* (London: Policy Studies Institute).

Beveridge, Sir W. (1942) *Social Insurance and Allied Services*, Cmd 6406, (London: HMSO).

Bevins, A. (1997) 'Blair is on a mission', *The Independent*, 15 December, p. 1.

Bhalla, A. and Blakemore, K. (1981) *Elderly of the Minority Ethnic Groups* (Birmingham: All Faiths for One Race).

Bhopal, R. and Donaldson, L. (1988) 'Health education for ethnic minorities – current provision and future direction', *Health Education Journal*, **47**(4): 137–40.

Bierstedt, R. (1950) 'An analysis of social power', *American Sociological Review*, December, pp. 730–8.

Bindoff, S.T. (1950) *Tudor England* (London: Penguin).

Bishop, N., Amina, M. and Williams, B. (1992) 'Black voluntary organisations in the care market', *Share*, **4**: 4–5.

Blackaby, D., Clark, K., Drinkwater, S., Leslie, D., Murphy, P. and O'Leary, N. (1998) *Earnings and Employment Opportunities for People with Disabilities: Secondary Analysis using the Census, General Household Survey and the Labour Force Survey* (Swansea: University of Wales, Swansea).

Blakemore, K. and Boneham, M. (1994) *Age, Race and Ethnicity, A Comparative Approach* (Buckingham: Open University Press).

Blakemore, K. and Drake, R.F. (1996) *Understanding Equal Opportunity Policies* (London: Prentice Hall and Harvester Wheatsheaf).

Blau, P. (1964) *Exchange and Power in Social Life* (London: John Wiley & Sons).

Blaxter, M. (1976) *The Meaning of Disability* (London: Heinemann).

Blomley, N. (1994) 'Mobility, empowerment and the rights revolution', *Political Geography*, **13**(5): 407–22.

Blumberg, L. (1991) 'For who among us has not spilled ketchup?' in Boylan, E., *Women and Disability* (London: Zed Books).

Boneham, M. (1989) 'Ageing and ethnicity in Britain: the case of elderly Sikh women in a Midlands town', *New Community*, **30**: 640–3.

Bookis, J. (1983) *Beyond the School Gate* (London, RADAR).

Booth, T. (1988) 'Challenging conceptions of integration' in Barton, L. (ed.) *The Politics of Special Educational Needs* (London: Falmer).

Borsay, A. (1990) 'Disability and attitudes to family care in Britain: towards a sociological perspective', *Disability, Handicap and Society*, **5**(2): 107–22.

Bourke, J. (1996) *Dismembering the Male: Men's Bodies, Britain and the Great War* (London: Reaktion Books).

Bowcott, O. (1996) 'No secure hospital place for stalker facing life', *The Guardian*, 23 October, p. 5.

Boylan, E. (1991) *Women and Disability* (London: Zed Books).

Bradsher, J.E. (1997) *Disability Among Racial and Ethnic Groups*, Disabilities Statistics Abstracts, No. 10, 30 January 1997 (California: University of California, Disability Statistics Center). Internet address http://dsc.uesf.edu/abs/ab10txt.htm

Bramley G, Bartlett, W. and Lambert, C. (1995) *Planning, the Market and Private Housebuilding* (London: UCL Press).

Brandon, D. (1988) 'Snouts among the troughs?', *Social Work Today*, 10 November, p. 27.

Brilliant, E. (1973) 'Private or public: a model of ambiguities', *Social Services Review*, **47**: 384–96.

Brindle, D. (1995) 'Two cats and a flat', *Search*, Spring, pp. 8–11.

Brindle, D. (1997) 'Care funds ruling "a devastating blow"', *The Guardian*, 21 March, p. 8.

Brisenden, S. (1986) 'Independent living and the medical model of disability', *Disability, Handicap and Society*, **1**(2): 173–8.

Brittain, F. (1947) *Arthur Quiller-Couch, A biographical study of 'Q'* (Cambridge: Cambridge University Press).

Brodie, I. and Berridge, D. (1996) *School Exclusion, Research Themes and Issues* (Luton: University of Luton Press).

Brown, C. (1984) *Black and White Britain: The Third PSI Survey* (London: Heinemann).

Brown, R. (1978) 'Bureaucracy as praxis: toward a political phenomenology of formal organisations', *Administrative Science Quarterly*, **23**: 365–78.

Brown, C. and Ringma, C. (1989) 'New disability services: the critical role of staff in a consumer directed empowerment model of service for physically handicapped people', *Disability, Handicap and Society*, **4**(3): 241–57.

Bryant, P. (1990) 'Community care – let's get it right', *Network Wales*, **70** (February): 11–12.

Buckle, J. (1971) *Work and Housing of Impaired Persons in Great Britain* (London: HMSO).

Bullard, D. and Knight, S. (eds) (1981) *Sexuality and Physical Disability: Personal Perspectives* (London: Mosby).

Burnett, J. (1986) *A Social History of Housing 1815–1985* (London: Routledge).

Burns, R. (1997) 'Disabled voters demand equal rights', *Big Issue Cymru*, May, p. 6.

Button, J. and Rosenbaum, W. (1990), 'Gray power, gray peril or gray myth? The political impact of the aging in local sunbelt politics', *Social Science Quarterly*, **71**(1): 25–38.

Cabinet Office (1994a) *Guidelines for the Implementation by Civil Service Departments and Agencies of a Guaranteed Interview Scheme for Disabled People* (London: Cabinet Office Equal Opportunities Division).

Cabinet Office (1994b) *Focus on Ability: A Practical Guide to Good Practice in Employment of Disabled People* (London: Cabinet Office Equal Opportunities Division).

Cameron, A. (1997) 'In search of the voluntary sector: a review article', *Journal of Social Policy*, **26**(1): 79–88.

Cameron, E., Badger, F., Evers, H. and Atkin, K. (1989) 'Black old women, disability and health carers' in Jeffreys, M. (ed.) *Growing Old in the Twentieth Century* (London: Routledge).

Campbell, J. and Oliver, M. (1996) *Disability Politics: Understanding Our Past, Changing Our Future* (London: Routledge).

Campling, J. (ed.) (1981) *Images of Ourselves* (London: Routledge & Kegan Paul).

Carby, H. (1982) 'Black feminism and the boundaries of sisterhood' in CCCS (ed.) *The Empire Strikes Back, Race and Racism in '70s Britain* (London: Hutchinson).

Carers National Association (1992) *Speak Up, Speak Out* (London: Carers National Association).

Cawson, A. (1982) *Corporatism and Welfare* (London: Heinemann).

Central Intelligence Agency (1997) *The World Factbook, 1996–7* (Washington: Brassey's).

Chamberlin, J. (1977) *On Our Own* (London: MIND Publications).

Chappell, A. (1992) 'Towards a sociological critique of the normalisation principle', *Disability, Handicap and Society*, **7**(1): 35–51.

Charities Aid Foundation (1997) *Charity Trends* (Tonbridge: CAF).

Chartered Institute of Public Finance Accountants (1996) *Housing Revenue Account Statistics, 1995 Commentary* (London: CIPFA Statistical Information Service).

Chote, R. (1994) 'A woman's work is rarely equal', *Independent on Sunday*, 22 May, p. 8.

Church, K. and Reville, D. (1988) *Report of Common Concerns: International Conference on User Involvement in Mental Health* (London: MIND).

Clark, J. (1997) 'Trading Places', *Telegraph Magazine*, 19 April, pp. 32–7.

Clarke, A. (1997) 'Disability Act may finally get some muscle' *The Independent*, Supplement, 26 November, p. 15.

Clements, L. (1996) 'A real act of care?', *Community Care*, 14–20 March, pp. 26–7.

Cochrane, R. and Bal, S. (1987) 'Migration and schizophrenia, an examination of five hypotheses', *Social Psychiatry*, **22**: 181–91.

Cocking, I. and Athwal, S. (1990) 'A special case for special treatment', *Social Work Today*, 8 February, pp. 12–13.

Cohen, P. (1994) 'Bearing witness', *Community Care*, 30 April, pp. 20–1.

Cole, I. and Furbey, R. (1994) *The Eclipse of Council Housing* (London: Routledge).

Commission for Racial Equality (1989) *Racial Equality in Social Services Departments: A Survey of Equal Opportunity Policies* (London: CRE).

Connell, R. (1995) *Masculinities* (Cambridge: Polity Press).

Connelly, N. (1989) *Race and Change in Social Services Departments* (London: Policy Studies Institute).

Cooper, G. (1997a) 'Councils may axe home helps, say law lords', *The Independent*, 21 March, p. 9.

Cooper, G. (1997b) '£200m for the disabled', *The Independent*, 3 July, p. 17.

Cooper, J. and Vernon, S. (1996) *Disability and the Law* (London: Jessica Kingsley).

Cornwall, A. and Lindisfarne, N. (eds) (1994) *Dislocating Masculinity* (London: Routledge).

Council for Advancement of Communication with Deaf People (1993) *Directory* (Durham: University of Durham).

Coward, R. (1994) 'The big issue: abortion', *The Guardian*, 16 September, p. 3.

Croft, S. and Beresford, P. (1990) *From Paternalism to Participation: Involving People in Social Services* (London: Open Services Project).

Crompton, R. (1993) *Class and Stratification: An Introduction to Current Debates* (Cambridge: Polity Press).

Crow, L. (1990) *Direct Action and Disabled People: Future Directions* (Manchester: Greater Manchester Coalition of Disabled People).

Crow, L. (1996) 'Including all of our lives: renewing the social model of disability' in Barnes, C. and Mercer, G. (eds) *Exploring the Divide: Illness and Disability* (Leeds: Disability Press).

D'Aboville, E. (1991) 'Social work in an organisation of disabled people' in Oliver, M. (ed.) *Social Work, Disabled People and Disabling Environments* (London: Jessica Kingsley).

Dahl, R. (1957) 'The concept of power', *Behavioural Science*, **2**: 201–5.

Dahl, R. (1961) *Who Governs?* (New Haven, CT: Yale University Press).

Dahrendorf, R. (1959) *Class and Class Conflict in Industrial Society* (London: Routledge & Kegan Paul).

Darvill, G. (1985) 'Provision for profit – where does that leave volunteers?', *Involve*, **46**: 2.

Darvill, G. (1987) 'Dancing along the lion's teeth', *Involve*, Winter 1986–87.

Daunt, P. (1991) *Meeting Disability, A European Response* (London: Cassell).

Davies, J. Dossett (1987) 'Standing up for pensioners', *Community Care*, 18 June, pp. 20–1.

Davies, P. Wynn (1997) 'Woman deaf since birth wins new deal for disabled', *The Independent*, 22 May, p. 10.

Davis, K. (1990) 'Issues in disability: integrated living' in *Private Troubles and Public Issues* (Milton Keynes: Open University Press).

Davis, K. (1993) 'On the movement', in Swain, J., Finkelstein, V., French, S. and Oliver, M. (eds) *Disabling Barriers, Enabling Environments* (London: Sage).

Dawson, C. (1995) *Employing Personal Assistants*, Social Care Research Findings, No. 61 (Norfolk: Independent Living Project).

De Jong, G. (1979) *The Movement for Independent Living: Origins, Ideology and Implications for Disability Research* (Michigan: University Center for Rehabilitation).

De Jong, G. (1983) 'Defining and implementing the independent living concept' in Crewe, N. and Zola, I. (eds) *Independent Living for Physically Disabled People* (London: Jossey-Bass).

Department for Education and Employment (1997) *£3.6 Million Boost for Disabled Access to Schools* [Press Release], 21 May.

Department of Employment (1990) *The Employment of People with Disabilities: A Review of the Legislation* (London: HMSO, IFF Research).

Department of Employment (1994) *The United Kingdom Response: Response by the United Kingdom Government to the European Commission's Paper on European Social Policy* (London: Department of Employment).

Department of the Environment (1977) *Housing Policy: A Consultative Document*, Cmnd 6851 (London: HMSO).

Department of the Environment (1992) *Planning Policy Guidance, No. 3* (London: Department of Environment).

Department of Health (1989a) *Caring for People: Community Care in the Next Decade and Beyond*, Cm 849 (London: HMSO).

Department of Health (1989b) *Working for Patients* (London: HMSO).

Department of Health (1990) *Caring for People: Community Care in the Next Decade and Beyond*, Policy Guidance (London: HMSO).

Department of Health (1991) *Implementing Community Care: Purchaser, Commissioner and Provider Roles* (The Price Waterhouse Report) (London: HMSO).

Department of Health (1996) *Health and Personal Social Services Statistics for England* (London: Stationery Office).

Department of Health and Social Security (1986) *Disabled Persons (Services, Consultation and Representation) Act* (London: HMSO).

Department of Health and Social Security (1994) *Civil Rights (Disabled Persons) Bill Compliance Cost Assessment* (London: DHSS).

Department of Social Security (1990) *The Way Ahead: Benefits for Disabled People*, Cmnd 917 (London: HMSO).

Department of Social Security (1996) *Social Security Statistics 1995* (London: HMSO).

Department of Social Security (1998) *New Ambitions for Our Country – A New Contract for Welfare* (London: Stationery Office).

Development and Equal Opportunities Division, Office of Public Service (1996a) *Equal Opportunities in the Civil Service – A Progress Report: Women, Race and Disability, 1993–95* (London: Office of Public Service).

Development and Equal Opportunities Division, Office of Public Service (1996b) *Civil Service Data Summary, 1996* (London: Office of Public Service).

Direct Action Network (1997) *DAN Descends on London*. Internet address http://disabilitynet.co.uk/groups/dan/index.htm

Disability Activist (1997) *The Disability Rights Activist*. Internet address http://www.teleport.com/~abarhyd

Disability Alliance (1991) *A Way Out of Poverty and Disability* (London: Disability Alliance).

Disability, Handicap and Society (1993) 'An open letter to the powers that be' (Author anonymous), *Disability, Handicap and Society*, **8**(3), pp. 317–27.

Disabled Peoples' International (1997) *DPI Member Profile*. Internet address http://www.dpi.org/indextxt.htm

Disweb (1997) *European Network of Women with Disabilities*. Internet address http://www.stakes.fi/sfa/disweba.htm

Dobson, R. (1996) 'Sense and sensitivity', *Community Care*, 9–15 May, p. 21.

Dodd, V. and Owens, B. (1996) 'CPS "shrugs off sex attacks on the vulnerable"', *The Independent on Sunday*, 2 June, p. 10.

Dourado, P. (1990) 'Grey power', *Community Care*, 5 July, pp. 16–19.

Dourado, P. (1991) 'Getting the message across', *Community Care*, **856**: 22–3.

Drake, R.F. (1992a) 'Consumer participation: the voluntary sector and the concept of power', *Disability, Handicap and Society*, **7**(3): 267–78.

Drake, R.F. (1992b) *A Little Brief Authority? A Sociological Analysis of Consumer Participation in Voluntary Agencies in Wales*, PhD Thesis (Cardiff: University of Wales, Cardiff).

Drake, R.F. (1994) 'The exclusion of disabled people from positions of power in British voluntary organisations', *Disability and Society*, **9**(4): 461–80.

Drake, R.F. (1996a) 'A critique of the role of the traditional charities' in Barton, L. (ed.) *Disability and Society: Emerging Issues and Insights* (London: Longman).

Drake, R.F. (1996b) 'Charities, authority and disabled people: a qualitative study', *Disability and Society*, **11**(1): 5–23.

Drake, R.F. and Owens, D.J. (1992) 'Consumer involvement and the voluntary sector in Wales: breakthrough or bandwagon?', *Critical Social Policy*, **33**: 76–86.

Driedger, D. (1989) *The Last Civil Rights Movement: Disabled Peoples' International* (London: Hurst).

Dungate, M. (1984) *A Multiracial Society: The Role of National Voluntary Organisations* (London: Bedford Square Press).

Dunn, J. and Fahy, T. (1990) 'Police admissions to a psychiatric hospital: demographic and clinical differences between ethnic groups', *British Journal of Psychiatry*, **156**: 373–8.

Eagles, J.M. (1991) 'The relationship between schizophrenia and immigration. Are there alternatives to psychosocial hypotheses?' *British Journal of Psychiatry*, **159**: 783–9.

Easton, D. (1965) *A Systems Analysis of Political Life* (New York, John Wiley & Sons).

Eder, K. (1993) *The New Politics of Class: Social Movements and Cultural Dynamics in Advanced Societies* (London: Sage).

Edley, N. and Wetherall, M. (1995) *Men in Perspective* (London: Prentice Hall).

Eigner, W., Knol, H., Neuer-Miebach, T., Rioux, M., Van de Vate, K. and Bunch, M. (1994) *Just Technology? From Principles to Practice in Bio-Ethical Issues* (New York, Ontario: Roeher Institute).

Ellis, B. and Smith, A. (1995) 'Report on the first project for disabled women' in *The Conference Report of the Disability Rights Symposium of the European Regions*, (Southampton: Disability Rights Symposium Planning Group) pp. 177–83.

Emanuel, J. and Ackroyd, D. (1996) 'Breaking down barriers' in Barnes, C. and Mercer, G. (eds) *Exploring the Divide: Illness and Disability* (Leeds: Disability Press).

Emerson, R. (1962) 'Power-dependence relations', *American Sociological Review*, **27**: 31–41.

Equal Opportunities Review (1997) 'Implementing the DDA: an EOR survey of employers', *Equal Opportunities Review*, **71** (January/February): 20–6.

Esmail, A. and Everington, S. (1993) 'Racial discrimination against doctors from ethnic minorities', *British Medical Journal*, **36**: 691–2.

European Commission (1996) *How is the European Union Meeting Social and Regional Needs?* (Brussels: European Commission).

Farleigh, A. (1990) 'Invisible communities', *Community Care*, **806**: 30–1.

Femia, J. (1985) *Gramsci's Political Thought: Hegemony, Consciousness and the Revolutionary Process* (Oxford: Oxford University Press).

Fenton, S. (1986) *Race, Health and Welfare: Afro Caribbean and South Asian People in Central Bristol* (Bristol: Department of Sociology, University of Bristol).

Fernando, S. (1988) *Race and Culture in Psychiatry* (London: Billing & Son).

Fernando, S. (1991) *Race and Culture* (Basingstoke: Macmillan/MIND).

Fiedler, B. (1988) 'A fair slice of the cake', *Community Care*, 4 February, pp. 30–1.

Field, S. and Jackson, H. (1989) *Race, Community Groups and Service Delivery* (London: HMSO).

Fielding, N. and Gutch, R. (1989) *Contracting In or Out? The Legal Context* (London: National Council for Voluntary Organisations).

Finkelstein, V. (1981) 'Disability and the helper/helped relationship. An historical view' in Brechin, A., Liddiard, P. and Swain, J. (eds) *Handicap in a Social World* (London: Hodder & Stoughton).

Fletcher, A. (1997) 'It's not the baby's responsibility to be perfect', *Amazons*, June, pp. 1, 4–5.

Foley, C. and Pratt, S. (1994) *Access Denied, Human Rights and Disabled People* (London: National Council for Civil Liberties).

Forrest, R. and Murie, A. (1991) *Selling the Welfare State* (London: Routledge).

Fowler, R., Hodge, B., Kress, G. and Trew, T. (1979) *Language and Control* (London: Routledge & Kegan Paul).

Francis, J. (1993) 'Pressure Group', *Community Care*, 24 June, pp. 14–15.

Fraser, D. (1984) *The Evolution of the British Welfare State* (London: Macmillan).

Freire, P. (1972) *Pedagogy of the Oppressed* (Harmondsworth: Penguin).

French, S. (1993) 'Disability impairment, or something in between?' in Swain, J., Finkelstein, V., French, S. and Oliver, M. (eds) *Disabling Barriers, Enabling Environments* (London: Sage).

Friend, J., Power, J. and Yewlett, C. (1974) *Public Planning: The Intercorporate Dimension* (London: Tavistock).

Fry, E. (1987) *Disabled People and the 1987 General Election* (London: Spastics Society).

Fulcher, G. (1989) 'Integrate and mainstream? Comparative issues in the politics of these policies' in Barton, L. *Integration: Myth or Reality?* (London: Falmer Press).

Gaventa, J. (1980) *Power and Powerlessness, Quiescence and Rebellion in an Appalachian Valley* (Oxford: Clarendon Press).

Gazdar, S. (1994) 'Ethnic minorities development project', *Disability Rights Bulletin*, Summer, p. 14.

Gazdar, C. (1997) 'Service is "dreadful"', *Community Care*, 26 June, p. 7.

George, M. (1993) 'Needs unveiled', *Community Care*, 23 September, pp. 14–15.

George, M. (1996) 'From cradle to grave: the future of social care', *Community Care*, 1 August, pp. i–viii.

George, V. and Wilding, P. (1984) *The Impact of Social Policy* (London: Routledge).

Gerschick, T. and Miller, A. (1993) 'Coming to terms: masculinity and physical disability', *American Sociological Association*, Annual Meeting, Miami, FL.

Giddens, A. (1968) 'Power in the recent writings of Talcott Parsons', *Sociology*, **2**: 257–72.

Giddens, A. (1993) 'Problems of action and structure' in Cassell, P. (ed.) *The Giddens Reader* (London: Macmillan).

Ginn, J. (1993) 'Grey power: age based organisations' response to structured inequalities', *Critical Social Policy*, **38**: 23–47.

Ginsburg, H. (1983) *Full Employment and Public Policy: The United States and Sweden* (Lexington: Lexington Books).

Ginsburg, N. (1992) 'Black people and housing policies' in Birchall, J. (ed.) *Housing Policy in the 1990s* (London: Routledge).

Glendinning, C. (1991) 'Losing ground: social policy and disabled people in Great Britain', *Disability, Handicap and Society*, **6**(1): 3–20.

Glendinning, C. and Miller, J. (1987) *Women and Poverty* (London: Harvester Wheatsheaf).

Glennerster, H., Power, A. and Travers, T. (1991) 'A new era for social policy: a new Enlightenment or a new Leviathan?', *Journal of Social Policy*, **20**(3): 389–414.

GMCODP (1997) EU Social Policy – ECU 10.8m in the 1996 Budget for the Disabled (Manchester: Greater Manchester Coalition of Disabled People). Internet address http://www.disabilitynet.co.uk/groups/gmcdp/index.html

Gooding, C. (1994) *Disabling Laws, Enabling Acts: Disability Rights in Britain and America* (London: Pluto Press).

Gooding, C. (1996) *Blackstone's Guide to the Disability Discrimination Act 1995* (London: Blackstone Press).

Gould, A. (1988) *Conflict and Control in Welfare Policy: The Swedish Experience* (London: Longman).

Gould, A. (1993) *Capitalist Welfare Systems: A Comparison of Japan, Britain and Sweden* (London: Longman).

Graham, P. (1992) *When I'm 64: in Interfering in People's Lives?* (Milton Keynes: Open University Press).

Gramsci, A. (1971) *Selections from the Prison Notebooks*, edited by Q. Hoare and G. Nowell Smith (London: Lawrence & Wishart).

Greengross, W. (1976) *Entitled to Love* (Guildford: National Marriage Guidance Council).

Griffiths, Sir R. (1988) *Community Care: Agenda for Action* (London: HMSO).

Gutch, R. (1989) *The Contract Culture: The Challenge for Voluntary Organisations* (London: National Council for Voluntary Organisations).

Ham, C. and Hill, M. (1984) *The Policy Process in the Modern Capitalist State* (Brighton: Wheatsheaf).

Handy, C. (1988) *Understanding Voluntary Organisations* (Harmondsworth: Penguin).

Hansard (1994) *Civil Rights (Disabled Persons) Bill* Friday, 6 May, Cols. 960–1017 (London: HMSO).

Harris, M. (1995) 'We can't lift every kerb', *The Daily Telegraph*, 9 February.

Harris, N. and Wikeley, N. (1995) 'Disability working allowance', *Journal of Social Welfare Law*, **2**: 276.

Harrison, M. (1995) *Housing, 'Race', Social Policy and Empowerment* (Aldershot: Avebury).

Haskey, J. (1991) 'The ethnic minority populations resident in private households – estimates by County and Metropolitan Districts of England and Wales', *Population Trends*, **63**: 22–35.

Hasler, F. (1993) 'Developments in the disabled people's movement' in Swain, J., Finkelstein, V., French S. and Oliver, M. (eds) *Disabling Barriers, Enabling Environments* (London: Sage).

Haveman, R. (1984) *Public Policy towards Disabled Workers: Cross National Analysis of Economic Impacts* (Cornell: Cornell University Press).

Haydon, S. (1997) 'Sweden owns up to racial purification', *The Independent*, 25 August, p. 10.

Healey, D. (1989) *The Time of My Life* (London: Penguin).

Heath, A. (1968) 'Economic theory and sociology: a critique of P.M. Blau's "Exchange and Power in Social Life"', *Sociology*, **2**: 273–92.

Heclo, H. (1972) 'Review article: policy analysis', *British Journal of Political Science*, **2**: 83–108.

Hicks, C. (1988) 'NHS colour blindness', *Health Service Journal*, **98**(5102): 590–1.

Higgens, P. (1992) *Making Disability* (Springfield, IL: Charles C. Thomas).

Hill, M. (1992) 'Conference Address', *Race and Disability: A Dialogue for Action* (London: Greater London Association of Disabled People).

Hill, M. (1997) *The Policy Process in the Modern State* (London: Prentice Hall).

Himmelweit, S. (1988) 'More than a woman's right to choose?', *Feminist Review*, **29**(Spring): 38–56.

Hinton, N. and Hyde, M. (1982) 'The voluntary sector in a remodelled welfare state' in Jones, C. and Stevenson, J. (eds) *The Yearbook of Social Policy in Britain, 1980–81* (London: Routledge & Kegan Paul).

Hirst, J. (1996) 'Direct benefit?', *Community Care*, 1–7 May, p. 10.

Hogwood, B. and Gunn, L. (1984) *Policy Analysis for the Real World* (Oxford: Oxford University Press).

Holland, B. and Lewando-Hundt, G. (1987) *Coventry Ethnic Minorities Elderly Survey, Method and Data and Applied Action* (Coventry: City of Coventry, Ethnic Development Unit).

Hood, J. (ed.) (1993) *Man, Work and Family* (London: Sage).

Hough, M. and Mayhew, P. (1984) *Taking Account of Crime: Key Findings from the 1984 British Crime Survey* (London: HMSO).

House Builders Federation (1995) 'The application of building regulations to help disabled people in new dwellings in England and Wales' (unpublished paper), quoted in Imrie, R. (1996) *Disability and the City: International Perspectives* (London: Paul Chapman Publishing).

House of Commons (1908) Building Accidents Committee. *Report of the Departmental Committee Appointed to Inquire into the Dangers Attendant on Building Operations*, Cd 3848.

Howe, G.M. (1963) *National Atlas of Disease Mortality in the United Kingdom* (London: Nelson).

Howe, G.M. (1986) 'Spatial inequalities in mortality experience in Wales', *Cambria, A Welsh Geographical Review*, **13**(1): 131–49.

Howitt, R. (1995) 'Disability rights in a European legislative framework', *The Conference Report of the Disability Rights Symposium of the European Regions*, (Southampton: Disability Rights Symposium Planning Group.

Hunt, A. (1978) *The Elderly at Home: A Study of People Age Sixty Five and Over Living in the Community in England in 1976* (London: HMSO).

Hunt, J. and Heyes, L. (1980) *Housing the Disabled* (Cwmbran: Torfaen Borough Council).

Hurst, R. (1995) 'Choice and empowerment – lessons from Europe', *Disability and Society*, **10**(4): 529–34.

Imrie, R. (1996) *Disability and the City: International Perspectives* (London: Paul Chapman Publishing).

Imrie, R. and Wells, P. (1993) 'Disablism, planning and the built environment', *Environment and Planning C: Government and Policy*, **11**(2): 213–31.

Institute for Fiscal Studies (1994) *For Richer, For Poorer: The Changing Distribution of Income in the UK 1961–1991* (London: Institute for Fiscal Studies).

Institute for Fiscal Studies (1997) *The State of Donation: Household Gifts to Charity 1974–1996* (London: Institute for Fiscal Studies).

Isherwood, J. (1994) 'Poll victor warns of "deep cuts" in Sweden', *Daily Telegraph*, 20 September, p. 13.

Jarrett, M. (1990) 'The black voluntary sector', *NCVO News*, **19**: 7–8.

Jenkins, W. (1978) *Policy Analysis: A Political and Organisational Perspective* (London: Martin Robertson).

Johnson, M. (1990) 'Defective fetuses and us', *Disability Rag*, March/April, p. 34.

Jones, K. (1955) *Lunacy, Law and Conscience 1744–1845* (London: Routledge).

Jones, K. (1991) *The Making of Social Policy in Britain 1830–1990* (London: Athlone).

Kallianes, V. and Rubenfeld, P. (1997) 'Disabled women and reproductive rights', *Disability and Society*, **12**(2): 203–21.

Kandola, R., Fullerton, J. and Ahmed, Y. (1995) *Managing the Mosaic: Diversity in Action* (London: Institute of Personnel Management).

Karacs, I. (1996) 'Welfare slashed in Kohl's EMU austerity drive', *The Independent*, 27 November, p. 8.

Katz, I. and Bunting, M. (1993) 'God's shock troops', *The Guardian*, 8 November, p. 2.

Keeble, P. (1984) *Disability and Minority Ethnic Groups: A Factsheet of Issues and Initiatives* (London: Royal Association of Disability and Rehabilitation).

Kestenbaum, A. (1995) *Local Authorities' Use of Independent Living Money*, Social Care Research Findings, No. 63 (London: Disablement Income Group).

Kestenbaum, A. (1996a) *Independent Living: A Review* (York: York Publishing Services).

Kestenbaum, A. (1996b) 'The state of independence', *Community Care*, 22–28 February, pp. 32–3.

Kleinman, M. and Piachaud, D. (1993) 'European social policy', *Journal of European Social Policy*, **3**(1): 1–19.

Knowles, C. (1991) 'Afro-Caribbeans and schizophrenia: how does psychiatry deal with issues of race, culture and ethnicity?', *Journal of Social Policy*, **20**: 173–90.

Knowsley, J. (1997) 'Gay pride as festival-goers get a message from Blair', *Sunday Telegraph*, 6 July, p. 2.

König, A. and Schalock, R. (1991) 'Supported employment: equal opportunities for severely disabled men and women', *International Labour Review*, **130**: 21–37.

Krauss-Mars, A.H. and Lachman, P. (1994) 'Breaking bad news to parents with disabled children – a cross cultural study', *Child: Care, Health and Development*, **20**: 101–13.

Kunz, C., Jones, R. and Spencer, K. (1989) *Bidding for Change?* (Birmingham: Birmingham Settlement).

Labour Party (1997) *Because Britain Deserves Better, New Labour's Election Manifesto 1997*. Internet edition, address http://www.labour.org.uk

Laing, W. (1993) *Empowering the Elderly: Direct Consumer Funding of Care Services* (London: Institute of Economic Affairs, Health and Welfare Unit).

Land, H. and Rose, H. (1985) 'Compulsory altruism for some or an altruistic society for all?' in Bean, P., Ferris, J. and Whynes, D. (eds) *In Defence of Welfare* (London: Tavistock).

Lane, D. (1981) 'Foreword' in Barton, L. and Tomlinson, S. *Special Education: Policy, Practices and Social Issues* (London: Harper & Row).

Langan, M. and Clarke, J. (1994) 'Managing in the mixed economy of care' in Clarke, J., Cochrane, A. and McLaughlin, E. (eds) *Managing Social Policy* (London: Sage).

LaPlante, M.P. (1997) 'How many Americans have a disability?', *Disability Statistics Abstract, No. 5, 30 January, 1997* (California: University of California, Disability Statistics Center). Internet address http://dsc.uesf.edu/abs/ab5txt.htm

LaPlante, M.P., Kennedy, J., Kaye, H.S. and Wenger, B.L. (1997) 'Disability and employment', *Disability Statistics Abstract*, No. 11, 30 January (California: University of California, Disability Statistics Center). Internet address http://dsc.uesf.edu/abs/ab11txt.htm

Laune, L. (1993) *Building Our Lives: Housing, Independent Living, and Disabled People* (London: Shelter).

Laurance, J. (1997) 'Stephen and Russell are gay, disabled and want a baby. Do they have a right to ask a surrogate to bear their child?', *The Independent*, 28 May, p. 3.

Laver, M. (1979) *The Politics of Private Desires* (Harmondsworth: Penguin).

Lawrance, J. and Blackhurst, C. (1989) 'Big spending Woopies turn on grey power', *Sunday Times*, 5 March, p. A5.

Lawrence, M. (1987) *Fed up and Hungry* (London: Women's Press).

Lawrence, R. (1983) 'Voluntary action: a stalking horse for the Right?', *Critical Social Policy*, **2**(3): 14–30.

Leach, B. (1989) 'Disabled people and the implementation of local authorities' equal opportunity policies', *Public Administration*, **67**(Spring): 65–77.

Leat, D. (1986a) 'Clearing out the myth cupboard', *Involve* **48**: 6–7.

Leat, D. (1986b) 'Local authorities and the voluntary sector, prospects for change', *Policy Studies*, **6**(4): 70–81.

Leat, D. (1986c) 'Privatization and voluntarization', *Quarterly Journal of Social Affairs*, **2**(3): 285–320.

Leat, D., Smolka, G. and Unell, J. (1981) *Voluntary and Statutory Collaboration: Rhetoric or Reality?* (London: Bedford Square Press).

Le Grand, J. and Robinson, R. (eds) (1984) *Privatisation and the Welfare State* (London: Allen & Unwin).

Le Grand, J., Propper, C. and Robinson, R. (1992) *The Economics of Social Problems*, 3rd edn (London: Macmillan).

Levin, P. (1997) *Making Social Policy* (Buckingham: Open University Press).

Levy, L., Andrews, C., Bynorth, M., Cobb, A. *et al.* (1986) *Finding our own Solutions* (London: MIND Publications).

Liberty (1994) *Women's Rights, Human Rights* (London: National Council for Civil Liberties).

Lifton, R.J. (1986) *The Nazi Doctors: Medical Killings and the Psychology of Genocide* (Basingstoke: Macmillan).

Lightfoot, L. (1995) 'Britons flock to rescue of China's girls', *Sunday Times*, 18 June, p. 9.

Lindblom, C. (1959) 'The science of "muddling through"', *Public Administration Review*, **19**: 78–88.

Lindblom, C. (1977) *Politics and Markets* (New York: Basic Books).

Lindow, V. (1990) 'Participation and power', *Openmind*, **44**: 10–11.

Lindqvist, B. (1995) 'The UN standard rules on the equalisation of opportunities for persons with disabilities', *The Conference Report of the Disability Rights Symposium of the European Regions* (Southampton: Disability Rights Symposium Planning Group).

Littlewood, R. (1992) 'Psychiatric diagnosis and racial bias: empirical and interpretative approaches', *Social Science Medicine*, **34**: 141–9.

Locker, D. (1983) *Disability and Disadvantage* (London: Tavistock).

Loney, M., Bocock, R., Clarke, J., Cochrane, A., Graham, P. and Wilson, M. (eds) (1992) *The State or the Market* (London: Sage).

Lonsdale, S (1990) *Women and Disability, The Experience of Physical Disability among Women* (London: Macmillan).

Lonsdale, S. and Walker, A. (1984) *A Right to Work: Disability and Employment* (London: Low Pay Unit).

Lowe, R. (1993) *The Welfare State in Britain since 1945* (London: Macmillan).

Lukes, S. (1974) *Power: A Radical View* (London: Macmillan).

Lund, B. (1996) *Housing Problems and Housing Policy* (London: Longman).

Lunt, N. and Thornton, P. (1993) *Employment Policies for Disabled People, A Review of Legislation and Services in Fifteen Countries* (London: Department of Employment).

Mabbot, J. (1992), *Local Authority Funding for Voluntary Organisations* (London: National Council for Voluntary Organisations).

MacAnGhaill, M. (1996) *Understanding Masculinities* (Buckingham: Open University Press).

McAvoy, B. and Donaldson, L. (eds) (1990) *Health Care for Asians* (Oxford: Oxford University Press).

McCarthy, M. (ed.) (1989) *The New Politics of Welfare* (London: Macmillan).

MacDonald, V. (1997) 'Down's babies used in vaccine experiments', *Sunday Telegraph*, 6 July, p. 4.

MacErlean, N. (1997) 'Benefits trap for disabled', *The Observer* (Money Matters), 7 September, p. 14.

MacFarlane, A. (1995) 'Building a supportive environment for older disabled people', *The Conference Report of the Disability Rights Symposium of the European Regions* (Southampton: Disability Rights Symposium Planning Group).

McGwire, S. (1997) 'MP in a wheelchair gets a lift at the House', *The Independent on Sunday*, 11 May, p. 11.

McLean, C., Carey, M. and White, C. (eds) (1996) *Men's Way of Being* (Oxford: Westview Press).

McLean, M. and Jeffreys, M. (1974) 'Disability and deprivation', in Wedderburn, D. (ed.) *Poverty, Inequality and Class Structure* (Cambridge: Cambridge University Press).

McLennan, G. (1989) *Marxism, Pluralism and Beyond* (Cambridge: Polity Press).

McNaught, A. (1988) *Race and Health Policy* (London: Croom Helm).

McPherson, C. (1991) 'Violence as it affects disabled women: a view from Canada' in Boylan, E. (ed.) *Women and Disability* (London: Zed Books).

McRae, H. (1996) 'Sweden's welfare meltdown has lessons for Labour', *The Independent*, 20 December, p. 19.

Malpass, P. and Murie, A. (1994) *Housing Policy and Practice*, 4th edn (London: Macmillan).

Manning, N. (1985) *Social Problems and Welfare Ideology* (Aldershot: Gower).

Mapp, S. (1997) 'Background factors', *Community Care*, 15–21 May, p. 25.

Mares, P., Henley, A. and Baxter, C. (1985) *Health Care in Multiracial Britain* (Cambridge: Health Education Council and National Extension College).

Marshall, T.H. (1950) *Citizenship and Social Class* (Cambridge: Cambridge University Press).

Marshall, T.H. (1963) *Sociology at the Crossroads and Other Essays* (London: Heinemann).

Martin, J. and White, A. (1988) *Surveys of Disabled of Disabled People in Great Britain: Report No. 2, The Financial Circumstances of Disabled Adults Living in Private Households* (London: OPCS).

Martin, J., Meltzer, H. and Elliot, D. (1988) *Surveys of Disabled People in Great Britain: Report No. 1, The Prevalence of Disability Among Adults* (London: OPCS).

Martin, J., White, A. and Meltzer, H. (1989) *Surveys of Disabled of Disabled People in Great Britain: Report No. 4, Disabled Adults: Services, Transport and Employment* (London: OPCS).

Matrix (1984) *Making Space: Women and the Man Made Environment* (London: Pluto Press).

Middlemas, K. (1979) *Politics in Industrial Society* (London: André Deutsch).

Mid Glamorgan Association of Voluntary Organisations (1991) *The Elderly Initiative Project in Merthyr Tydfil and the Cynon Valley, Annual Report* (First Year) (Pontypridd: MGAVO).

Mid Glamorgan Association of Voluntary Organisations (1992a) *Services for Older People Living in Merthyr Tydfil* (Pontypridd: MGAVO).

Mid Glamorgan Association of Voluntary Organisations (1992b) *Services for Older People Living in the Cynon Valley* (Pontypridd: MGAVO).

Mid Glamorgan Association of Voluntary Organisations (1993) *The Elderly Initiative Project in Merthyr Tydfil and Cynon Valley April 1990 – March 1993* (Pontypridd: MGAVO).

Mid Glamorgan Health Authority (1985) *Mid Glamorgan Deprivation and Health: The Need for Health Care* (Cardiff: Mid Glamorgan Health Authority).

Midwinter, E. (1992) *Citizenship: From Ageism to Participation, Carnegie Inquiry into the Third Age*, Research Paper Number 8 (Dunfirmline: Carnegie United Kingdom Trust).

Miliband, R. (1969) 'The capitalist state: reply to Nicos Poulantzas', *New Left Review*, **59**: 53–60.

MIND (National Association for Mental Health) (1989) *The Right to Vote* (Preston: North West MIND).

Ministry of Health (1951) *Circular* 32/51 (London: HMSO).

Ministry of Health (1959) *Report of the Working Party on Social Workers in the Local Authority Health and Welfare Services* (London: HMSO).

Ministry of Health (1960) *Circular* 15/60 (London: HMSO).

Mitchell, D. (1990) 'Contracts for equality', *Social Services Insight*, **5**(21): 15.

Modood, T., Berthoud, R., Lakey, J., Nazroo, J., Smith, P., Virdee, S. and Beishon, S. (1997) *Ethnic Minorities in Britain* (London: Policy Studies Institute).

Momm, W. and König, A. (1989) 'Community integration for disabled people: a new approach to their vocational training and employment', *International Labour Review*, **128**(4): 497–509.

Moore, C. and Bloomer, K. (1977) *Body, Memory and Architecture* (New Haven: Yale University Press).

Morgan, D. (1992) *Discovering Men* (London: Routledge).

Morrell, J. (1990) *The Employment of People with Disabilities: Research into the Policies and Practices of Employers* (London: Department of Employment).

Morris, J. (1988) *Freedom to Lose: Housing Policy and People with Disabilities* (London: Shelter).

Morris, J. (ed.) (1989) *Able Lives* (London: Women's Press).

Morris, J. (1990) *Our Homes, Our Rights: Housing, Independent Living and Physically Disabled People* (London: Shelter).

Morris, J. (1991) *Pride Against Prejudice* (London: Women's Press).

Morris, J. (1992) 'Us and them? Feminist research, community care, and disability', *Critical Social Policy*, **11**(3): 22–39.

Morris, J. (1993) *Independent Lives: Community Care and Disabled People* (London: Macmillan).

Morris, J. (1997) 'Now know your rights', *Community Care*, 12–18 June, p. 25.

Moyes, A.M. (1981) 'Health Facilities and Disease Mortality', *The National Atlas of Wales*: Section 7.

Müller-Hill, B. (1988) *Murderous Science: Elimination by Scientific Selection of Jews, Gypsies and Others, Germany 1933–1945* (Oxford: Oxford University Press).

Müller-Hill, B. (1994) 'The idea of the final solution and the role of experts' in Cesarani, D. (ed.) *The Final Solution: Origins and Implementation* (London: Routledge).

Murray, N. (1992) 'Listening to the silent minority', *Community Care*, 20 August, pp. 12–13.

Nathwani, A. (1987) *Disability in the Asian Communities* (London: Greater London Association of Disabled People).

National Association of Health Authorities (1988) *Action not Words: A Strategy to Improve Health Services for Black and Minority Ethnic Groups* (London: National Association of Health Authorities).

Newman, O. (1973) *Defensible Space* (London: Architectural Press).

O'Day, B. (1995) 'The Americans with Disabilities Act: from civil rights to enabling practice', *The Conference Report of the Disability Rights Symposium of the European Regions* (Southampton: Disability Rights Symposium Planning Group).

Office for National Statistics (1996) *New Earnings Survey, Part A: Streamlined Analyses: Description of the Survey* (London: HMSO).

Office of Population, Censuses and Surveys (1971) *The Prevalence of Disability in Great Britain* (London: HMSO).

Office of Population, Censuses and Surveys (1986) *Social Trends* (London: HMSO).

Office of Population, Censuses and Surveys (1991) *Labour Force Survey 1988 and 1989* (London: HMSO).

Office of Population, Censuses and Surveys (1993) *The United Kingdom Census, 1991* (London: HMSO).

Oliver, M. (1989) 'Conductive education: if it wasn't so sad it would be funny', *Disability, Handicap and Society*, **4**(2): 197–200.

Oliver, M. (1990) *The Politics of Disablement* (London: Macmillan).

Oliver, M. (1991a) 'Disability and participation in the labour market' in Brown, P. and Scase, E. (eds) *Poor Work* (Milton Keynes: Open University Press).

Oliver, M. (1991b) 'Reappraising special needs education', *European Journal of Special Needs Education*, **6**(1).

Oliver, M. (1996) *Understanding Disability* (London: Macmillan).

Oliver, M., Zarb, G., Moore, M., Silver, J. and Salisbury, V. (1988) *Walking into Darkness: The Experience of Spinal Cord Injury* (London: Macmillan).

Ossowski, S. (1963) *Class Structure in the Social Consciousness* (London: Routledge & Kegan Paul).

Owen, F. (1977), *Profiles of the Elderly: Their Health and the Health Services* (Mitcham: Age Concern).

Owen, M.J. (1991) 'What's so important about the wrapping paper on our souls?' in Boylan, E. (ed.) *Women and Disability* (London: Zed Books).

Owens, D., Harrison, H. and Boot, D. (1991) 'Ethnic factors in voluntary and compulsory admissions', *Psychological Medicine*, **21**: 185–96.

Pagel, M. (1988) *On Our Own Behalf* (Manchester: Greater Manchester Coalition of Disabled People).

Painz, F. (1993) *Parents with a Learning Disability*, Social Work Monographs (Norwich: University of East Anglia).

Pakulski, J. and Waters, M. (1996) *The Death of Class* (London: Sage).

Pampel, F. and Williamson, J. (1989) *Age, Class, Politics and the Welfare State* (Cambridge: Cambridge University Press).

Parry, R.L. (1996) 'Lepers still suffer under Japanese prejudice', *The Independent*, 10 February, p.16.

Parsons, T. (1964) 'Some reflections on the place of force in social processes' in Eckstein, H. (ed.) *Internal War* (New York: Free Press).

Passigli, S. (1973) 'On power, its intensity and distribution', *European Journal of Political Research*, **1**: 163–77.

Patel, N. (1990) *A Race Apart* (London: King's Fund).

Pearson, M. (1986) 'The politics of ethnic minority health studies' in Rothwell, T. and Phillips, D. (eds) *Health, Race and Ethnicity* (London: Croom Helm).

Pearson, N. (1990) *Putting People First: Consumer Consultation and Community Care* (Cardiff: Welsh Consumer Council).

Pearson, R. (1988) *Social Services in a Multi-Racial Society* (London: Department of Health, Social Services Inspectorate).

Phaure, S. (1991) *Who Really Cares? Models of Voluntary Sector Community Care and Black Communities* (London: London Voluntary Service Council).

Phillipson, C. and Walker, A. (1986) *Ageing and Social Policy* (Aldershot: Gower).

Potts, P. (1989) 'Working Report: The People's Republic of China' in Barton, L. (ed.) *Integration: Myth or Reality* (London: Falmer Press).

Poulantzas, N. (1969) 'The problem of the capitalist state', *New Left Review*, **58**: 67–78.

Prescott-Clarke, P. (1990) *Employment and Handicap* (London: Social and Community Planning Research).

Priestly, M. (1995) 'Commonality and difference in the movement: an association of blind Asians in Leeds', *Disability and Society*, **10**(2): 157–70.

RADAR (Royal Association for Disability and Rehabilitation) (1993) *Disability and Discrimination in Employment* (London: RADAR).

Rao, N. (1991) *From Providing to Enabling* (York: Joseph Rowntree).

Rees, G. and Rees, T.L. (1980) *Poverty and Social Equality in Wales* (London: Croom Helm).

Reich, W. (1975) *The Mass Psychology of Fascism* (Harmondsworth: Penguin).

Reuters (1997) 'Swiss sterilisation scandal', *The Independent*, 28 August, p. 10.

Richards, R. (1987) *A Geographical Analysis of Patterns of Mortality and Ill-Health in Wales*, Unpublished PhD Thesis (Swansea: University College of Swansea).

Riddell, S. (1996) 'Theorising special educational needs in a changing political climate' in Barton, L. (ed.) *Disability and Society: Emerging Issues and Insights* (London: Longman).

Rights Now (1994a) *What Price Civil Rights? The Facts Behind the Myths of the Cost Compliance Assessment* (London: Rights Now).

Rights Now (1994b) *Accounting for Discrimination: Estimating the Costs of Excluding Disabled People from the Workforce* (London: Rights Now).

Riker, W. (1964) 'Some ambiguities in the notion of power', *American Political Science Review*, **58**: 341–9.

Roberts, M. (1991) *Living in a Man-Made World: Gender Assumptions in Modern Housing Design* (London: Routledge).

Robinson, C.A. and Wenger, G.C. (1992) *An Overview of Projects Funded under the Welsh Office Elderly Initiative 1987–1991* (Bangor: Centre for Social Policy Research and Development, University of Wales, Bangor).

Rock, P. (1996) 'Eugenics and euthanasia: a cause for concern for disabled people, particularly disabled women', *Disability and Society*, **11**(1): 121–8.

Ronnby, A. (1985) *Socialstaten* (Lund: Studentlitteratur).

Rosen, M. (1996) *On Voluntary Servitude: False Consciousness and the Theory of Ideology* (Cambridge: Polity Press).

Roulstone, A. (1993) 'Access to new technology in the employment of disabled people' in Swain, J., Finkelstein, V., French, S. and Oliver, M. (eds) *Disabling Barriers, Enabling Environments* (London: Sage).

Rowlingson, K. and Berthoud, R. (1994) *Evaluating the Disability Working Allowance* (London: Policy Studies Institute).

Rowlingson, K. and Berthoud, R. (1996) *Disability, Benefits and Work: An Evaluation of Disability Working Allowance*, DSS Research Report No. 54 (London: Stationery Office).

Royal Town Planning Institute (1988) *Access for Disabled People*, Practice Advice Note No. 3 (London: Royal Town Planning Institute).

Roys, P. (1988) 'Racism and welfare: social services' in Bhat, A., Carrhill, R. and Ohri, S. (eds) *Britain's Black Population, A New Perspective* (Aldershot: Gower).

Rufford, N. (1995) 'China moves to ban babies with defects', *Sunday Times*, 5 February, p. 17.

Ryan, S. (1994) 'Handicap test may harm unborn babies', *Sunday Times*, 12 June, p. 4.

Sainsbury, S. (1970) *Registered as Disabled* (London: Bell).

Sainsbury, S. (1993) *Normal Life: A Study of War and Industrially Injured Pensionsers* (Aldershot: Avebury).

Sainsbury, S. (1995) 'Disabled people and the personal social services' in Gladstone, D. (ed.) *British Social Welfare: Past, Present and Future* (London: UCL Press).

Samhall (1995) *Samhall's Annual Report 1994* (Tullinge: Samhall).

Sandler, D. (1997) 'NatWest accused by disabled customer', *Independent on Sunday* (Travel and Money Section), 20 April, p. 15.

Saunders, P. (1990) *A Nation of Home Owners* (London: Unwin Hyman).

Savage, M. and Warde, A. (1993) *Urban Sociology, Capitalism and Modernity* (London: Macmillan).

Savill, A. (1994) 'Swedes cling to nanny state's apron', *The Independent*, 18 September.

Saxton, M. (1984) 'Born and unborn, the implications of reproductive technologies for people with disabilities' in Arditti, R., Klein, D. and Minden, S. (eds) *Test-tube Women: What Future for Motherhood* (London: Pandora Press).

Scase, R. (1992) *Class* (Buckingham: Open University Press).

Schofield, A.N. (1955) *Parliamentary Elections* (London: Shaw & Sons).

Schuchardt, E. (1991) 'The crisis as an opportunity to learn' in Boylan, E. (ed.) *Women and Disability* (London: Zed Books).

Schwarzmantel, J. (1994) *The State in Contemporary Society* (Hemel Hempstead: Harvester Wheatsheaf).

Scott, V. (1994) *Lessons from America, A Study of the Americans with Disabilities Act* (London: Royal Association for Disability and Rehabilitation).

SCRCSSP (Steering Committee for the Review of Commonwealth/State Service Provision, Commonwealth of Australia) (1997) *Report on Government Service Provision* (Melbourne: Commonwealth of Australia).

Seattle Rape Relief (1979) *Information Concerning Sexual Exploitation of Mentally and Physically Handicapped Individuals* (Washington: Developmental Disabilities Project, Seattle Rape Relief).

Sedley, A. (1989) *The Challenge of Anti-Racism: Lessons from a Voluntary Organisation* (London: Family Services Unit).

Seebohm, F. (Chairman) (1968) *Report of the Committee on Local Authority and Allied Personal Social Services*, Cmnd 3703 (London: HMSO).

Shah, R. (1992) *The Silent Minority: Children with Disabilities in Asian Families* (London: National Children's Bureau).

Shakespeare, T. (1993) 'Disabled people's self-organisation: a new social movement?', *Disability, Handicap and Society*, **8**(3): 249–64.

Shakespeare, T. (1997) *Choices and Rights: Eugenics, Genetics and Disability Equality* (unpublished paper).

Shakespeare, T., Gillespie-Sells, K. and Davies, D. (1996) *The Sexual Politics of Disability* (London: Cassell).

Sheard, J. (1986) *The Politics of Volunteering* (London: Advance).

Shu, J., Goldlust, J., Mckenzie, F., Struik, A. and Khoo, S. (1996) *Australia's Population Trends and Prospects 1995* (Canberra: Australian Government Publishing Service).

Silo, J. (1991) 'A deaf teacher: a personal odyssey' in Taylor, G. and Bishop, J. (eds) *Being Deaf: The Experience of Deafness* (London: Pinter and Open University).

Simon, H. (1957) *Administrative Behaviour* (New York: Macmillan).

Simpson, F. and Campbell, J. (1996) *Facilitating and Supporting Independent Living* (London: Disability Income Group).

Sjöberg, M. (1994) *New Rights for Persons with Functional Impairments* (Stockholm: Swedish Institute).

Sjostrom, J. (1984) *Social Politiken* (Stockholm: Arbeterkultur).

Slee, R. (1993) 'The politics of integration – new sites for old practices?', *Disability, Handicap and Society*, **8**(4): 351–60.

Smith, S. (1989) *The Politics of 'Race' and Residence* (Cambridge: Polity Press).

Social Care Network (1990) County Intermediary Bodies Meeting on Consumer Representation, unpublished minutes, 26 July.

Social Security Advisory Committee (1988) *Benefits for Disabled People: A Strategy for Change* (London: HMSO).

Socialstyrelsen (1995) *The Disability Reform, Summary of the 1995 Report* (Stockholm: Socialstyrelsen).

Spastics Society (1993) *The School Survey: Within Reach – Access for Disabled Children to Mainstream Education* (London: Spastics Society and National Union of Teachers).

Statens Institut för Handikappfrågor i Skolan (1995) *The Swedish Public School System and Disabled Students* (Härnösand: National Swedish Agency for Special Education).

Stevens, J. (1997) *Disability, What It's Really Like* (London: BBC World Service). Internet address http://www.bbc.co.uk/worldservice/education/disable2.htm

Stocking, B. (1990) 'Health services for black and ethnic minorities', *King's Fund News*, **13**(3): 1.

Stuart, O. (1992) 'Race and disability, just a double oppression?', *Disability, Handicap and Society*, **7**(2): 177–88.

Stubbings, P. (1982) 'The volunteer: hero or victim of social policy', *Involve*, **18**: 2–3.

Stubbings, P. (1983) 'Next time you drive that old lady to the shops', *Involve*, **23**: 2–3.

Stubbings, P. (1984) 'The smile on the face of the tiger', *Involve*, **35**: 2.

Stubbings, P. (1985) 'More volunteering – less work', *Involve*, no. 46, October.

Sutherland, A.T. (1981) *Disabled We Stand* (London: Souvenir Press).

Swedish Institute (1995) *Disability Policies in Sweden* (Stockholm: Swedish Institute).

Swedish Institute (1996) *Fact Sheets on Sweden* (Stockholm: Swedish Institute).

Taylor, A.J.P. (1965) *English History 1914–1945* (Oxford: Clarendon Press).

Taylor, M. (1995) 'Voluntary action and the state' in Gladstone, D. (ed.) *British Social Welfare: Past, Present and Future* (London: UCL Press).

Tengström, A. (1996) *Report from the joint HELIOS/ENIL Seminar on Personal Assistance* (Stockholm: STIL and European Network on Independent Living). Internet address http://www.independentliving.org/ENIL

Thane, P. (1982) *The Foundations of the Welfare State* (London: Longman).

Thomas, C.J. (1988) *The Relationship Between Social Conditions and Ill-Health in South Wales 1981–1983*. Conference Paper: The Valleys, A Programme for the People: Maesteg, 18 November.

Thompson, J. (1983) 'Volunteers – the Tories' fifth column?', *Involve*, **27**: 1–2.

Thompson, P. (1992) '"I don't feel old": subjective ageing and the search for meaning in later life', *Ageing and Society*, **12**: 23–47.

Thornton, P. and Lunt, N. (1995) *Employment for Disabled People, Social Obligation or Individual Responsibility?* (York: Social Policy Research Unit, University of York).

Tinker, A. (1984) *The Elderly in Modern Society*, 2nd edn (Harlow: Longman).

Tonkin, B. (1987) 'Sowing the seeds of success', *Community Care*, 30 July, pp. 16–21.

Trevillian, S. (1988) 'Griffiths and Wagner: which future for community care?', *Critical Social Policy*, **24**: 65–73.

Tucker, B.P. (1994) 'Overview of the DDA and comparison with the ADA', *Australian Disability Review*, **3**(94): 23–37.

Tullock, G. (1997) 'The economic theory of bureaucracy' in Hill, M. (ed.) *The Policy Process: A Reader*, 2nd edn (London: Prentice Hall).

Union of Physically Impaired against Segregation (UPIAS) (1976) *Fundamental Principles of Disability* (London: UPIAS and the Disability Alliance).

United Nations (1997) *Monthly Bulletin of Statistics* [Statistics Division, Department for Economic and Social Information and Policy Analysis] (New York: United Nations).

United States Department of Justice (1996) *Certification of State and Local Building Codes* (Washington: Department of Justice). Internet address http://www.usdoj.gov/crt/ada/certcode.htm

Upper Afan Valley Elderly People's Project (1993) *Report and Recommendations* (Port Talbot: Upper Afan Valley Elderly People's Project).

Vernon, A. (1996) 'A stranger in many camps: the experiences of disabled black and ethnic minority women', in Morris, J. (ed.) *Encounters with Strangers* (London: Women's Press), pp. 48–69.

Wagner, Lady G. (1988) Positive Choice: *The Report of the Independent Review of Residential Care* (London: HMSO).

Walker, A. (1989) 'Community care' in McCarthy, M. (ed.) *The New Politics of Welfare* (London: Macmillan).

Walker, B. (1981) *Welfare Economics and Urban Problems* (London: Hutchinson).

Walker, C. (1996) 'Levelling the odds', *Community Care*, 23–29 May, p. 25.

Walker, C., Ryan, T. and Walker, A. (1995) *Disparities in Service Provision for People with Learning Difficulties Living in the Community* [Social Care Research Findings, No. 75], (York: Joseph Rowntree Foundation).

Walker, C., Ryan, T. and Walker, A. (1996) *Fair Shares for All* (London: Pavilion Publishing).

Walker, D. (1996) 'A decision fairly reached', *The Independent*, 10 May, p. 18.

Ward, L. (1987) *Talking Points: The Right to Vote* (No Place: CMH Campaign for Mentally Handicapped People).

Ward, R. (1982) 'Race, housing and wealth', *New Community*, $X(1)$: 3–15.

Watson, F. (1930) *Civilization and the Cripple* (London: Bale).

Weaver, J. (1976) 'The elderly as a political community', *Western Political Quarterly*, **26**: 610–19.

Webb, T. (1996) 'End of an era', *Helios News UK*, **4**: 1–2.

Weber, M. (1947) *The Theory of Social and Economic Organisations* (Glencoe: Free Press).

Welsh Office (1983) *All Wales Strategy for the Development of Services for Mentally Handicapped People* (Cardiff: Welsh Office).

Welsh Office (1985a) *Symposium on Services for the Elderly* (Cardiff: Welsh Office).

Welsh Office (1985b) *A Good Old Age: An Initiative on the Care of the Elderly in Wales* (Cardiff: Welsh Office).

Welsh Office (1987) *All Wales Strategy for the Development of Services for Mentally Handicapped People: Review of Progress since March, 1983* (Cardiff: Welsh Office).

Welsh Office (1988) *The Valleys: A Programme for the People* (Cardiff: Welsh Office).

Welsh Office (1989) *Still a Small Voice: Consumer Involvement in the All Wales Strategy* (Cardiff: Welsh Office).

Welsh Office (1990a) *Guidance on Social Care Plans* (Cardiff: Welsh Office).

Welsh Office (1990b) *Community Care: Draft Guidance on Assessment and Case Management* (Cardiff: Welsh Office).

Wenger, C. (1980) *Mid Wales: Deprivation or Development – A Study of Patterns of Employment in Selected Communities* (Cardiff: University of Wales Press).

Wenger, C. (1984) *The Supportive Network: Coping with Old Age* (London: Allen & Unwin).

Wenger, C. (1988a) *Help in Old Age – Facing up to Change* (Bangor: Centre for Social Policy Research and Development, University of Wales, Bangor).

Wenger, C. (1988b) *Old People's Health and Experience of the Caring Services, Accounts from Rural Communities in North Wales* (Liverpool: Liverpool University Press).

Wenger, C. (1990) *Access to Cars and Telephones in Old Age: Keeping in Touch in Rural Areas* (Bangor: Centre for Social Policy Research and Development, University of Wales, Bangor).

Wenger, C. and Shahtahmasebi, S. (1990) *Ageing and Dependency in Rural Areas: Eight Years of Domiciliary Visiting of the Old Elderly* (Bangor: Centre for Social Policy Research and Development, University of Wales, Bangor).

Which (1990) 'No go', *Which*, June, pp. 347–50.

White, D. (1972) 'The problem of power', *British Journal of Political Sciences*, **2**: 479–90.

Whiteley, P. (1996) 'Growing pains', *Community Care*, 11–17 January, pp. 20–1.

Williams, R. (1988) 'The black experience of social services', *Social Work Today*, **19**(19): 14–15.

Williamson, J.B. (1982) *The Politics of Aging* (Springfield, IL: Charles C. Thomas).

Wilson, F. (1990) 'Neo-corporatism and the rise of new social movements' in Dalton, R.J. and Kuechler, M. (eds) *Challenging the Political Order* (Cambridge: Polity Press).

Wilson, G. (1993) 'Users and providers: different perspectives on community care services', *Journal of Social Policy*, **22**(4): 507–26.

Wilson, M. and Francis, J. (1997) *Raised Voices: African-Caribbean and African Users' Views and Experiences of Mental Health Services in England and Wales* (London: MIND).

Winkler, F. (1987) 'Consumerism in health care: beyond the supermarket model', *Policy and Politics*, **15**(1): 1–5.

Winkler, J. (1977) 'The corporate economy, theory and administration' in Scase, R. (ed.) *Industrial Society: Class, Cleavage and Control* (London: George Allen & Unwin).

Winward, J. (1990) 'Information is power' in McConnell, C. (ed.) *Involving the Disadvantaged Consumer in the Management of Public Services* (London: Community Projects Foundation).

Wollaston, H.W. (ed.) (1970) *Parker's Conduct of Parliamentary Elections* (London: Charles Knight).

Wright, J. (1993) *Asian and Disabled: A Study into the Needs of Asian People with Disabilities in the Bradford Area* (Bradford: Barnardo's Keighley Project).

Young, C. (1990) 'Black and ethnic minority users and carers in rural areas', *ARVAC Bulletin*, no. 43: 4–5.

Young, I. (1990) *Justice and the Politics of Difference* (New York: Princeton University Press).

Younghusband, E. (1947) *Report on the Employment and Training of Social Workers* (Dunfermline: Carnegie United Kingdom Trust).

Younghusband, E. (1951) *Second Report on the Employment and Training of Social Workers* (Dunfermline: Carnegie United Kingdom Trust).

Younghusband, E. (1978) *Social Work in Britain 1950–1975* (London: George Allen & Unwin).

Zarb, G. (1991a) 'Creating a supportive environment: meeting the needs of people who are ageing with a disability' in Oliver, M. (ed.) *Social Work, Disabled People and Disabling Environments* (London, Jessica Kingsley).

Zarb, G. (1991b) 'Forgotten but not gone: the experience of ageing with disability', Paper presented to British Society of Gerontology Annual Conference (Manchester: UMIST) .

Zarb, G. (1993) 'The dual experience of ageing with a disability' in Swain, J., Finkelstein, V., French, S. and Oliver, M. (eds) *Disabling Barriers, Enabling Environments* (London: Sage).

Zarb, G. and Nadash, P. (1995) *Direct Payments for Personal Assistance*, Social Policy Research Findings No. 64 (London: Policy Studies Institute).

Zarb, G. and Oliver, M. (1991) *Ageing with a Disability: Dimensions of Need, Preliminary Findings* (London: Thames Polytechnic).

Zarb, G. and Oliver, M. (1992) *Ageing with a Disability: Dimensions of Need* (London: Spinal Injuries Association).

Zarb, G., Oliver, M. and Silver, J. (1990) *Ageing with a Spinal Cord Injury* (London: Spinal Injuries Association).

Index